PRAISE FOR *MASTERING ATTRIBUTION IN FINANCE*

'There are only a few individuals with the requisite qualifications to undertake the task of writing a book on performance attribution, and Andrew Colin clearly ranks among them. His expertise and experience as a developer, designer, and lecturer provide him with the necessary credentials. The result is a book that masterfully covers all aspects of the subject, both broadly and deeply. This book deserves to rest upon the shelves of any performance measurement or investment professional eager to learn and understand more about this subject.'

David Spaulding, DPS, CIPM
CEO, The Spaulding Group

'An excellent step forward in the explanation of the dark art of fixed income attribution! The material is methodical and strikes an appropriate balance between academic theory and practical implementation.'

Carl Bacon CIPM
Chairman, StatPro Group

'Yet again, Andrew Colin produces a book that brings together the details of attribution, blending both detailed theoretical concepts and practical examples. A must have for any attribution specialist.'

Andrew Kophamel CFA, CIPM, FRM
Head of Performance, Asia Pacific, Aberdeen Asset Management

Mastering Attribution in Finance

Mastering Attribution in Finance

A practitioner's guide to risk-based analysis of investment returns

ANDREW COLIN

PEARSON

Harlow, England • London • New York • Boston • San Francisco • Toronto • Sydney
Auckland • Singapore • Hong Kong • Tokyo • Seoul • Taipei • New Delhi
Cape Town • São Paulo • Mexico City • Madrid • Amsterdam • Munich • Paris • Milan

PEARSON EDUCATION LIMITED
Edinburgh Gate
Harlow CM20 2JE
United Kingdom
Tel: +44 (0)1279 623623
Web: www.pearson.com/uk

First published 2016 (print and electronic)

ISBN: 978-1-292-11402-6 (print)
978-1-292-11404-0 (PDF)
978-1-292-11405-7 (ePub)

British Library Cataloguing-in-Publication Data
A catalogue record for the print edition is available from the British Library

Library of Congress Cataloging-in-Publication Data
Names: Colin, Andrew, author.
Title: Mastering attribution in finance: a practitioner's guide to risk-based analysis of investment returns / Andrew Colin.
Description: Harlow, England: Pearson Education, 2016. | Includes bibliographical references and index.
Identifiers: LCCN 2015038612 | ISBN 9781292114026
Subjects: LCSH: Portfolio management. | Rate of return—Mathematical models. | Investments. | Fixed-income securities. | Technical analysis (Investment analysis)
Classification: LCC HG4529.5 .C65 2016 | DDC 332.6--dc23
LC record available at http://lccn.loc.gov/2015038612

Print edition typeset in 11.5pt Garamond 3 LT Pro by Lumina Datamatics

NOTE THAT ANY PAGE CROSS REFERENCES REFER TO THE PRINT EDITION

ScoutAutomatedPrintCode

For Linda, Thomas and Rachel

Contents

About the author xvi

Acknowledgements xvii

Preface xix

1 An introduction to attribution 1

1.1 Securities, portfolios and risk 3

1.2 Types of risk 3

1.3 Return and attribution 4

1.4 Strategy tagging 5

1.5 Types of attribution 5

1.6 Book structure 6

Part 1 EQUITY ATTRIBUTION 9

2 The basics of performance measurement 11

2.1 Introduction 13

2.2 Defining return 13

2.3 Compounded returns 14

2.4 Time-weighted and money-weighted returns 15

2.5 Portfolio returns 17

2.6 Transactions and cash flows 17

2.7 Sector returns 19

2.8 Calculating portfolio returns over successive intervals 20

2.9 Futures cash offsets 20

2.10 Edge cases 22

2.11 External returns 22

2.12 Benchmarks 24

2.13 Active return 25

2.14 Stochastic attribution 25

2.15 Liability-driven investment (LDI) 26

3 Equity attribution 27
3.1 Introduction 29
3.2 Brinson attribution 29
3.3 Single-level Brinson attribution 33
3.4 Multiple-level asset allocation 38
3.5 Off-benchmark securities 43
3.6 Successive portfolio attribution 43
3.7 Security-level attribution 45

4 Currency attribution 49
4.1 Introduction 51
4.2 Currency attribution returns 51
4.3 Performance and attribution on unhedged portfolios 52
4.4 Attribution on an unhedged portfolio 53
4.5 Portfolio hedging 55
4.6 Currency forwards 56
4.7 Hedging and risk 57
4.8 Naïve attribution on a hedged portfolio 58
4.9 Measuring hedge returns 59
4.10 Brinson attribution on a hedged portfolio 60
4.11 Problems with the Brinson approach when hedging is active 60
4.12 Calculating base and return premiums 63
4.13 The Karnosky-Singer attribution model 65
4.14 Running Karnosky-Singer attribution on an unhedged portfolio 65

5 Smoothing algorithms 67
5.1 Why returns do not combine neatly over time 69
5.2 The importance of internally consistent return contributions 71
5.3 Path-independence 71
5.4 Carino smoothing 73
5.5 Geometric smoothing 76
5.6 Foreign exchange return and smoothing 79
5.7 Summary 79

Part 2 FIXED INCOME ATTRIBUTION 81

6 An overview of fixed income risks 83
6.1 Introduction 85

6.2 What is a bond? 85
6.3 Pricing conventions 86
6.4 Maturity 87
6.5 Coupons 87
6.6 Discounted cash flows and net present value 88
6.7 Pricing a bond from its discounted cash flows 88
6.8 Bond yield and carry return 88
6.9 Prices and yields 89
6.10 Return of a bond 90
6.11 Credit effects 91
6.12 The three Cs 92

7 Yield curves in attribution 93
7.1 Introduction 95
7.2 Why interest rates vary by term 95
7.3 Interpolation 96
7.4 Par curves and zero curves 97
7.5 Credit spreads 99

8 Pricing, risk and the attribution equation 101
8.1 Introduction 103
8.2 Pricing securities from first principles 103
8.3 Calculating return using the perturbational equation 103
8.4 Residuals 107
8.5 Stand-alone portfolios 108

Part 3 SOURCES OF FIXED INCOME RETURN 109

9 Carry return 111
9.1 Introduction 113
9.2 Carry-based investment strategies 113
9.3 Types of yield 114
9.4 Calculating carry return 115
9.5 Pros and cons of YTM 116
9.6 Decomposing carry 116
9.7 Which yield to use? 116
9.8 Decomposing carry return 117
9.9 Yield for non-bond securities 120
9.10 Using yield to maturity in attribution reports 120

10 Sovereign curve attribution 121
10.1 Introduction 123
10.2 Yield curve models 123
10.3 Parallel shift and modified duration, and why they matter 124
10.4 Measuring twist 127
10.5 Taxonomy of curve shifts 128
10.6 Sources of yield curve data 134

11 Sector and credit return 135
11.1 Credit spreads 137
11.2 Sectors and credit ratings 138
11.3 Building sector curves 140
11.4 Attribution using sector curves 142
11.5 Attribution on Euro bond portfolios 143
11.6 Attribution on credit portfolios 145
11.7 Credit attribution without a credit curve 145

12 Other security-specific sources of return 147
12.1 Paydown 149
12.2 Convexity 150
12.3 Rolldown 152
12.4 Liquidity return 153

13 Balanced attribution 155
13.1 Introduction 157
13.2 Calculating balanced attribution 157

14 Duration allocation attribution 161
14.1 Introduction 163
14.2 Return of a single fixed income security 166
14.3 Calculating duration returns 166
14.4 Discussion 179

Part 4 ATTRIBUTION ON FIXED INCOME SECURITIES 181

15 Bonds 183
15.1 Introduction 185
15.2 Bond pricing formulae 185

15.3 Types of bonds 186
15.4 Repos 189

16 Money market securities 191
16.1 Introduction 193
16.2 Money market yield curves 193
16.3 Money market curve decomposition 193
16.4 Cash 194
16.5 Bank bills and discount securities 195
16.6 Accrual securities 197
16.7 Floating rate notes 197
16.8 Interest rate and credit risk 198
16.9 FRN types 198
16.10 Yields and discount margins 198
16.11 FRN durations 199
16.12 Decomposing the return of an FRN 200
16.13 Yield curve attribution 200
16.14 Attribution with complete data 201
16.15 Attribution with incomplete data 201
16.16 Treatment of FRNs in commercial systems 201
16.17 FRNs and securitisation 202
16.18 Currency forwards 202
16.19 Repurchase agreements (repos) 203
16.20 Money market benchmarks 203

17 Inflation-linked securities 205
17.1 Introduction 207
17.2 Overview of the inflation-linked bond market 207
17.3 What is an inflation-linked bond? 208
17.4 The Canadian model for inflation-linked debt 208
17.5 Inflation ratios 209
17.6 Real yields and nominal yields 209
17.7 Pricing an inflation-linked bond 211
17.8 Real yield term structure 211
17.9 Pricing an inflation-linked bond 212
17.10 Modified duration and return of inflation-linked gilts 213
17.11 Break-even yields in attribution 215
17.12 Inflation swaps 215
17.13 Practical considerations 216

18 Futures 217
18.1 Introduction 219
18.2 How futures work 219
18.3 Attribution on bond futures 224
18.4 Futures contracts on other fixed income securities 227
18.5 Heuristics for dealing with futures 227

19 Annuities and amortising securities 229
19.1 Introduction 231
19.2 Prepayments 232
19.3 Mortgage-backed securities 232

20 Swaps 235
20.1 Introduction 237
20.2 Two-leg swaps 237
20.3 Single-leg swaps 238
20.4 Modelling swaps 238
20.5 Types of swap 239
20.6 Credit default swaps 239

21 Options and callable bonds 241
21.1 Introduction 243
21.2 Measuring yield on bonds with embedded options 243
21.3 Optionality in practice 245

22 Collateralised and securitised debt 247
22.1 Introduction 249
22.2 Securitisation 249
22.3 Collateralised debt 249
22.4 Attribution on securitised debt 250

Part 5 ATTRIBUTION IN PRACTICE 251

23 Popular attribution models 253
23.1 The Campisi model 255
23.2 Duration attribution 256
23.3 The Tim Lord model 256
23.4 Key rate attribution 257
23.5 Top-down attribution 258

24 Reporting 261
24.1 Treatment of residuals 263
24.2 Unattributed return 263

Afterword 265
Appendices 267
A A summary of the Karnosky-Singer attribution model 269
B Explicit pricing of an FRN 271
C Attribution on Australian and New Zealand bond futures 272
D Parametric and non-parametric yield curve models 274
E Replicating the return of a hedged benchmark 275
F Duration-weighted yields 278
G Combining duration allocation returns 279
H Sources of yield curve data 280
Bibliography 281
Index 283

About the author

Andrew Colin is a leading authority in the field of investment performance attribution. He has worked at Citigroup, the Commonwealth Bank, Zurich Investment Management, JP Morgan, StatPro and the Queensland University of Technology, and has also managed many consulting projects in defence and applied statistics.

He holds a PhD in mathematics from the University of St Andrews, is a Fellow of the Institute of Mathematics and its Applications, and holds Chartered Mathematician accreditation. He is currently adjunct professor in the faculty of business at the University of Tasmania.

Andrew is founder of Flametree Technologies (www.flametreetechnologies.com), a company that builds advanced attribution and risk management tools. You can contact him at andrew.colin@flametreeia.com.

Acknowledgements

For feedback on the manuscript: Carl Bacon, Dan Griffiths, Jakub Kalarus, Katalin Kiss, Andrew Kophamel, Ilker Kumlu, David Spaulding, Chen Sui, Stephen Thorpe, Andrew Turner.

For their help and support: Adam Clements, my parents, Joanna Deane, Susan Deane, Chris Maden.

Thanks to the many classes to whom I have presented this material in various forms.

For his limitless patience and good humour: my co-founder Graeme Condie.

For suggesting the title 'Fixed Income Attribution 2: Electric Boogaloo', opening my eyes to LaTeX, superlative editing and many useful suggestions: Thomas Colin.

To the editorial team at Pearson Education, in particular Emma Steel for her expert copy-editing.

To my family, for their unstinting love and support.

Most of all, to Linda. Words are not enough. Thanks, hon.

Any mistakes that remain are, naturally, my responsibility.

Preface

> **'Begin at the beginning,' the King said gravely, 'and go on till you come to the end: then stop.'**
>
> Lewis Carroll, *Alice in Wonderland*

The purpose of this book is to provide a comprehensive, up-to-date account of how attribution is used in the equity and fixed income markets. My specific aims are:

- to present a structured overview of the field at all levels, including unpublished or difficult to find material that should be part of every attribution analyst's toolset;
- to provide a fresh, accessible introduction to the ideas behind performance and attribution. Relatively little material is available for newcomers to this field. While I have tried not to compromise on the required mathematics, I hope that the book also conveys insight into why things are done in a particular way;
- to fill some of the gaps in my previous book (Colin, 2005), particularly around the areas of top-down attribution and attribution on specific types of fixed income security.

The book is a personal view of the subject, and some of my views and definitions differ from other presentations. Where appropriate, I have tried to indicate where differences in usage for terms, such as *residual*, are common.

Where possible, all concepts are supported with worked examples.

WHO SHOULD READ THIS BOOK?

Anyone who needs to calculate, provide or interpret an attribution report will find this book interesting, including:

- portfolio managers;
- client portfolio managers;

- asset consultants;
- marketing teams;
- senior management;
- front, middle and back office personnel;
- investors;
- software vendors.

Most of these individuals will be familiar with the ideas behind performance measurement and simple Brinson attribution, and may now wish to broaden their knowledge to cover advanced equity and fixed income attribution. In addition to comprehensive introductory material they will find a detailed presentation of all these topics, and more, in the following pages.

In particular, this book is, as far as I am aware, the first to describe the different types of fixed income security from the perspective of an attribution analyst. Even experienced quantitative analysts may find the emphasis on performance and return, rather than pricing or risk, of interest.

UNDERSTANDING YOUR CLIENT'S REQUIREMENTS

It is particularly important to understand what your clients need and expect from attribution, and this can require extensive interaction with portfolio managers, client managers, marketing staff and others. Many performance measurement staff find it intimidating to engage these skilled and busy people. This book will supply you with the background knowledge to ask them the right questions.

UNDERSTANDING YOUR TOOLS

One of the difficulties currently affecting this field is the availability and cost of good attribution software.

Few commercial systems fully match the requirements of a sophisticated fund manager, and most require deep background knowledge and extensive configuration before they can begin to produce useful results. Many resemble an Acme Sculpture Set, containing a block of marble, a photograph of the Venus de Milo and a chisel. You are provided with a database and some pretty input screens. To actually get the system running and producing useful results requires a considerable amount of time, skill and additional expertise, much of which probably has to be purchased from your software vendor or external consultants at a large multiple of the software's original cost.

The material in the following pages should take you a long way towards being able to configure and run such a system yourself.

PRAGMATISM

Attribution requires a healthy dose of pragmatism, since it is all too easy to spend vast amounts of time and effort on measuring attribution effects that have no appreciable impact on the final report. Where possible, I have indicated where you can take short cuts or even ignore conventional wisdom entirely without significantly distorting your results.

Accurate performance reports remain a business-critical requirement, but the need for complete accuracy in attribution often comes second to being able to tell a story about which risks drove a portfolio's returns. For this reason, attribution often sits uneasily with performance measurement, and a certain amount of doublethink may be required when working out what users actually need.

MARKET STANDARDS

Attribution is a field in its early days, and unlike performance measurement there are no market standards for calculation and reporting of attribution effects.

To some degree, this is inevitable. There are as many investment processes as there are managers, with each requiring its own tailored reports. Therefore, there can be no one 'right' way to run attribution. The only hard-and-fast rule is that an attribution report must reflect the decisions made in managing the underlying portfolio.

However, the building blocks of attribution are well defined. Concepts such as *allocation return*, *selection return*, *duration return*, *credit spread return*, *duration allocation return* and *sector curve return* all form part of the common vocabulary of the attribution analyst, and tend to be combined in standard ways. If agreement can be reached on how to measure the underlying market movements, such as parallel yield curve shift, then attribution standards may yet be in reach.

My view is that attribution should provide tools to allow the user to set up their own attribution reports in terms of these concepts. In the following chapters, I will explain how each of these building blocks work, and how to combine them to arrive at the holy grail of performance measurement: accurate, timely, useful attribution reports.

Andrew Colin
Eudlo, November 2014

1

An introduction to attribution

1.1 Securities, portfolios and risk

1.2 Types of risk

1.3 Return and attribution

1.4 Strategy tagging

1.5 Types of attribution

1.6 Book structure

1.1 SECURITIES, PORTFOLIOS AND RISK

The aim of a managed fund is to invest in appropriate financial instruments so that the fund's value is maintained, or increased, over time. In this context, value can either be tracked in absolute terms or measured relative to a reference entity called a *benchmark*.

For convenience, the securities in a fund are usually grouped into entities called *portfolios*. One can then talk of the return of the portfolio as a whole, rather than the returns of its constituent assets.

1.2 TYPES OF RISK

Managed funds that hold assets such as cash, equities, investment trusts and derivatives are usually managed via *stock selection* and *asset allocation* decisions. Informally, a stock selection decision is *which* securities to hold, while asset allocation decisions are *how much* of each security to hold.[1] Stock selection decisions apply at the security level, while asset allocation decisions are made by varying the relative weights of subsets of holdings between the portfolio and the benchmark.

In addition, many funds also hold fixed income securities, which supply exposure to additional sources of market risk such as *yield*, *interest rate risk*, *credit risk* and *inflation*.

Lastly, exposure to securities that are denominated in overseas currencies generates *exchange rate risk*, which may be hedged and controlled using securities such as forwards.

Almost every investment portfolio has exposure to multiple concurrent risks, which occurs when

- the securities that make up the portfolio are inherently exposed to multiple risks. For instance, a corporate bond generates simultaneous returns from yield, sovereign curve risk and credit risk;
- the manager deliberately uses multiple risks as part of an investment strategy.

It is up to the manager to decide to which risks they want to be exposed, and to implement suitable investment strategies that put these decisions into practice.

Just as importantly, the manager should be able to hedge their portfolio so that it is not exposed to other, unwanted risks. For instance, an equity manager may decide to take only stock selection decisions, and not to have any asset allocation exposures. In this case, the fund's asset allocation return

[1] These terms are defined explicitly in Chapter 3.

should always be zero, and the attribution report will verify that this decision was implemented successfully.

Asset allocation hedges are relatively easy to implement, as they simply require that each portfolio sector weight is equal to the corresponding benchmark sector weight. Other types of hedge, such as immunisation of the portfolio against non-parallel yield curve shifts, can be much more difficult to implement and may require considerable expertise and investment in risk-management tools.

1.3 RETURN AND ATTRIBUTION

A statement of the fund's overall return will show the aggregate sum of the returns from each investment decision, decomposed by time or by market sector. What it will not show are the fund's returns, decomposed by risk. *The purpose of attribution is to disentangle this single return into the multiple returns generated by each risk.* In other words, attribution measures which of your investment decisions about the portfolio's underlying risks worked, and which did not. This is critical business intelligence for anyone involved in selecting, managing or marketing investments.

The ability to run attribution presupposes an ability to run accurate performance calculation. There is little use in being able to decompose the return of a security or a portfolio if that return is wrong.

Fortunately, accurate reporting of results can usually be assumed. The introduction of the Global Investment Performance Standards (GIPS) has ensured comparability of portfolio returns between managers and against benchmarks.

The capability to run attribution puts the manager in full control of their investments. Running attribution shows the following:

- the manager's skill at identifying and managing risks;
- where the manager took risks;
- when the manager took risks;
- how well the manager's hedging strategies worked.

Without this information, the manager is effectively flying blind. They may be making profits, but it is probably not clear where or why, and this lack of transparency will make it difficult or impossible to isolate the manager's core investment strengths.

This is the true value of attribution. It allows the manager to ensure that a portfolio is following the manager's investment strategy, to verify that no unexpected risks are driving returns down and to take remedial action if necessary. As a result, attribution is generally recognised as an important requirement for any investment institution.

1.4 STRATEGY TAGGING

Many portfolios implement simultaneous investment strategies by dividing their investments into different subportfolios, each designed to profit from a particular perceived market opportunity. These can vary in complexity from the simple (go long Russia) to the complex (volatility plays, yield curve barbell trades and the like). The overall return of the portfolio is generated by the return of all its underlying strategies, and the decomposition of a portfolio's returns by investment strategy (as distinct from market sector or risk) is generally called *strategy tagging*.

In principle, the calculation of returns from each strategy is straightforward, and only requires standard performance measurement tools. If one regards the holdings assigned to each strategy as a separate subportfolio, then the return of that subportfolio will show the value added by the strategy.

In practice, few managers have successfully implemented strategy tagging systems. The difficulties are largely due to workflow issues and the mechanics of logging individual trades against the correct strategy.

A particular difficulty is that some trades may involve one security but multiple strategies. For instance, if Strategy A requires the purchase of 500 bond future contracts, while Strategy B requires the sale of the same number of contracts, then the net result is that no physical trade need be made; yet each strategy requires a dummy trade, and the deal entry system should allow such trades to be recorded.

Strategy tagging is closely related to attribution but does not require any of its underlying machinery. Some managers regard strategy tagging analysis as more valuable than attribution analysis.

1.5 TYPES OF ATTRIBUTION

Attribution techniques fall neatly into two well-defined categories:

- equity attribution;
- fixed income attribution.

Each category has its own algorithms, literature and jargon. The conventional view is that equity attribution is mostly about the Brinson algorithm, while fixed income attribution is mostly about yield curves. While not strictly true, this is a useful distinction, and the book follows the same pattern.

1.5.1 Equity attribution

Equity attribution is usually driven by asset allocation and stock selection decisions. Individual equity returns are driven by both corporate and macroeconomic factors. From the attribution analyst's perspective, there is no direct relationship between these market factors and security prices, and various statistical tools, such as factor analysis, can be used to find the core drivers of return, if required. Such topics are outside the scope of this text.

1.5.2 Fixed income attribution

The price and return of fixed income securities are driven by a combination of structural and market factors. Typically, these include:

- the cash flows of the security, including any guaranteed payments to the owner, such as coupons and repayment of principal;
- the risk-free yield curve;
- credit curves, where appropriate;
- the resulting yield of the security;
- other minor effects such as roll-down, convexity and paydown;
- security-specific factors, such as the creditworthiness and financial strength of the issuer.

In most cases the relationship between a security's return and the change in its underlying curve(s) is well understood. The factors that drive performance can then be described as the sum of different movements in these curves, such as parallel shift, changes at a particular maturity and global movements in a credit curve.

Fixed income attribution decomposes the return of individual securities into return from each factor, and then recombines these returns over the portfolio so that their total contribution to return may be measured.

Fixed income portfolios can also generate excess return by varying their interest rate risks against benchmark at the sector or aggregate level. The effect this *duration allocation* decision has on the portfolio's outperformance may then be measured. The topic is covered in detail in Chapter 14.

1.6 BOOK STRUCTURE

The book is divided into five sections. Part 1 concentrates on equity attribution, while Parts 2 to 5 cover fixed income attribution. The threads come together again occasionally, as when we discuss mixed and hybrid attribution techniques, which can be applied to both types of security, but generally the techniques required for fixed income and equity attribution are quite different.

Part 1 is a self-contained guide to equity attribution.

> Chapter 2 covers the basics of performance measurement.
>
> Chapter 3 examines the Brinson model, including attribution on nested allocation decisions.
>
> Chapter 4 is about currency attribution and the Karnosky-Singer model for hedged portfolios.
>
> Chapter 5 describes the rationale and techniques underlying smoothing of portfolio returns.

Part 2 introduces the concepts behind fixed income return.

> Chapter 6 provides an overview of how a bond is priced and how its returns can be decomposed in terms of fixed income-specific factors. This material acts as an introduction to the concepts of fixed income attribution, and provides context for Part 3.
>
> Chapter 7 covers the role of the yield curve as a fundamental driver of fixed income returns.
>
> Chapter 8 is about ways in which movements in underlying market drivers can be translated to attribution returns, including first-principles pricing and the perturbational equation.

Part 3 describes, in detail, the sources of risk that drive the returns of fixed income securities, which include:

> carry return (Chapter 9);
>
> sovereign or risk-free curve return, and the ways in which movements in the yield curve can be decomposed and described (Chapter 10);
>
> sector and credit curve return (Chapter 11);
>
> other sources of return such as convexity, roll-down and pay-down (Chapter 12);
>
> mixed or balanced attribution, in which top-down allocation returns are combined with bottom-up fixed income effects (Chapter 13);
>
> macro-level allocation decisions (Chapter 14).

Part 4 describes how to perform attribution on the main fixed income security types:

> bonds (Chapter 15);
>
> money market securities (Chapter 16);
>
> inflation-linked securities (Chapter 17);

futures (Chapter 18);

sinking securities, including MBS and amortising debt (Chapter 19);

swaps (Chapter 20);

options and callable bonds (Chapter 21);

collateralised and securitised debt (Chapter 22).

Part 5 covers some practical aspects of attribution:

popular attribution models (Chapter 23);

tools and techniques for attribution reporting (Chapter 24).

Part 1

EQUITY ATTRIBUTION

2. The basics of performance measurement
3. Equity attribution
4. Currency attribution
5. Smoothing algorithms

2

The basics of performance measurement

2.1 Introduction
2.2 Defining return
2.3 Compounded returns
2.4 Time-weighted and money-weighted returns
2.5 Portfolio returns
2.6 Transactions and cash flows
2.7 Sector returns
2.8 Calculating portfolio returns over successive intervals
2.9 Futures cash offsets
2.10 Edge cases
2.11 External returns
2.12 Benchmarks
2.13 Active return
2.14 Stochastic attribution
2.15 Liability-driven investment (LDI)

2.1 INTRODUCTION

This chapter provides a high-level overview of performance calculation for both individual securities and portfolios of securities.

Routine performance calculations are almost always carried out by specialist software packages that can handle the large volumes of data involved. However, even if you never need to calculate performance manually, an appreciation of how performance numbers work and are used is necessary to understand attribution.

Security and portfolio performance is well described elsewhere (Bacon, 2008), and any reader of this book is already likely to have a good understanding of the basics of the subject. The material is therefore presented at a relatively high level.

2.2 DEFINING RETURN

The concept of *return* is suggested by questions such as:

- If I had invested \$100 in a particular stock, what would my investment be worth after a year?
- Would I have been better off investing in another security?
- If I had invested twice as much, what would my profit have been?

Return is defined as the rate of increase r in the value of an investment. Alternatively, return is the ratio of money gained or lost (whether realised or unrealised) on an investment, relative to the amount of money initially invested. In algebraic terms, r is given by

$$r = \frac{\delta P}{P} \tag{2.1}$$

where P is the value of the investment at the outset, and δP its change in value.

The advantages of expressing profit as a dimensionless quantity r, rather than as a P/L (profit and loss) in currency terms, are twofold:

- Return allows different investments to be compared on a common basis. Investible portfolios typically range in size from individual securities to managed funds containing many thousands of securities from completely different markets, but both generate a return that can be measured and compared.
- The use of a return measure allows quality of investments to be compared when amounts invested are quite different. In particular, the use of return makes it possible for the portfolio to be compared to a reference portfolio

(or benchmark), as well as against its peers, which would not be possible if only currency P/L were available.[1]

2.3 COMPOUNDED RETURNS

Consider an investment that pays 12% annually. To calculate its rate of return when payments are reinvested, we also need to know its *frequency of compounding*, since the value of the amount invested will change over each compounding interval.

- If the investment is held for a year and pays a single lump sum of 12% at the end of this interval, its annual return is 12.0%.
- If interest is paid at six-monthly intervals, then the return is calculated over two intervals.

  At the end of the first six months, the value of an invested dollar investment is $1 + (1 \times 0.06) = 1.06$. Therefore, the starting value for the investment over the second six-month interval is 1.06, and the overall return is 6% compounded twice: $r = (1 + 0.06)^2 - 1 = 12.36\%$.
- If interest is paid at one-monthly intervals, the return is $12\% \div 12 = 1\%$ compounded 12 times: $r = (1 + 0.01)^{12} - 1 = 12.68\%$.

In the limit where the compounding interval goes to zero, the return r is given by

$$r = \lim_{n \to \infty} \left(1 + \frac{r}{n}\right)^n - 1 = e^r - 1 \tag{2.2}$$

where e is the constant 2.71828... In this case the return is $e^{0.12} - 1 = 12.75\%$.

Investments often have their aggregated returns calculated using continuously compounded return. The reason is that its use makes return very straightforward to calculate over multiple intervals:

$$1 + r = (1 + r_a)(1 + r_b) = e^a e^b = e^{a+b} \tag{2.3}$$

In other words, the continuously compounded return of an investment over multiple intervals is simply the sum of the continuously compounded returns over each interval.[2]

---

[1] Use of a benchmark is just one way of measuring skill. As discussed later, benchmarks are typically constructed using quite different criteria from those used to manage portfolios.

[2] While searching for a mortgage in the early 1990s I asked various UK high street lenders about their compounding rate policies. I was appalled to find that many lenders only compounded borrowings annually, despite requiring monthly payments – to the disadvantage of the consumer. Conversely, Australian lenders compounded on a weekly basis, resulting in substantially shorter mortgage lifetimes for the same equivalent payments.

2.4 TIME-WEIGHTED AND MONEY-WEIGHTED RETURNS

2.4.1 Time-weighted return

The most commonly used way to calculate return is based on the approach shown in (2.1). If there are no cash flows over the calculation interval, return r is given by

$$r = \frac{EMV - BMV}{BMV} = \frac{\delta P}{P} \tag{2.4}$$

This expression is typically expanded to handle the effects of cash inflows or outflows over the calculation interval $\{t, t + 1\}$, as well as the effects of income from dividends or bond coupons:

$$r = \frac{EMV - BMV - CF + Income}{BMV} \tag{2.5}$$

or, equivalently

$$r_{t,t+1} = \frac{P_{t+1} - P_t - CF_{t,t+1} + I_{t,t+1}}{P_t} \tag{2.6}$$

where

- $BMV = P_t = P$ is the value of the investment at the start of the calculation interval;
- $EMV = P_{t+1}$ is the value of the investment at the end of the calculation interval;
- $\delta P = EMV - BMV$ is the change in the value of the investment over the calculation interval;
- $CF = CF_{t,t+1}$ is the aggregated value of any cash flows occurring over the interval;
- $Income = I_{t,t+1}$ is any income accruing from the investment over the interval.

All these expressions are approximations to the true return, which requires complete revaluation of every portfolio asset each time a transaction occurs.

In practice it is difficult to measure the exact return of a portfolio, since prices are typically only sampled at particular fixed times, typically the start and end of each day. For transactions at other times of day, some form of approximation is required. The dollar P/L is never in question, but the rate of return can be, due to the resulting uncertainty in the portfolio's revaluation.

These expressions represent *time-weighted* return, which is the industry standard for performance measurement. Time-weighted return is not sensitive to contributions or withdrawals.

Example

A bond has a price of 104.5 at the start of a month, 102.0 at the end of the month, and generates a coupon payment of $3 during the month. There are no other cash flows. Its return over the month is

$$r = \frac{102.0 - 104.5 + 3}{104.5} = \frac{0.5}{104.5} = 0.478\%$$

2.4.2 Money-weighted return

Money-weighted return is also occasionally encountered. Money-weighted return is the discount rate for a portfolio that makes the present value of its inflows equal to its outflows. Like time-weighted return, money-weighted return can measure the return of a security, a sector or a portfolio over an arbitrary period in which cashflows occur.

This is a rather opaque definition, so consider an example. We buy one share of a stock for $100 that pays a $5 dividend six months after it was purchased and another $5 dividend 12 months after it was purchased. The share is then sold just after the second dividend was paid at a price of $95. What was its money-weighted rate of return?

Here, the outflow for the investor is $100, and the inflows are the two $5 dividends and the sale price of $95. Therefore, the money-weighted rate of return will be the rate r that satisfies the following expression:

$$\frac{\$5}{(1 + r)^{0.5}} + \frac{\$5}{(1 + r)^{1}} + \frac{\$95}{(1 + r)^{1}} = \$100$$

Equations of this type are seldom analytically tractable and must be solved numerically. In this case, $r = 5.137\%$. Compare this to the time-weighted rate of return:

$$\frac{\$95 - \$100 + \$5 + \$5}{\$100} = 5.000\%$$

Apart from its calculation overhead, the main reason money-weighted return is not widely used is that it overweights the contribution to return made during periods when holdings are highest. Since holdings in a portfolio are typically outside the manager's control, this can distort the overall returns and give a misleading view of the manager's skill. Intuitively, one expects any measure of return to be unaffected by the size of the investment held. This is not necessarily the case for money-weighted returns.

2.5 PORTFOLIO RETURNS

Portfolios typically hold more than one security; this could be for a number of reasons, including:

- risk diversification;
- having multiple investment strategies in play;
- matching a set of known liabilities;
- matching the cashflows of a benchmark.

Each security i in a portfolio has a market value MV_i, a weight w_i and a return r_i. The weight is the security's proportion of the overall portfolio value:

$$w_i = \frac{MV_i}{\sum_i MV_i} \tag{2.7}$$

where the sum is over the entire portfolio.

This implies that the sum of the security weights over the portfolio is always 1:

$$\sum_i w_i = 1 \tag{2.8}$$

Note that weights can be *negative*. This most commonly occurs when a portfolio holds derivatives such as currency forwards, futures or swaps, which may have negative market values. In this case, the sum of the weights of the other securities in the portfolio will be greater than one.

Given the weight and return of each security in the portfolio, the portfolio's overall return R is the sum-product of its security weights and returns:

$$R = \sum_i w_i r_i \tag{2.9}$$

Defining the performance contribution c_i of security i as $c_i = w_i r_i$, we can rewrite (2.9) as

$$R = \sum_i c_i \tag{2.10}$$

In other words, the return of a portfolio over a given interval is the sum of its performance contributions over that interval. This apparently trivial observation is more useful than it might seem, as is shown in Section 2.6.1.

2.6 TRANSACTIONS AND CASH FLOWS

Typically, the composition of a portfolio changes over time. This may be due to:

- security transactions (buying or selling stocks);
- cash flows (dividends and coupons);

- revaluation (stock splits);
- internal changes within a security (sinking bond paydowns);
- changes from one security type to another (bonds maturing, bonds being called, convertible bonds turning into equity).

All these cases can be handled by the equations above.

2.6.1 Performance contribution, or weight and return?

The 'obvious' way to provide information about the securities that make up a portfolio is to supply their weights and returns, since the two are independent. However, many performance systems work with performance contributions and returns instead. There are two main reasons:

- *Accurate intraday contributions*

  A continuous view of the holdings and valuation of the managed portfolio is seldom available. Instead, the analyst must work with snapshots of the portfolio, usually at the start or end of the day, and include the effects of trades and other cash flows between these points.

  At some point a trader will buy into a stock after the market opens and sell it out before the market closes. The stock will generate a contribution to the portfolio's overall performance, but its weight at the beginning and the end of the calculation interval will be zero. In this case, a conventional use of weights and returns will report the security's return contribution as zero when it is not.

- *Highly leveraged securities*

  The other reason to work with performance contributions is that they often convey a clearer picture of the source of portfolio returns. A highly leveraged swap may have a very large return but a small exposure. In this case it may not be clear whether the swap is making any impact on the portfolio's overall return. The swap's performance contribution provides a much more transparent way to assess its impact on the portfolio's return.

A disadvantage of using return contributions is that weight must now be calculated as

$$w_i = \frac{c_i}{r_i} \tag{2.11}$$

The sum of the w_i terms may differ slightly from 1 on days where there is significant intraday trading, but this is always preferable to reporting the wrong overall return.

2.7 SECTOR RETURNS

2.7.1 The concept of a sector

It is often useful to categorise securities as belonging to a particular sector, or partition, within a portfolio. Commonly used sectors include:

- country of issuance;
- industry sector;
- currency;
- pricing model;
- credit rating.

Sector classifications may vary over time. For instance, a bond may be re-rated, in which case the credit sector to which it belongs will change.

There can be many different ways to categorise a given security. For instance, a bond may be issued in euros (currency), issued by Finland (country), and be a AA-rated security (credit rating).

Performance analysts often view portfolios in terms of hierarchies of classification, starting at broad-brush levels (country) and proceeding through succeeding levels of detail (credit rating, sector) to extremely specific classifications, such as issuer ticker.

The amount invested in each sector is typically referred to as its asset allocation. Asset allocation decisions are a common way to modify a portfolio's exposure against a benchmark, and Chapter 3 shows ways to measure the return such decisions generate.

The overall statement of which security belongs to which sectors is called the portfolio's *classification structure*. Classification structures are often complex and may show information at many levels. A portfolio may use multiple classification structures, depending on the user's reporting requirements.

2.7.2 Sector weights and returns

The weight w_S and return r_S of a sector S over a single time interval are given by

$$w_S = \sum_{i \in S} w_i \tag{2.12}$$

$$r_S = \frac{\sum_{i \in S} w_i r_i}{\sum_{i \in S} w_i} \tag{2.13}$$

2.8 CALCULATING PORTFOLIO RETURNS OVER SUCCESSIVE INTERVALS

While contribution to return in a portfolio aggregates additively, it aggregates geometrically over multiple time intervals.

For instance, suppose a stock shows a return of 10% over one month and 20% over the following month. Using (2.3), the stock's aggregated return R over both months is given by geometric aggregation:

$$R = (1 + 10\%) \times (1 + 20\%) - 1 = 32\%$$

Conversely, suppose a portfolio holds 50% of a stock that returns 10% over a month, and the remaining 50% in another stock that returns -20%. From (2.9), the return of the portfolio R_p over the month is given by additive aggregation:

$$R_p = (50\% \times 10\%) + (50\% \times -20\%) = -5\%$$

The fact that returns combine differently, depending on whether the aggregation is over time or sector, can and does cause difficulties. Chapter 5 describes various ways in which performance managers address this issue.

2.9 FUTURES CASH OFFSETS

In addition to physical cash holdings, many portfolios show large cash balances due to *futures offset holdings* (or *notional cash*). Futures offsets exist because, unlike a physical security, the market exposure of a futures contract is always zero, and this must be taken into account when calculating the portfolio's exposures and risks.[3]

To put this another way, a future is a derivative that promises the same dollar profit and loss of the underlying security, but without the requirement to actually hold the security in the portfolio. If the future is modelled as a security with a non-zero market exposure, an equal but opposite amount to this market exposure should also be held in cash to ensure that the futures holding does not change the overall market value of the portfolio.

Futures offsets are *not* the same as margin, which is cash put up by the owner of the contract and deposited at the futures exchange to cover counterparties against potential losses. The analyst should always remain aware

[3] In this respect, a futures contract is like the Cheshire Cat's grin in *Alice in Wonderland*, which persists even if the cat is not present. The futures contract gives the benefit of the market exposure of a security, without the security being present.

that futures offsets are an accounting convenience rather than an actual asset, and that they should not be combined with actual cash assets.

To see how a futures offset works, consider a portfolio containing a single bond and a single future. The effective exposures, market exposures and returns of both securities are shown in Table 2.1. The market exposure of each security is its actual value (which is zero for futures), and the effective exposure is its value for the purpose of calculating profit and loss.

Table 2.1

Exposures, risks and returns of sample portfolio without cash offsets

Security	Effective exposure	Market value	Rate of return
Bond	$1,000,000	$1,000,000	1%
Future	$1,000,000	$0	2%
TOTAL	$2,000,000	$1,000,000	3%

Consider the return R made by this portfolio. Using the holdings in Table 2.1,

$$R = \frac{\sum_i EE_i \times r_i}{\sum_i MV_i} = \frac{(\$1 \times 1\%) + (\$1 \times 2\%)}{(\$1 + \$0)} = 3\%$$

where MV_i is the market exposure of security i, EE_i its effective exposure and r_i its return.

An alternative approach ignores the fact that the market value of the futures contract is zero. Instead, the future is treated as a bond with the same characteristics, and a *cash offset* with an equal and opposite market exposure to that of the bond is added to the portfolio. In this case we work solely with effective exposures:

Table 2.2

Exposures, risks and returns of sample portfolio with cash offsets

Security	Effective exposure	Rate of return
Bond	$1,000,000	1%
Future	$1,000,000	2%
Cash offset	–$1,000,000	0%
TOTAL	$1,000,000	3%

Using the holdings in Table 2.2, the portfolio's return is now given by the alternative expression

$$R = \frac{\sum_i EE_i \times r_i}{\sum_i EE_i} = \frac{(\$1 \times 1\%) + (\$1 \times 2\%) - (\$1 \times 0\%)}{(\$1 + \$1 - \$1)} = 3\%$$

where EE_i is the effective exposure of security i. The result is identical to the return of the portfolio without cash offsets.

The advantage of using cash offsets to model returns for futures is that no special consideration need be given to the fact that the market exposure of futures contracts is always zero, which simplifies the calculation of returns.

The disadvantage is that the accounting system has to generate extra cash offset transactions that will have various sizes as the market value of the futures position varies. In addition, the cash offsets must always be grouped with the futures holdings so that holdings of physical cash are not incorrectly stated.

Arguably, a better and simpler way to model the zero-exposure feature of futures is to treat them as special types of security with zero market exposure, and to use this market exposure when calculating portfolio return. In this case, no futures offset holdings need ever be used.

For better or worse, futures offsets are now an established feature of many commercial performance systems.

2.10 EDGE CASES

The difficulty in running performance does not usually lie in applying these equations. The main issues tend to be edge cases, such as very highly leveraged portfolios or portfolio valuations that are zero or negative. In addition, there are the perennial workflow problems of bad pricing data, reversed trades and the like.

2.11 EXTERNAL RETURNS

The three sources of return described in the next sections (trading, pricing, swing) are all often shown on performance reports, but do not strictly belong in an attribution report as they are not generated by the interaction between market movements and investment strategies.

2.11.1 Trading return

Trading return measures any additional return made by buying or selling a security at a different rate to the end-of-day revaluation rate.

For instance, suppose that a dealer buys a bond in the middle of the day at 99.50. The price rises over the rest of the day to close at 100.00, which is its revaluation price. In this case he has added

$$r_{dealing} = \frac{100.00 - 99.50}{99.5} = 0.503\%$$

to the subsequent return of the security by buying at a lower price than its official value for that day.

Trading return is generated by the skill, market knowledge and contacts of the trader.

2.11.2 Price return

Price return is generated when the portfolio and benchmark record a different return for the same security over the same interval. It is measured as the difference between the two returns.

A non-zero price return is a frequent occurrence that may arise from:

- portfolio and benchmark prices being sampled at different times of day;
- use of different pricing sources;
- illiquid markets.

If there is a difference between portfolio and benchmark returns, we conventionally regard the benchmark return as definitive and assign the pricing return to the portfolio. However, this need not always be the case.

For instance, an illiquid bond market may not have any trades in a particular security for several days, so the benchmark price must be estimated. Suppose that a security is then traded in the marketplace. Both parties agree on a price, which may be quite different to the theoretical price, which has been determined using factors that may be out of date. In this case, a difference will arise between the portfolio and benchmark return, but the portfolio price is the true one, and any pricing return should be assigned to the benchmark.

2.11.3 Swing return

Some traded funds are valued each day using a net asset value (NAV), which assigns a monetary value to each share. The value is typically a function of the number of shares on issue and the market value of the assets in the fund at the end of the last valuation period. When buying or selling in or out of the fund, the amount paid is typically reckoned in terms of this NAV, rather than the market price of the fund's assets.

If a shareholder in the fund sells out their holdings, transaction costs will be incurred. These costs should be borne by the investor who is selling, rather than by the ongoing investors.

To ensure that shareholders are not penalised by such events, the fund's NAV can be adjusted to compensate for the cost of these transactions:

- Large inflows $\Rightarrow$ price adjusted upwards.
- Large outflows $\Rightarrow$ price adjusted downwards.

The mechanism to compensate for such events is as follows. If net inflows exceed a given percentage of the fund's asset value, the NAV per share will be changed, or swung, by a predetermined amount. The performance impact of swing pricing is typically from 30 to 60 basis points (bp) per year.

The result is that the return calculated from NAV values can differ from the return calculated using mid-rate prices. Any difference between the two should be attributed to swing pricing.

Calculation of swing return requires both the overall return of the fund, which is calculated using market pricing and a history of transactions, and the return calculated from the published NAV.

2.12 BENCHMARKS

A benchmark is a reference portfolio that has its composition and return available to investors and managers, often for a substantial fee.

Benchmarks are usually published by large financial institutions or data vendors, and can vary in size from a few tens of securities to many thousands.

Benchmark holdings are usually set up in terms of the amount of a security on issue. For instance, the FTSE 100 is an index of the 100 companies listed on the LSE (London Stock Exchange) that have the largest market capitalisations.

Some investors also use *composite benchmarks*, which are constructed by combining several benchmarks together in varying proportions to meet a predefined risk objective.

Benchmark data requirements for the equity performance analyst are often straightforward. For a simple comparison of overall return, one only needs a single time series measuring the benchmark's return. Even for a Brinson analysis, only the sector weights and returns are required.

In contrast, a detailed fixed income attribution analysis requires security-level weights and returns for both the portfolio and the benchmark. This vastly increased data requirement is often one of the major costs and causes of difficulty in running attribution.

The situation may be eased if the market reaches agreement on the types of fixed income attribution to be used. In this case, benchmark vendors may decide to publish summary attribution analyses for benchmarks as a supplement to their full holdings. To date no benchmark vendor has made such data available, perhaps because there are as yet no agreed, standardised approaches to calculating quantities such as parallel curve movements.

Benchmarks may also be hedged to reduce foreign exchange exposures while retaining exposures to selected overseas markets. This topic is covered in Chapter 4.

Which benchmark, or combination of benchmarks, to use is conventionally decided when a fund is set up. The selected benchmark should always match the aims and investment strategies of the fund. For instance, if the fund manager has a mandate to invest in small-cap stocks in emerging markets, a blue-chip index would be inappropriate, as the performance of stocks in the latter category is not necessarily a measure of how the former market is performing.

A comprehensive guide to fixed income benchmarks can be found in Brown (1994).

2.13 ACTIVE RETURN

The return that a portfolio generates over and above its benchmark is called its *active return*.

Many managers like to publish their positive active returns, as these are held to be evidence of a superior investment strategy. However, a random investment strategy can also generate positive active returns, so this measure on its own should not be taken as *prima facie* evidence of investment skill. An active return can still be positive even if a portfolio lost money.

2.14 STOCHASTIC ATTRIBUTION

An alternative way of measuring skill shown in running a portfolio is as follows:

- Build the set of all possible portfolios available to the manager.
- Calculate the return of each.
- Form a cumulative returns graph showing the frequency of each return. This will usually have the familiar shape of a normal distribution.
- Observe where the return of the managed portfolio lies on this graph.

If 99% of all portfolios showed return between 0% and 1%, then a return of 2% is clearly exceptional as it is several standard deviations away from a return that might have been generated by chance alone. Conversely, a return of 0.1% is more likely to have been a random occurrence, and is much less indicative of investor skill.

Naturally, it is seldom practical to build every possible portfolio. However, statistical sampling and Monte Carlo simulation can give excellent approximations to the distribution of expected returns.

In practice the main obstacles to this type of attribution are ensuring that the portfolios generated are realistic. For instance, investment compliance rules may place strict limits on the types, amounts and turnover of investments.

A particularly appealing feature of this type of attribution is that it does not require a benchmark.

2.15 LIABILITY-DRIVEN INVESTMENT (LDI)

Many portfolios are managed with the aim of maintaining a stream of cash flows to fund future liabilities. For instance, a pension fund will forecast the regular payments required to its members over the remainder of their expected lifetimes. In this case the portfolio's benchmark can be regarded as a portfolio of future payment streams.

In contrast to managing a portfolio against a benchmark, where the aim is to outperform, LDI aims to minimise risks by matching the portfolio's future cash flows to its liabilities as closely as possible.

For cases in which cash flows are known precisely, fixed income securities such as bonds (which pay known cash flows) may be used for matching liabilities. In other cases the manager may prefer to use over-the-counter (OTC) instruments such as inflation-linked swaps, which can be precisely tailored to the fund's liability requirements.

Attribution analysis is particularly useful for LDI, as it provides detailed insight into how well the portfolio of assets matched its liabilities over varying market conditions.

3

Equity attribution

3.1 Introduction
3.2 Brinson attribution
3.3 Single-level Brinson attribution
3.4 Multiple-level asset allocation
3.5 Off-benchmark securities
3.6 Successive portfolio attribution
3.7 Security-level attribution

3.1 INTRODUCTION

This chapter describes the basic concepts required to understand and run *market value attribution*, in which the excess returns made by a portfolio against its benchmark are decomposed into returns generated by asset allocation and stock selection decisions.

The most commonly used algorithms used in this area are associated with Gary Brinson, who was first author on two widely cited papers on applying the technique to portfolios of equities (Brinson and Fachler, 1985; Brinson et al., 1986). For this reason, they are often collectively labelled as *Brinson* attribution.

Brinson attribution is typically used to analyse returns of equity portfolios, but it can be applied to other security types. For instance, in a fixed income portfolio one might firstly use Brinson attribution to calculate how much return was made by the decision to allocate capital by country, and then to use fixed income attribution techniques to decompose returns from each country.[1] For this reason the more general term *market weight attribution* is probably preferable to *Brinson attribution*, although the latter term remains in common use.

The Brinson approach ignores all types of risk apart from market exposure, and its indiscriminate use can be highly misleading in a fixed income context, where there may be numerous other sources of risk in play. With this caveat, it remains one of the most widely used tools in portfolio attribution.

3.2 BRINSON ATTRIBUTION

3.2.1 Asset allocation

The first type of return measured by Brinson attribution is value added by overweighting some sectors and underweighting others. This process is called *asset allocation*, or just *allocation*. The process may be repeated at finer and finer levels of detail until the investor no longer has a view, at which point individual stocks are selected within each sector.

For instance, if one believes that the returns for German equities will be better than those for the global equity market, then it makes sense to overweight one's exposure to Germany by placing a larger proportion of one's assets in German securities than lie in the benchmark. Should Germany's stock market then outperform global equities, this overweighting

[1] See Chapter 13.

will cause that part of the portfolio to outperform the German sector in the benchmark.[2]

The 'overweight Germany' decision can be refined further by looking at individual German sectors, such as industry or security type, and making asset allocation decisions for them as well. These decisions are separate to the country allocation decision and contribute additional return.

3.2.2 Sector classification

Brinson analysis requires that every security be assigned to one or more *sectors*. Examples of commonly used sectors are *country*, *industry* and *security type*.

The choice of an appropriate sector classification scheme is subjective and defined by the user, but should always reflect the terms in which investment decisions were made.

Consider a manager who decides to use a country classification scheme and to overweight US equities and underweight UK equities. There is little point in basing a subsequent analysis on a different classification scheme, such as market capitalisation sectors, because the portfolio's investment decisions were not made in those terms. Here, the report will not convey any additional insight into the investment process.

- If the sector was overweight against benchmark, and the sector return was positive, then the asset allocation decision added value.
- Less obviously, if the sector was underweight against benchmark, and the sector return was negative, then the underweighting decision also added value, because this part of the portfolio has not gone down in value as much as the benchmark. Although the sector has decreased in value for both portfolio and benchmark, the portfolio sector has not decreased as much as the benchmark, and so value has still been added.
- Conversely, overweighting a sector with negative return, or underweighting a sector with positive return, will subtract value.

In practice, asset allocation decisions tend only to be made at broader sector levels, since the manager may not hold views on the relative strengths of competing sectors at finer levels of detail. Macroeconomic forecasts may suggest overweighting Eurozone countries, but will have little to say about whether to favour (for instance) telecoms stocks over airlines within the Eurozone.

[2] This ignores any return gained or lost from exchange rate movements. Such currency returns are covered in Chapter 4.

3.2.3 Stock selection

Asset allocation decisions are not the only source of return in a managed portfolio. Once the manager has made their allocation decisions, the investment process changes to choosing individual stocks, with the constraint that the total market value of the stocks held in each sector must be determined by the asset allocation decision for that sector. The return made by picking individual stocks within each sector is called *stock selection return.*[3]

Stock selection and asset allocation form two entirely different types of return. Asset allocation forms a continuous, constrained set of decisions, while stock selection is a binary, yes/no decision.

Asset allocation and stock selection decisions are often made by different groups of people within the same investment firm, with each group exercising different skill sets. As a result, it is quite possible for a fund to make a good decision when selecting sectors, but a bad decision in terms of which stocks were actually held within the sector. In this case, the attribution report will show a positive asset allocation return and a negative stock selection return for that sector.

Conventionally, asset allocation return is only measured at the sector level, but stock selection return may be attributed down to the individual security level. For an in-depth discussion of this point, see Section 3.7.

Asset allocation decisions continue to be made within each sector, for the manager must still choose the relative proportions of the stocks held. In fact, stock selection return is just a particular form of aggregated asset allocation return. It measures the return of all asset allocation decisions below the level of the individual sector.

3.2.4 Bottom-up attribution

Managing stocks in this way is only one of many ways to run a portfolio. Many private investors allow their portfolio to build up a collection of individual investments over time, without necessarily holding any formal view on which sectors have the best prospects.

Funds managed in this way use a *bottom-up* investment process. Here, the manager concentrates solely on the characteristics of individual stocks, rather than on any global sector outlook. Implicit asset allocation decisions are being made, but they arise as a side effect of how much of each stock has been purchased.

---

[3] In principle, one could define sectors at such a level of detail that each one had one or zero stocks in them. All returns would then be due to asset allocation decisions, and no return would be due to stock selection decisions at all. In practice, this is most unlikely to happen, since most managers do not have a sufficiently detailed view of the markets to support such an investment process.

In this case, a Brinson analysis is inappropriate as it does not match the underlying investment process. The manager is better served by reporting on the performance contributions from each stock, which will sum to the overall performance of the portfolio.

3.2.5 Top-down and bottom-up attribution

Brinson attribution is best suited to measuring return from a *top-down* investment process, in which initial investment decisions are made in terms of entire market sectors, followed by later decisions on individual stocks.

In contrast, a *bottom-up* investment process makes investment decisions in terms of individual securities, without regard to any broader allocation implications.

In practice, most investment decisions are both top-down and bottom-up to varying degrees, although this is not always recognised or acknowledged.

3.2.6 Hedging against Brinson risks

To see how the results of a Brinson attribution analysis can be fed back into the investment process, consider the following cases:

1. *A portfolio consistently shows negative asset allocation returns and positive stock selection returns.*

   Here, the manager's strength lies in stock selection, and the result suggests that overall returns will be boosted by taking a neutral asset allocation position.

   This is relatively straightforward, and is simply a matter of ensuring that the market weights of the various sectors in the portfolio are identical to those in the benchmark, so that no over- or underweighting is occurring.

2. *A portfolio consistently shows positive asset allocation returns and negative stock selection returns.*

   In this case, returns can be increased by continuing to make asset allocation decisions, but taking neutral stock selection decisions.

   One way to do this is to invest in exactly the same securities in each sector that lie in the benchmark, in the same relative proportions. This may be difficult if the benchmark is composed of thousands of stocks or contains many small or illiquid issues. It may be easier to set up a replicating portfolio for each sector that generates the same return as the benchmark sector, but with fewer stocks. In either case, the aim is for the portfolio sector to show exactly the same return as the benchmark sector, and to allow their relative weights to vary.

3.3 SINGLE-LEVEL BRINSON ATTRIBUTION

This section deals with Brinson attribution when only one level of asset allocation decision is made. For cases where more than one level is active, see Section 3.4.

The most common versions of the Brinson attribution algorithm are the Brinson-Fachler algorithm (Brinson and Fachler, 1985) and the Brinson-Hood-Beebower algorithm (Brinson et al., 1986). Both are often encountered, so it is useful to have an appreciation of how they work.

3.3.1 The Brinson-Fachler model

Consider a portfolio where the manager makes a single asset allocation decision in terms of allocations to sectors. The asset allocation and stock selection returns r_S^{AA} and r_S^{SS} generated by sector S are given by

$$r_S^{AA} = (w_S^P - w_S^B)(r_S^B - r^B) \tag{3.1}$$

$$r_S^{SS} = (r_S^P - r_S^B)w_S^B \tag{3.2}$$

where w_S^P and w_S^B are the weight of the sector in the portfolio and the benchmark, $r_S^P$and r_S^B are the returns of the sector in the portfolio and benchmark, and r^B is the overall return of the benchmark. The sector weights and returns are given by

$$w_S^P = \sum_{i \in S} w_i^P \tag{3.3}$$

$$w_S^B = \sum_{i \in S} w_i^B \tag{3.4}$$

$$r_S^P = \frac{\sum_{i \in S} w_i^P r_i}{\sum_{i \in S} w_i^P} \tag{3.5}$$

$$r_S^B = \frac{\sum_{i \in S} w_i^B r_i}{\sum_{i \in S} w_i^B} \tag{3.6}$$

and the benchmark return by

$$r^B = \sum_{i \in B} w_i^B r_i \tag{3.7}$$

where the sums are over individual securities in sector S.

Equations (3.1) and (3.2) may be interpreted as follows:

- The first term in (3.1) is the active weight of the sector. If the relative weight of sector S is the same in portfolio and benchmark, there is no active allocation position and no allocation return will be made.
- The second term in (3.1) measures the amount by which sector S outperforms the benchmark as a whole. Here the return of the benchmark sector is used, as this is outside the control of the investor, and acts as a reference return.
- The first term in (3.2) is the active return of the sector. If the portfolio sector shows a higher return than the benchmark, this term is positive.
- The second term in (3.2) is the weight of the sector in the benchmark. The inclusion of this term allows the active return made from stock selection decisions to be weighted by the exposure of the sector in the benchmark. Again, we use the benchmark sector weight as a reference.

Each of these expressions measures the effect of a single type of investment decision. Equation (3.1) measures the effect of the portfolio sector having different weights to the benchmark, while (3.2) measures the effect of the portfolio sector having a different return to the benchmark.

3.3.2 The Brinson-Hood-Beebower model

The Brinson-Hood-Beebower model is similar to the Brinson-Fachler model, except that the asset allocation term is slightly different. Here, the asset allocation term (3.1) becomes

$$r_S^{AA} = (w_S^P - w_S^B)r_S^B \tag{3.8}$$

From the user's perspective, the only difference between the two models is that the sector-level asset allocation returns are different. Both models give the same total asset allocation return. To see why, note that the asset allocation term from the Brinson-Fachler model can be rearranged as follows:

$$r^{AA} = \sum_S (w_S^P - w_S^B)(r_S^B - r^B) \tag{3.9}$$

$$= \sum_S (w_S^P - w_S^B)r_S^B + \left(\sum_S w_S^P - \sum_S w_S^B\right)r^B \tag{3.10}$$

Since

$$\sum_S w_S^P = \sum_S w_S^B = 1 \tag{3.11}$$

the second term in (3.10) is zero, giving the result

$$r^{AA} = \sum_S (w_S^P - w_S^B)(r_S^B - r^B) = \sum_S (w_S^P - w_S^B) r_S^B \qquad (3.12)$$

In other words, the asset allocation terms in the Brinson-Hood-Beebower and the Brinson-Fachler models always sum to the same return, even though the individual sector returns may be different.

The Brinson-Hood-Beebower model provides less intuitive results than does the Brinson-Fachler approach. For instance, using the data in Table 3.1, Laker (2003) shows that the Brinson-Hood-Beebower expression (3.8) results in a contribution to asset allocation from Germany of (80% − 60%) × 1.0% = 0.20%, which is positive. This is clearly incorrect because the decision to overweight Germany lost value; the portfolio was overweight a sector that performed below the benchmark. A better solution is to use equation (3.1), which includes the effect of relative return against benchmark, and so provides results that are more in line with expectations.

Table 3.1

Sector weights and durations

Country	w^P	w^B	r^P	r^B
Germany	80%	60%	2.25%	1.0%
France	20%	40%	6.0%	9.0%
TOTAL	100.0%	100.0%	3.0%	4.2%

3.3.3 Interaction

The main flaw of the Brinson-Fachler and Brinson-Hood-Beebower attribution algorithms is that they do not account for all the active return α generated by a portfolio against its benchmark, given by

$$\alpha = R_P - R_B - \sum_{S \in P} w_S^P r_S^P - \sum_{S \in B} w_S^B r_S^B \qquad (3.13)$$

where R_P, w_S^P, r_S^P are the overall return, weight of sector S, and return of sector S in the portfolio, with benchmark quantities defined similarly.

Any unaccounted-for return δ is given by the portfolio return, minus the asset allocation return, the stock selection return and the benchmark return:

$$\begin{aligned} \delta &= \sum w_S^P r_S^P - \left[\sum w_S^B r_S^B + \sum (w_S^P - w_S^B) r_S^B + \sum (r_S^P - r_S^B) w_S^B\right] \\ &= \sum (w_S^P r_S^P - w_S^B r_S^B + w_S^P r_S^B - w_S^B r_S^B + r_S^P w_S^B - r_S^B w_S^B) \\ &= \sum (w_S^P - w_S^B)(r_S^P - r_S^B) \end{aligned} \qquad (3.14)$$

The quantity δ is called the *interaction* return, given on a sector basis by

$$r_S^{interaction} = (w_S^P - w_S^B)(r_S^P - r_S^B) \tag{3.15}$$

and the active return α_s of each sector is then the sum of the asset allocation, the stock selection and the interaction returns:

$$\alpha_S = r_S^P - r_S^B = r_S^{AA} + r_S^{SS} + r_S^{interaction} \tag{3.16}$$

Interaction can be seen as a cross term, generated by the product of the active return and the active weight. If both are small, then the interaction will be correspondingly smaller.

The value of interaction, and what it actually measures, remains a topic of active debate. Bacon (2008) observes that

> **Interaction is not part of the investment decision process; you are unlikely to identify in any asset management firm individuals responsible for adding value through interaction.**

Many managers, having calculated their asset allocation return, take a pragmatic view and regard whatever is left over (including interaction) as stock selection return. Combining stock selection and interaction into one term gives

$$\begin{aligned} r_S^{SS} &= w_S^B(r_S^P - r_S^B) + (w_S^B - w_S^B)(r_S^P - r_S^B) \\ &= w_S^P(r_S^P - r_S^B) \end{aligned} \tag{3.17}$$

This is equation (3.2) with the critical difference that benchmark weights have been replaced with portfolio weights. With this minor change, the sum of these new stock selection returns and the existing asset allocation returns equals the overall active return.[4]

It is a matter of preference, and the expectations of your clients, whether to show interaction return in a separate category. If one prefers to hide interaction, then combining it with stock selection is probably the best way to do it. The alternative is to distribute interaction return across all other returns on a pro-rata basis, for which there is no theoretical justification.

For simplicity, we use equation (3.17) to calculate stock selection for the remainder of the chapter. However, the reader should be aware of the role interaction can play in active returns, particularly when active weights and returns are large.

Colin (2005) presents a market allocation approach based on the construction of an intermediate portfolio P' composed of only the stocks in the

[4] This expression also arises naturally out of the successive-portfolio approach, as shown in Section 3.6.1.

portfolio, but with the same relative holdings that they have in the benchmark. This is similar to the construction of a semi-notional portfolio in the Brinson framework, but at the security level instead of the sector level. The result does not generate any interaction returns and does not require a sector scheme, so it may be seen as an extension of the asset allocation model.

To illustrate the meaning and impact of the various terms in equations (3.1) and (3.17), consider the following example.

Sample Brinson-Fachler calculation

Table 3.2 shows weights and returns for US and Japanese equities and bonds in a sample portfolio and benchmark. The portfolio has outperformed the benchmark by 5.825% − 5.725% = 0.1%.

Table 3.2

Country and asset type weights and returns

Country	Asset type	w^P	r^P	w^B	r^B
US	Equities	17.0%	5.0%	15.0%	7.5%
	Bonds	39.5%	10.0%	40.0%	9.5%
Japan	Equities	12.5%	2.0%	10.0%	1.0%
	Bonds	31.0%	2.5%	35.0%	2.0%
TOTAL		100.0%	5.825%	100.0%	5.725%

To run a country-level Brinson-Fachler analysis, we first calculate country weights and returns, using equations (3.3)–(3.7).

Asset allocation return is then calculated using equation (3.1). The asset allocation return made by overweighting the US was

$$r_{US}^{AA} = (56.5\% - 55.0\%) \times (8.9545\% - 5.725\%) = 0.0484\%$$

The asset allocation return made by underweighting Japan is shown in Table 3.3:

Table 3.3

Country weights and returns

Country	w_S^P	r_S^P	w_S^B	r_S^B
US	56.5%	8.4956%	55.0%	8.9545%
Japan	43.5%	2.3563%	45.0%	1.7778%
TOTAL	100.0%	5.825%	100.0%	5.725%

$$r_{Japan}^{AA} = (43.5\% - 45.0\%) \times (1.7778\% - 5.725\%) = 0.0592\%$$

US securities were overweighted and overperformed the benchmark, while Japanese securities underperformed but were underweighted, so both sectors added value relative to benchmark. The total return contribution from asset allocation at the country level was 0.0484% + 0.0592% = 0.1077%.

Stock selection return is finally calculated using equation (3.17). The return made by picking US stocks was

$$r_{US}^{SS} = 56.5\% \times (8.4956\% - 8.9545\%) = -0.2593\%$$

and the return made by picking Japanese stocks was

$$r_{Japan}^{SS} = 43.5\% \times (2.3563\% - 1.7778\%) = 0.2516\%$$

The total return due to stock selection at the country level was −0.2593% + 0.2516% = −0.0076%. The total active return (asset allocation plus stock selection) is 0.1077% − 0.0076% = 0.10%. As expected, this is the difference between the portfolio and benchmark returns.

Sample Brinson-Hood-Beebower calculation

To run a country-level Brinson-Hood-Beebower analysis on the same portfolio and benchmark, the asset allocation returns are calculated using equation (3.8) instead of (3.1). With this approach, return made by overweighting the US was

$$r_{US}^{AA} = (56.5\% - 55.0\%) \times 8.9546\% = 0.1343\%$$

and return made by underweighting Japan was

$$r_{Japan}^{AA} = (43.5\% - 45.0\%) \times 1.7778\% = -0.0267\%$$

The total asset allocation return was 0.1343% − 0.0267% = 0.1077%. The individual sector-level allocation returns are different from those calculated using a Brinson-Fachler approach, but their sum is the same. Stock selection returns are calculated in the same way as for the Brinson-Fachler model, combined with interaction return if required.

3.4 MULTIPLE-LEVEL ASSET ALLOCATION

Consider a portfolio that is managed as follows:

- First, the fund's senior managers make a global decision on what proportion of the fund's capital should be invested in the US, and what proportion in Japan. The fund only invests in these two countries.
- For each country, a sub-committee then makes a range of separate asset allocation decisions about the relative exposures to be taken to bonds and equities within each country.
- At the last stage of the investment process, the individual fund managers decide which securities to buy within the constraints imposed by these two sets of decisions.

Here, the managers are following a top-down investment process with *two* levels of asset allocation decision, rather than the one level presented in the previous section. Both the country allocation and the security type allocation decision can add or subtract value, as well as the stock selection decision.

Many levels of asset allocation decision may be involved in managing larger portfolios. This section describes how to extend the Brinson framework to measure the returns made at multiple decision levels.

The weights and returns of the sectors in a sample portfolio and benchmark are as shown in Table 3.4, which is the same portfolio used earlier to illustrate single-level attribution. Over the calculation period, the portfolio outperforms by 10 basis points.

Security weights and returns

Table 3.4

Sector 1	Sector 2	w^P	r^P	w^B	r^B
US	Equities	17.0%	5.0%	15.0%	7.5%
	Bonds	39.5%	10.0%	40.0%	9.5%
Japan	Equities	12.5%	2.0%	10.0%	1.0%
	Bonds	31.0%	2.5%	35.0%	2.0%
TOTAL		100.0%	5.825%	100.0%	5.725%

3.4.1 Calculating single-level asset allocation returns

The simplest way to run asset allocation attribution is to assume that all allocation decisions were taken together. In this example the manager had four sectors in which to invest: US equities, US bonds, Japanese equities and Japanese bonds.

Asset allocation return is given by the standard Brinson expression

$$r_S^{AA} = (w_S^P - w_S^B)(r_S^B - r^B) \tag{3.18}$$

where the terms have the same meaning as before.

Using the weights and returns in Table 3.4, the total return r^{AA} from asset allocation is

$$\begin{aligned} r^{AA} &= (15.0\% - 15.0\%) \times (7.5\% - 5.725\%) \\ &+ (39.5\% - 40.0\%) \times (9.5\% - 5.725\%) \\ &+ (12.5\% - 10.0\%) \times (1.0\% - 5.725\%) \\ &+ (31.0\% - 35.0\%) \times (2.0\% - 5.725\%) \\ &= 0.04750\% \end{aligned}$$

However we decompose these returns, the total asset allocation return should always equal this figure.

3.4.2 Calculating multiple-level asset allocation returns

In many cases, asset allocation decisions are made at terms of successive levels of detail. In the following example, the decision is made first at the country level and then at the security type level.

The effects of the upper-level decisions constrain lower-level actions. For instance, if 60% of the portfolio's capital is initially assigned to the US, it is not possible to assign 80% to US bonds at a later stage of the investment process.

3.4.3 Top-level asset allocation returns

The first step in calculating multi-level asset allocation return is to run a standard Brinson analysis using weights and returns from the top-level sector. In this case, the top-level sector is *country*, so the appropriate asset allocation returns are as calculated in the earlier section.

3.4.4 Lower-level asset allocation returns

The next step is to calculate the asset allocation returns by security type. This is a little more involved. We cannot simply repeat the process in the previous step using weights and returns aggregated over each security type, because the weights of each security in the managed portfolio result from *two* asset allocation decisions, not one: the country allocation and the security type allocation. To measure the return added by security type allocation, we have to isolate the portion made by country allocation, and ensure it is not included in the result.

To achieve this result requires a simple trick. The benchmark is temporarily reweighted so that, *at the country level*, it becomes identical to the portfolio. With this adjustment in place, there is no country overweighting or underweighting in play. Returns from country allocation will be zero, so any remaining asset allocation returns will be due to industry allocation.

More specifically, the weight of each security in the benchmark is adjusted so that when aggregated at the country level:

- the weight of each country in the benchmark is adjusted to match the weight of each country in the portfolio;
- the relative weights of securities remain unchanged within each country sector.

In the earlier example, US securities have an overall weight of 56.5% in the portfolio, but 55.0% in the benchmark. To remove the effect of this US overweighting, the benchmark weight of US securities is increased to 56.5% as well, ensuring that the weight of US securities in portfolio and benchmark become the same.

This is easily accomplished by multiplying the benchmark weight of all US securities by 56.5% ÷ 55.0%, but leaving the portfolio weights unchanged. The sum of the adjusted weights of the US securities in the benchmark now equals 56.5%, as required, but their relative proportions within the US remain the same.

Similarly, the benchmark weight of all Japanese equities is multiplied by 43.5% ÷ 45.0%.

These new, rescaled weights can be used to give the returns due to the second-level asset allocation decision. In this example, the new benchmark sector weights $\widetilde{w}_S^B$ are assigned the values shown in Table 3.5.

Table 3.5

Adjusted portfolio weights

Sector 1	Sector 2	$\widetilde{w}_S^B$
US	Equities	$15.0\% \times \frac{56.5\%}{55.0\%} = 15.41\%$
	Bonds	$40.0\% \times \frac{56.5\%}{55.0\%} = 41.09\%$
Japan	Equities	$10.0\% \times \frac{43.5\%}{45.0\%} = 9.67\%$
	Bonds	$31.0\% \times \frac{43.5\%}{45.0\%} = 33.83\%$

Note that the weight of US securities in the benchmark has now changed from 15.0% + 40.0% = 55.0% to 15.41% + 41.09% = 56.50%, which equals the portfolio's exposure to this asset class. However, the relative exposures of equities versus bonds within each sector remain unchanged, since the weights of both types of security have been adjusted by the same amount.

Asset allocation at the security type level now proceeds as before, but at the sector level. The asset allocation return for each sector is given by

$$r_i^{AA} = (w_i^P - \widetilde{w}_S^B)(r_i^P - r_S^B) \tag{3.19}$$

where r_S is the benchmark sector return, rather than the overall benchmark return, and $\widetilde{w}_S^B$ is the rescaled benchmark weight.

- The sector-level asset allocation return for US equities is (17.0% − 15.41%) × (7.5% − 8.9545%) = −0.0231%.
- The sector-level asset allocation return for US bonds is (39.5% − 41.09%) × (9.5% − 8.9545%) = −0.0087%.
- The sector-level asset allocation return for Japanese equities is (12.50% − 9.67%) × (1.0% − 1.7778%) = −0.0220%.
- The sector-level asset allocation return for Japanese bonds is (31.0% − 33.83%) × (2.0% − 1.7778%) = −0.0063%.

At this level, asset allocation return was negative for all asset types, since the managers either overweighted underperforming sectors or underweighted overperforming sectors against the corresponding benchmark sectors. The total asset allocation return from the lower-level decisions was −0.0231% − 0.0087% − 0.0220% − 0.0063% = −0.0602%.

The overall asset allocation return from decisions at both levels was 0.06020% + 0.04750% = 0.1077%, which gives the same result as for the single-level asset allocation calculation.

3.4.5 Stock selection returns for multi-level calculations

We have now calculated the asset allocation return at both country and security type levels. The only remaining return is due to stock selection and interaction returns, which we combine for simplicity, using equation (3.17) as before. The final results are shown in Table 3.6, where:

- r_1^{AA} are the asset allocation returns made at sector level 1 (country);
- r_2^{AA} are the asset allocation returns made at sector level 2 (security type);
- r^{SS} are the stock selection returns.

The sum of the attribution returns is the active return of 10 basis points, as expected.

Table 3.6 **Results of multi-level attribution**

Sector 1	Sector 2	r_1^{AA}	r_2^{AA}	r^{SS}	Total
US	Equities	0.0484%	−0.0231%	−0.4250%	−0.3997%
	Bonds		−0.0087%	0.1975%	0.1888%
Japan	Equities	0.0592%	−0.0220%	0.1250%	0.1622%
	Bonds		−0.0063%	0.1550%	0.1487%
TOTAL		0.1077%	−0.0602%	0.0525%	0.1000%

The same principle applies if more than two levels of asset allocation are required, or when different parts of the portfolio are managed to different depths. Suppose that no further asset allocation decisions are made for equities, but that a further subdivision is made within bonds so that an allocation between government and corporate bonds also forms part of the investment decision. In this case, the returns from asset allocation decisions are measured at the country and security type levels for equities, but at the country, security type and government/corporate allocation levels for bonds.

3.5 OFF-BENCHMARK SECURITIES

A common point of contention is the treatment of securities that are present in the portfolio but not in the benchmark. Should the return contribution of such securities be assigned to stock selection or to asset allocation? The arguments run along the following lines:

- The use of this off-benchmark stock implies that the investor wanted to invest in a sector that was not present in the benchmark. Therefore, this was an asset allocation decision.
- The investor chose this particular stock over all others. Therefore, this was a stock selection decision.

Opinions vary, and it may be necessary to assign the return of off-benchmark stocks to either category depending on the views of your audience.

3.5.1 Order dependence of asset allocation variables

For portfolios that are managed at two or more levels, the order in which asset allocation investment decisions are taken will affect the return at each level, even though the sum of the returns will be the same. This can become an important point to stress when explaining results to managers who may not have a rigorously defined investment process, particularly if it is not possible to say which of two sectors took precedence in their investment process.

If the user prefers not to make arbitrary assumptions about the order in which asset allocation decisions were taken, one approach is to consider all sectors at the same time. For instance, if the country sectors are $\{US, Japan\}$ and the industry sectors are {Finance, Industrials}, then the sectors to use for attribution are $\{US \mid Finance, US \mid Industrials, Japan \mid Finance, Japan \mid Industrials\}$. Asset allocation can then be carried out on this one-level sector definition, leaving the user free to aggregate and group the results as required.

3.6 SUCCESSIVE PORTFOLIO ATTRIBUTION

A commonly encountered idea in attribution is the idea of *successive portfolios*.

Starting with the benchmark, a number of successive notional portfolios are constructed with each applying the cumulative change from a different source of risk. The process is continued until all sources of risk have been included and the exposures of the benchmark has become those of the portfolio, at which point attribution stops. The differences in price between these intermediate portfolios are then used to calculate the returns due to the various risks.

The idea of moving from benchmark to portfolio via a series of successive portfolios, with each risk measured by the difference in performance between one portfolio and the next, is elegant and appealing. However, it does make the analysis path-dependent, in that the returns may depend on the order in which the interim portfolios were constructed.

The successive portfolio approach may also be used for fixed income attribution, where there are many more sources of risk.

3.6.1 Brinson attribution as an example of successive portfolio attribution

The best-known successive portfolio algorithm is the Brinson model, although it is not always identified as such.

Start with the benchmark, whose return r^B is given by

$$r^B = \sum_{i \in B} w_i^B r_i^B \tag{3.20}$$

Construct a new intermediate portfolio I made up of a set of sectors that have the portfolio's weights but the benchmark's returns. The difference between the return of this portfolio and the benchmark is generated by the weightings in the portfolio being different to those in the benchmark; in other words, to asset allocation.

The return r^I of this portfolio is given by

$$r^I = \sum_{i \in B} w_i^P r_i^B \tag{3.21}$$

so the return due to asset allocation is given by

$$r^{AA} = r^I - r^B = \sum_{i \in B} (w_i^P - w_i^B) r_i^B \tag{3.22}$$

Next, construct a new portfolio with the same weights as this notional portfolio, but the same returns as the portfolio. This time, the difference between the two portfolios is generated by the returns of each sector in the portfolio being different to those from the benchmark. Different returns arise from picking different stocks, so this is called stock selection return and is given by

$$r^{SS} = r^P - r^I = \sum_{i} (r_i^P - r_i^B) w_i^P \tag{3.23}$$

The new notional portfolio is now the same as the managed portfolio, since at the sector level its weights and returns are identical. Therefore, attribution can stop at this point. The sum of the two attribution effects $R_{SS} + R_{AA}$ is the total active return, as expected.

Note that (3.23) is just the same as (3.17), which is the sum of the theoretical stock selection and interaction terms. This is another justification for combining stock selection and interaction returns into one term.

3.7 SECURITY-LEVEL ATTRIBUTION

The conventional view of asset allocation returns is that they have no meaning at security level. Unlike stock selection, asset allocation is a macro-level decision that is made at sector level within a managed portfolio, so asset allocation returns should only be reported at the corresponding sector level.

While this is certainly true, it is often convenient to calculate asset allocation returns in terms of their contribution at security level, and then to aggregate the results to the sector level for reporting purposes. This allows the same data structures to be used to model both stock selection and multiple levels of asset allocation return, which can result in a considerable saving of time and effort.

This section shows how to calculate both asset allocation and stock selection returns at security level, so that they aggregate to the correct values at sector and portfolio levels. Once sector-level allocation returns have been calculated, the underlying security-level allocation returns need not be displayed.

Finally, we cover the corrections required to calculate multiple-level asset allocation correctly at the level of the individual security.

3.7.1 The Brinson model at the sector level

Recall that the standard Brinson approach to market weight attribution is to calculate asset allocation returns at the sector level as follows:

$$r_S^{AA} = (w_S^P - w_S^B)(r_S^B - r^B) \tag{3.24}$$

where the terms have the same meaning as for (3.1).

3.7.2 The Brinson model at the security level

Brinson-style attribution may be calculated at the security level using the following set of equations:

$$r_i^{AA} = (w_i^P - w_i^B)(r_S^B - r^B) \tag{3.25}$$

$$r_i^{SS} = w_S^B\left[\frac{w_i^P}{w_S^P} - \frac{w_i^B}{w_S^B}\right](r_i - r_S^B) \tag{3.26}$$

$$r_i^{INT} = (w_i^P - w_i^B)(r_i - r_S^B) \tag{3.27}$$

where, for security i and its sector S:

- r_i^{AA} is the return due to asset allocation;
- r_i^{SS} is the return due to stock selection;
- r_i^{INT} is the return due to interaction;
- w_i^P and w_i^B are the weights of the security in portfolio and benchmark, respectively;
- w_S^P and w_S^B are the weights of the sector in portfolio and benchmark, respectively;
- r_i is the return of the security;
- r^B is the return of the benchmark;
- r_S^B is the return of sector S in the benchmark.

If these security-level returns are aggregated by sector, the results will be identical to an analysis that calculates sector weights and returns first and uses the standard Brinson analysis.

3.7.3 Combined security-level stock selection and interaction terms

If a separate interaction term is not required, it may be combined with the security-level stock selection term as follows:

$$r_i^{AA} = (w_i^P - w_i^B)(r_S^B - r^B) \tag{3.28}$$

$$r_i^{SS} = (w_i^P - w_i^B)(r_i - r_S^B) \tag{3.29}$$

where r_i^{SS} is now the sum of the returns from equations (3.26) and (3.27). We use this contraction of stock selection and interaction into a single term throughout the remainder of the chapter, but the reader should note that stock selection returns can always be decomposed further as shown above.

3.7.4 Multiple levels of asset allocation at the security level

Asset allocation can be performed over several levels, using the sectors defined at each level. For instance, one might manage a portfolio by first making allocation decisions by *country*, and then by *industry*. In this case the sector for level 1 is *country*, and the sector for level 2 is *industry*.

The contribution to asset allocation return by security i at each level is defined recursively by

$$r_i^{AA} = \left(w_i^P - w_i^B\left[\frac{w_S^{'P}}{w_S^{'B}}\right]\right)(r_S^B - r_S^{'B}) \tag{3.30}$$

where w_i^P and w_i^B are the weights of security i in portfolio and benchmark, r_S^B is the return of the benchmark sector to which security i belongs, and r'^B_S, w'^P_S and w'^B_S are the returns and weights of the higher-level sector to which S belongs. For instance, in Table 3.7 security A belongs to sector *Telecoms*, which belongs in turn to country *UK*.

Table 3.7

Simple multi-level security classification

Country	Industry	Security
UK	Telecoms	A
UK	Finance	B
US	Telecoms	C

The term in square brackets in (3.30) is a correction to remove the effect of upper-level asset allocation decisions. If this correction factor is omitted, the summed asset allocation returns will still be correct, but the individual returns will be incorrect.

The correction factor is 1 at the first level of an attribution hierarchy. Equivalently, the summed upper-level weights are identical (100% for portfolio and benchmark), so no correction is applied at the uppermost level. This is as expected, since there is no need to remove the effect of previous allocation decisions.

There are as many asset allocation terms as there are asset allocation variables. For instance, an analysis that uses country and industry as allocation variables will generate two asset allocation returns for each security.

The combined selection and interaction term r_i^{SS} is given by

$$r_i^{SS} = (w_i^P - w_i^B)(r_i^P - r_S^B) \tag{3.31}$$

where the terms have the same meaning as above, and r_i is the return of security i. There is only one stock selection return for each security, irrespective of the number of asset allocation decisions taken.

4

Currency attribution

4.1 Introduction

4.2 Currency attribution returns

4.3 Performance and attribution on unhedged portfolios

4.4 Attribution on an unhedged portfolio

4.5 Portfolio hedging

4.6 Currency forwards

4.7 Hedging and risk

4.8 Naïve attribution on a hedged portfolio

4.9 Measuring hedge returns

4.10 Brinson attribution on a hedged portfolio

4.11 Problems with the Brinson approach when hedging is active

4.12 Calculating base and return premiums

4.13 The Karnosky-Singer attribution model

4.14 Running Karnosky-Singer attribution on an unhedged portfolio

4.1 INTRODUCTION

Any portfolio with holdings in overseas assets is subject to exchange rate risk. Since most exchange rates fluctuate constantly, such changes may make a substantial contribution to performance, depending on the amounts of overseas assets held and the volatility of the foreign exchange (FX) markets.

This chapter is about ways to measure exchange rate return, the assignment of returns to risks taken and the complications involved when one hedges foreign exchange positions to modify the portfolio's risk profile.

In previous chapters I introduced the idea of a sector. In this chapter, the only sector used is *country* or *currency*.

4.2 CURRENCY ATTRIBUTION RETURNS

So far, I have talked about the return of a security or a portfolio as a single quantity. When currency exposures are active, there are two types of return to consider instead of one:

- *Local currency return*: the return of an asset expressed in the home, or local, currency of the asset. All returns described so far are local currency returns.
- *Base currency return*: the return of an asset expressed in the base, or denominating, currency of the portfolio. For instance, if an asset is denominated in GBP but the portfolio in which it is held is denominated in USD, then it will have two measures of return: a local currency GBP return and a base currency USD return.[1]

Assuming continuous compounding, the base currency return r_{BASE} of an asset is given by

$$r_{BASE} = r_{LOCAL} + r_{FX} \tag{4.1}$$

where r_{LOCAL} is its local currency return, and r_{FX} is the foreign exchange return due to changes in the exchange rate between the local and base currencies.

For example, suppose that you have US dollars to invest. Your research tells you that over the coming year the prospects for the Indonesian stock market are particularly good, but there is a significant risk that the Indonesian rupiah will devalue against the US dollar during the same period.

Nevertheless, you convert your dollars into rupiah and purchase Indonesian stock. Should the Indonesian stock market go up 10% (the

[1] In the fixed income world it is quite common for bonds issued by one country to be denominated in the currency of another. The generic term for such a security is a *Eurobond*.

local currency return), but the value of the rupiah drop 20% over the same interval (the foreign exchange return), then the base currency return of your investment is $10\% - 20\% = -10\%$. The overall result is a loss, even if you were right about the gains to be made in the Indonesian market.

4.3 PERFORMANCE AND ATTRIBUTION ON UNHEDGED PORTFOLIOS

Consider the following AUD-denominated portfolio, which has exposure to several foreign currencies. In Table 4.1 the columns show, in order: country, portfolio weights (w^P), local portfolio returns (r^P_{LOCAL}), benchmark weights (w^B), local benchmark returns (r^B_{LOCAL}) and benchmark return from exchange rate movements (r^{FX}) over the calculation interval.[2]

Table 4.1 **Weights and returns for demonstration portfolio**

Country	w^P	r^P_{LOCAL}	w^B	r^B_{LOCAL}	r^{FX}
Germany	60%	6.80%	25%	7.00%	1%
UK	10%	12.25%	25%	10.50%	–3%
Japan	10%	10.50%	25%	9.50%	–1%
Australia	15%	9.00%	25%	8.40%	0%
Cash	5%	8.00%	0%	7.50%	0%
Total	100.00%	8.105%	100.00%	8.850%	–0.750%

The aggregate local currency returns for portfolio and benchmark are shown at the bottom of the third and fifth columns. Note that the difference between these figures is not the actual active portfolio return, as they ignore the impact of exchange rate shifts.

While base and local currency *returns* are often different, base and local currency *weights* are always the same, as their relative holdings are unchanged no matter how return is measured. For this reason, we use a single measure of weight when calculating local and base currency portfolio returns.

The true active return of the portfolio is calculated by comparing the base currency returns r^P_{base} and r^B_{base} for each country. These are derived by summing the local currency returns r^P_{local} and r^B_{local} with the exchange rate return r^{FX} over each sector, as shown in Table 4.2.

[2] This data is intentionally identical to that provided in the monograph by Karnosky and Singer (1994) and Laker (2003), to allow the approaches of different authors to be compared.

Table 4.2

Base currency returns

Country	r^P_{base}	r^P_{base}
Germany	6.80% + 1.00% = 7.80%	7.00% + 1.00% = 8.00%
UK	12.25% − 3.00% = 9.25%	10.50% − 3.00% = 7.50%
Japan	10.50% − 1.00% = 9.50%	9.50% − 1.00% = 8.50%
Australia	9.00% + 0.00% = 9.00%	8.40% + 0.00% = 8.40%
Cash	8.00% + 0.00% = 8.00%	7.50% + 0.00% = 7.50%
Total	8.305%	8.100%

The base currency returns for portfolio and benchmark are given by the sum-product of the country weights with the corresponding base currency country returns:

$$r^P_{base} = (60\% \times 7.80\%) + (10\% \times 9.25\%) + (10\% \times 9.50\%) + (15\% \times 9.00\%) + (5\% \times 8.00\%) = 8.305\%$$

$$r^B_{base} = 25\% \times 8.00\%) + (25\% \times 7.50\%) + (25\% \times 8.50\%) + (25\% \times 8.40\%) + (0\% \times 7.50\%) = 8.100\%$$

The true overall outperformance, in base currency terms, is therefore 8.305% − 8.100% = 0.205%.

To see this result in a different way, treat the portfolio as two subportfolios; one with exposure to local markets, but no exposure to currency; and another with no local market component, but exposure to currency movements.

- The local contribution to return for the portfolio is 8.105%.
- The local contribution to return for the benchmark is 8.850%.
- Currency return from the portfolio is (60% × 1%) + (10% × −3%) + (10% × −1%) + (0% × 9.00%) + (0% × 8.00%) = 0.200%.
- Currency return from the benchmark is (25% × 1%) + (25% × −3%) + (25% × −1%) + (25% × 0%) + (0% × 0%) = −0.750% .

The overall portfolio return is 8.105% + 0.200% = 8.305%. The overall benchmark return is 8.850% − 0.750% = 8.100%. The active outperformance is 0.205%, as before.

If a security is denominated in the portfolio's base currency return, its local and base currency returns will be identical and it will not generate FX returns. For instance, the example portfolio above is denominated in AUD, so the FX returns from its AUD holdings were zero.

4.4 ATTRIBUTION ON AN UNHEDGED PORTFOLIO

Just as for a single-currency portfolio, we can run attribution on a portfolio with foreign exchange exposures to decompose its active returns by sources of risk.

One way to do this is to convert everything to base currency returns and run standard Brinson attribution, using

$$r_S^{AA} = (w_S^P - w_S^B)(r_S^B - r^B) \tag{4.2}$$

for the asset allocation return of sector S, and

$$r_S^{SS} = w_S^P(r_S^P - r_S^B) \tag{4.3}$$

for the stock selection and interaction return of the same sector, where w_S^P, w_S^B, r_S^P, r_S^B are the weights and base currency returns of sector S in portfolio and benchmark, respectively, and r^B is the base currency return of the benchmark. These expressions give the results shown in Table 4.3.

Table 4.3 **Brinson attribution using base currency returns**

Country	r^{AA}	r^{SS}
Germany	–0.035%	–0.120%
UK	0.090%	0.175%
Japan	–0.060%	0.100%
Australia	–0.030%	0.090%
Cash	–0.030%	0.025%
Subtotal	–0.065%	0.270%
Total		0.205%

Although correct, this analysis does not separate the returns generated by exchange rate movements from asset allocation and stock selection returns. For a clearer view of the effects of the manager's investment decisions, one should treat this multi-currency portfolio as two subportfolios, one containing securities with returns measured in local currency and one containing FX positions. This allows the value added by local currency investment decisions to be separated from the value added by exchange rate movements.

For the example shown in Table 4.1, the local currency asset allocation return for sector S is again given by the standard Brinson expression

$$r_S^{AA} = (w_S^P - w_S^B)(r_S^B - r^B) \tag{4.4}$$

and the local currency stock selection return by

$$r_S^{SS} = w_S^P(r_S^B - r^B) \tag{4.5}$$

where the weights have the same definitions as above, but the returns are now in local currency terms.

When running Brinson attribution on currency holdings, the FX return of portfolio and benchmark sectors is always the same, so the stock selection term will always be zero.[3] For this reason we do not show a stock selection return for the portfolio's foreign exchange exposure, and instead use

$$r_S^{FX} = (w_S^P - w_S^B)(r_S^{FX} - r^{FX}) \tag{4.6}$$

for the currency asset allocation return, where r_S^{FX} is the FX return of country S, and r^{FX} is the benchmark's FX return, given by

$$r^{FX} = \sum_S w_S^B r_S^{FX} \tag{4.7}$$

For instance, the attribution and stock selection returns for Germany are as follows:

$$r^{AA} = (60\% - 25\%) \times (7.000\% - 8.850\%) = -0.648\%$$
$$r^{SS} = 60\% \times (6.80\% - 7.00\%) = -0.120\%$$
$$r^{FX} = (60\% - 25\%) \times (1\% - 0.750\%) = 0.613\%$$

where all values are taken from Table 4.3. Overall, the results are as shown in Table 4.4.

Table 4.4

Brinson attribution using local and FX returns

Country	r^{AA}	r^{SS}	r^{FX}
Germany	−0.648%	−0.120%	0.613%
UK	−0.248%	0.175%	0.338%
Japan	−0.097%	0.100%	0.038%
Australia	0.045%	0.090%	−0.075%
Cash	−0.068%	0.025%	0.038%
Subtotal	−1.015%	0.270%	0.950%
Total			0.205%

This approach to running attribution on a multi-currency portfolio is called *naïve* attribution – not because it is wrong, but because it omits some important factors that can affect attribution when we hedge a portfolio.

4.5 PORTFOLIO HEDGING

Although the returns to be made in overseas investments might look attractive, the portfolio manager may not want to take the associated currency risk by investing in assets that have exchange rates that may move against them.

[3] An exception to this can occur if different FX revaluation rates are used for portfolio and benchmark. Returns from this effect are covered in Chapter 2 under the section 'Price return'.

Fortunately, there are ways to remove this currency risk, albeit at a cost. A technique called *hedging* involves holding additional securities that have an equal and opposite currency exposure to the assets held in the portfolio. If the exchange rate falls, the value of the hedge security will rise by an equal amount, so the net effect on the hedged asset's return from the change in exchange rates will be zero.

A portfolio that has holdings in overseas assets automatically has exposure to exchange rates. However, by using hedging we can change the exchange rate exposure to anything we want.

4.6 CURRENCY FORWARDS

One way to hedge foreign exchange exposures is to use a *forwards contract*.[4] A forwards contract is simply an agreement to exchange two currencies for a given length of time. In effect, we borrow one and lend the other, paying interest on the first and receiving interest on the second. The cost of the contract depends on the length of time for which the currencies are to be exchanged and their respective interest rates, but the net result is that, for the period during which the forwards contract is active, one has an additional FX exposure.

Forwards are usually traded in terms of a forward exchange rate. However, for attribution on hedge positions it is more useful to consider the cost of the contract in terms of the underlying interest rates.

A forwards contract always has a known expiration date. If the portfolio manager wishes to keep a currency hedge in place after this date, they enter into a new agreement with a counterparty. This is called *rolling the contract*.

Example: hedging Indonesian rupiah into US dollars

Consider the earlier example of buying Indonesian rupiah (IDR)-denominated securities with USD.

At the same time that the trader converts their US dollars into Indonesian equities, they take out a forward position in USD against rupiah so that the positive IDR exposure in stocks is offset by a negative IDR exposure in the forward contract.

In other words, the trader has bought IDR securities, so has an IDR currency exposure. To eliminate this exposure the trader needs to sell some other IDR and buy USD. This can be done by:

- borrowing IDR, and paying the Indonesian interest rate on the amount borrowed;
- buying USD, and receiving the USD interest rate on the same amount.

[4] Other alternatives include the use of currency swaps, currency futures contracts and currency options.

This aggregate position (short IDR, long USD) is the forward hedge. At the time of writing the IDR interest rate is much higher than the USD (5.75% vs 0.25%); so it only makes sense to follow this strategy if the expected annual return from investing in Indonesia exceeds the interest rate differential between the two countries (5.75% – 0.25% = 5.5%). The difference is called the *cost of hedging*.

However, suppose the trader goes ahead with this strategy. If the IDR falls, then the decrease in the value of the stocks due to this exchange rate movement will be exactly offset by an increase in the value of the forward hedge. The net impact of the change in exchange rates will be zero. The trader will still benefit from any returns in IDR stocks in local terms, although there will be a hedging cost of 5.5% of the exposure to pay. Therefore, this strategy only makes sense if the expected annual returns of the underlying asset exceed 5.5%.[5]

It is possible to hedge only part of a position. For instance, one might want to keep a partial exposure to the IDR in order to benefit from any appreciation in the currency. In this case, one might hedge only 50% of the exposure, at half the cost of the full hedge.

4.7 HEDGING AND RISK

The reasons why one might hedge can vary widely. In addition to removing risk, one may also seek to add it.

- A *defensive* or *hedging* strategy involves taking as little FX risk as possible. A *perfect hedge* is one that reduces FX risk to zero.
- An *active* or *speculative* strategy involves the active taking of risks in addition to the equity selection decisions, for instance, by seeking to profit from an expected forthcoming change in exchange rates.
- A *mixed* strategy involves a combination of defensive and active risks. For instance, the manager might seek to hedge away currency risk in most areas, but to take a small number of active currency bets for selected countries.
- A portfolio may need to be hedged if its benchmark is also hedged, to ensure that the same constraints are followed.[6]

[5] The counterpart to this strategy is a *carry trade*. As long as exchange rates do not change, a trader can make a profit by buying a (risky) high-yielding currency and selling a (safer) low-yielding one.

[6] Many data suppliers supply customised hedged benchmarks to match the investment mandates of their customers. While the constituents and overall returns of the benchmarks are supplied, it is relatively rare for the hedges to be published. This is a considerable nuisance for attribution analysts, who need to know all the security exposures in both portfolio and benchmark in order to run attribution. Appendix B shows one way around this problem.

Exchange rate strategy often is seen as a specialised area of expertise, since managers who specialise in asset allocation or stock selection may prefer not to manage currency exposures as well. For this reason, currency decisions are often outsourced to 'currency overlay' managers (Record, 2003).

4.8 NAÏVE ATTRIBUTION ON A HEDGED PORTFOLIO

The approaches described so far can also be used to analyse the returns of a hedged portfolio.

A hedged portfolio is essentially three portfolios in one: a portfolio with local returns generated by changes in the local prices of its constituent securities, another portfolio driven by returns generated by exchange rate movements and a third portfolio of hedging instruments. By allowing hedging, we have decoupled the currency allocation decision from the asset allocation and stock selection decisions.

Suppose that the portfolio shown in Table 4.1 has been hedged using currency forwards to give the exposures shown in Table 4.5. The second column *C* shows the hedge position. This is the actual currency exposure of the portfolio, as distinct to its market exposure. The third column *F* shows the forward positions required in each currency to give the net hedge, given the portfolio's physical exposures.

Table 4.5 **Weights and returns for demo portfolio**

Country	C	F	w_P	r_P^{local}	w_B	r_B^{local}	r_{FX}
Germany	60%	10%	–50%	6.80%	25%	7.00%	1%
UK	10%	55%	45%	12.25%	25%	10.50%	–3%
Japan	10%	25%	15%	10.50%	25%	9.50%	–1%
Australia	15%	10%	–5%	9.00%	25%	8.40%	0%
Cash	5%	0%	–5%	8.00%	0%	7.50%	0%
Total	100.00%	100%	0%	8.105%	100.00%	8.850%	–0.750%

To ensure the currency exposures are as shown, set up forwards positions equal to the hedge position, minus the portfolio position. For instance, the UK's hedge exposure is 10% in the portfolio, but the securities held in the portfolio contribute 55%. Therefore the UK forward position is 10% – 55% = –45%.

The hedging comes at a cost. Since we are borrowing in some currencies and lending in others, there are interest payments involved, which will affect the returns of the various positions in the portfolio. Therefore, the base currency return of a hedged asset from a given country will be affected by:

- its local currency return;
- the return generated by changes in exchange rates;

- the interest (or cash) rate of the local currency;
- the interest (or cash) rate of the base currency.

Without hedging, the portfolio's currency exposure is exactly the same as its market exposure. The portfolio has no hedge currency exposures, so interest rates do not enter into the returns calculation.

With hedging, the market exposure can differ from the currency exposures. The portfolio's return is now driven by a combination of market returns, FX movements and cash returns.

4.9 MEASURING HEDGE RETURNS

A country's return from interest $r_S^{INTEREST}$ is the active weight w_S^C of that country in the hedge, times the cash rate r_S^{CASH} for that country:

$$r_S^{INTEREST} = w_S^C r_S^{CASH} \tag{4.8}$$

Active weight is measured relative to the portfolio, not the benchmark, since it is the portfolio that is hedged, not the benchmark. The active weight w_S^C of the hedge is given by

$$w_S^C = w_S^H - w_S^P \tag{4.9}$$

where w_S^H is the portfolio hedge weight and w_S^P is the portfolio market weight in the portfolio.

For this portfolio, return due to movements in FX rates is given by $(-50\% \times 1\%) + (45\% \times -3\%) + (15\% \times -1\%) + (-5\% \times 0\%) + (-5\% \times 0\%) = -2.00\%$ while return due to hedging exposures is $(-50\% \times 5\%) + (45\% \times 11.25\%) + (15\% \times 9\%) + (-5\% \times 7.5\%) + (-5\% \times 7.5\%) = 3.163\%$ (see Table 4.6). The second and third columns are the returns in local terms, as before. The fourth (*Local*) column is the cash return, or the interest earned by holding exposures in these currencies. The contribution from each country is the active hedge weight for that country, times the return of that country's currency. The fifth (*FX*) column is the FX return times the active hedge weight.

Table 4.6

Returns of hedged portfolio

Country	r_S^P	r_S^B	Local	FX
Germany	7.800%	8.000%	5.000%	1.000%
UK	9.250%	7.500%	11.250%	–3.000%
Japan	9.500%	8.500%	9.000%	–1.000%
Australia	9.000%	8.400%	7.500%	0.000%
Cash	8.000%	7.500%	7.500%	0.000%
Subtotal	8.305%	8.100%	3.163%	–2.000%
Total				1.368%

The overall active return of the hedged portfolio is therefore given by $r^P - r^B = 8.305 - 8.100 + 3.163 - 2.000 = 1.368$.

To view the value added by the hedged currency position, examine the individual performance contributions in Table 4.7.

Table 4.7

Performance contributions from currency

Country	$r^{FX} + r^{CASH}$	w^H	$w^H(r^{FX} + r^{CASH})$
Germany	1% + 5%	–50%	–3.000%
UK	11.25% – 3%	45%	3.713%
Japan	9.00% – 1%	15%	1.200%
Australia	7.500% + 0.0%	–5%	0.375%
Cash	7.50% + 0.0%	–5%	–0.375%
Total		0%	1.163%

4.10 BRINSON ATTRIBUTION ON A HEDGED PORTFOLIO

The results from the earlier attribution without the hedge in place can now be combined with the results shown in Table 4.7 to give the overall Brinson attribution.

The presence of the new hedge makes no difference to the local currency asset allocation and stock selection returns. Currency hedging only gives rise to asset allocation returns, since the stock selection returns are identical for portfolio and benchmark. Table 4.8 shows the results of combining Tables 4.4 and 4.7.

Table 4.8

Brinson attribution using local and FX returns

Country	r^{AA}	r^{SS}	r^{FX}
Germany	–0.648%	–0.120%	0.613%
UK	–0.248%	0.175%	0.338%
Japan	–0.097%	0.100%	0.038%
Australia	0.045%	0.090%	–0.075%
Cash	–0.068%	0.025%	0.038%
Subtotal	–1.015%	0.270%	0.950%
Total			0.205%

4.11 PROBLEMS WITH THE BRINSON APPROACH WHEN HEDGING IS ACTIVE

An issue with applying this attribution model to hedged portfolios is that its results are not always consistent with intuition.

Recall that Table 4.4 showed the results of overweighting Germany (60% vs 25%) in an unhedged portfolio. Germany underperformed in local currency terms (7.00% vs 8.85%), so the Brinson approach indicates that overweighting Germany was a bad decision, and generated an active return of −0.648%.

However, if we allow hedging the situation becomes more complex. In addition to the local sector returns and the FX returns, hedging also generates extra cost and benefits due to the availability of additional interest rate exposures.

In fact, hedging can fundamentally change the outcome of this analysis because it alters the average level of return. Without hedging, the return from a non-base currency position is

$$r_{base} = r_{local} + r_{FX} \tag{4.10}$$

When hedging from one currency to another is available, the return from a hedged position becomes

$$r_{base} = r_{local} + r_{foreign} - r_{domestic} + r_{FX} \tag{4.11}$$

To illustrate the extra opportunities that can arise when hedging is available, consider the highest return that could have been made on the sample portfolio in Table 4.1.

Without hedging, the best strategy would have been to invest entirely in Japanese equities for a return of 10.50% local return - 1% FX return = 9.5% base return.

Suppose instead that we bought German equities and simultaneously hedged out of Deutsche Mark (DEM) and into GBP. In this case, the return would have been the sum of:

- 6.80%: Local currency return made by investing in Germany;
- 11.25%: Interest made on UK cash holdings via the hedge contract;
- -5%: Interest paid on DEM cash borrowings via the hedge contract;
- -3%: FX movements,

which totals 10.25%, substantially more than the 9.5% to be made by investing in unhedged assets.

The interplay between local return, FX return, and the interest returns paid or received from the various hedging currencies can make it difficult to see the best combination of local markets and hedging strategy. For this illustrative portfolio, a list of all possible investment and hedging strategies is shown in Table 4.9, sorted in descending order of net return, which shows that the strategy we used earlier as an example (buy German equities, hedge into GBP) was in fact the best possible.

Table 4.9 **All combinations of markets and hedging**

Rank	Strategy	Base return	Local	Base	FX	Net
1	German equities hedged into GBP	7.00%	11.25%	5.00%	3%	10.25%
2	German equities hedged into JPY	7.00%	9.00%	5.00%	1%	10.00%
3	German equities hedged into AUD	7.00%	7.50%	5.00%	0%	9.50%
4	Australian equities hedged into GBP	8.40%	11.25%	7.50%	3%	9.15%
5	Australian equities hedged into JPY	8.40%	9.00%	7.50%	1%	8.90%
6	Japanese equities hedged into GBP	9.50%	11.25%	9.00%	3%	8.75%
7	Japanese equities in JPY (no hedge)	9.50%	9.00%	9.00%	1%	8.50%
8	Australian equities in AUD (no hedge)	8.40%	7.50%	7.50%	0%	8.40%
9	Australian cash hedged into GBP	7.50%	11.25%	7.50%	3%	8.25%
10	German equities in DEM (no hedge)	7.00%	5.00%	5.00%	–1%	8.00%
11	Japanese equities hedged into AUD	9.50%	7.50%	9.00%	0%	8.00%
12	Australian cash hedged into JPY	7.50%	9.00%	7.50%	1%	8.00%
13	UK equities in GBP (no hedge)	10.50%	11.25%	11.25%	3%	7.50%
14	Australian cash (no hedge)	7.50%	7.50%	7.50%	0%	7.50%
15	UK equities hedged into JPY	10.50%	9.00%	11.25%	1%	7.25%
16	Australian equities hedged into DEM	8.40%	5.00%	7.50%	–1%	6.90%
17	UK equities hedged into AUD	10.50%	7.50%	11.25%	0%	6.75%
18	Japanese equities hedged into DEM	9.50%	5.00%	9.00%	–1%	6.50%
19	Australian cash hedged into DEM	7.50%	5.00%	7.50%	–1%	6.00%
20	UK equities hedged into DEM	10.50%	5.00%	11.25%	–1%	5.25%

The moral is that with the ability to hedge, the range of possible outcomes changes. The reference return that the manager should be trying to beat is no longer the average *unhedged* return, but the average *hedged* return – which can be quite different.

By allowing hedging, we have moved the goalposts. Unless all interest rates are the same across all currencies, there will be combinations of markets and hedging positions that will give higher returns than those available from the original range of unhedged markets. The availability of these new opportunities should be reflected when we come to measure the manager's skill.

In particular, Table 4.9 shows that, once the ability to hedge exposures is taken into account, overweighting Germany should have been regarded as a good decision. *This is not reflected in the results based on the naive approach, which suggests the exact opposite.*

4.12 CALCULATING BASE AND RETURN PREMIUMS

A simple transformation makes it straightforward to work out which investment strategy gives the best hedged returns, without considering every individual case.

1. Instead of using local currency return, replace r_{local} with $r_{local} - r_{cash}$ when calculating asset allocation returns. This quantity is called the *local return premium* (or just the *return premium*).
2. Instead of using FX return, replace r_{FX} with $r_{FX} + r_{cash}$. This quantity is called the *hedged Eurodollar rate* (or the *base return*).[7]

To see why this makes sense, consider where our returns come from when local market positions and currency exposures can be managed separately.

- The true return made from holding a currency is its FX return, plus the interest payable on that currency. This is the return generated by holding assets in a particular country without making any investment decisions.
- The true return from holding a market exposure is that market's return, minus the interest payable to holding an exposure in that currency. This is the excess, real return one gains from investing in a market, over and above the risk-free rate.

Therefore, *the appropriate returns to use for performance and attribution of hedged portfolios are the return premium and the base return, rather than the local market and FX returns.*

[7] I find these terms confusing, but mention them here so that you can follow other literature on this topic.

Suppose that a position is unhedged. In this case, the FX exposure will be the same as the market exposure. The return for each market is then simply the local return plus the FX return, since the cash rates cancel out.

In Table 4.10, *Base return* is given by $r_{Cash} + r_{FX}$ and *Return premium* by $r_B^{local} - r_{Cash}$. All totals are averaged using benchmark weights.

Table 4.10 **Sector-level and aggregated adjusted returns**

Sector	w_B	r_{FX}	r_B^{local}	r_{Cash}	Base return	Return premium
Germany	25%	1%	7.0%	5.00%	6.00%	2.00%
UK	25%	–3%	10.50%	11.25%	8.25%	–0.75%
Japan	25%	–1%	9.50%	9.00%	8.00%	0.50%
Australia	25%	0%	8.40%	7.50%	7.50%	0.90%
Total	100.00%	–0.75%	8.85%	8.19%	7.438%	0.663%

By inspection, the highest possible local return is made by investing in Germany (2%) since this the largest available figure in the *Return premium* column. Similarly, hedging into GBP gives the highest base return of 8.25%, since this is the largest figure in the *Base return* column.

Together, the active return from the combination of both strategies is 2% + 8.25% = 10.25%. Similarly, the lowest return is made by investing in the UK (−0.75%) and hedging into DEM (6%) giving an active return of 5.25%. Both results are consistent with Table 4.9.

The ability to hedge into other currencies, and transfer currency risk, can increase the opportunities available to increase return, and this should be acknowledged in any attribution analysis. The technique was introduced in a seminal 1994 monograph by Dennis Karnosky and Brian Singer (Karnosky and Singer, 1994).

The core insight behind Karnosky and Singer's approach to hedged currency attribution is that spot exchange rates are insufficient to decide whether currency decisions in a hedged portfolio were successful.

Instead, if we use (local currency return) minus (cash rate) as the return in an asset allocation calculation for country exposure, and (FX return) plus (cash rate) as the return in an asset allocation calculation for FX return, then the results will reflect the merit (or otherwise) of the various investment decisions made *when the ability to hedge is taken into account.*

For instance, in our demo portfolio we were overweighting Germany, which we now know to have been a good decision when the portfolio can be hedged. The local return premium for Germany was 7% – 5% = 2%, which is greater than the average local return premium of 0.66%. So this position added (60% − 25%) × (2.00% − 0.66%) = 0.468, rather than the -0.648% indicated by the earlier approach.

4.13 THE KARNOSKY-SINGER ATTRIBUTION MODEL

A formal statement of the Karnosky-Singer algorithm is given in Appendix A, but the results applied to the sample hedged portfolio in Table 4.5 are shown in Table 4.11.

Table 4.11

Results of Karnosky-Singer attribution

Country	r^{AA}	r^{FX}	r^{SS}
Germany	0.468%	0.216%	–0.120%
UK	0.212%	0.244%	0.175%
Japan	0.024%	0.000%	0.100%
Australia	–0.024%	–0.009%	0.090%
Cash	–0.033%	0.000%	0.025%
	0.648%	0.450%	0.270%

To illustrate the calculation, consider Germany.

- Market asset allocation return r_{AA} is

$$r_{AA} = (w_S^P - w_S^B) \times (r_S^L - \overline{r_S^L})$$
$$= (60\% - 25\%) \times (2.000\% - 0.663\%) = 0.468\%$$

where r_S^L is the return premium for sector S, and $\overline{r_S^L}$ is the sum-product of the benchmark weights and the return premiums, given in Table 4.10.

- Stock selection return r^{SS} is

$$r_{SS} = w_S^P \times (r_S^P - r_S^B) = 60\% \times (6.80\% - 7.00\%) = -0.120\%$$

- Currency allocation return r^{FX} is

$$r^{FX} = (w_S^H - w_S^B) \times (r_S^{FX} - \overline{r_S^{FX}})$$
$$= (10\% - 25\%) \times (6.00\% - 7.438\%) = 0.216\%$$

where r_S^B is the base premium for sector S, and $\overline{r_S^{FX}}$ is the sum-product of the benchmark weights and the base premiums – also read from Table 4.10.

4.14 RUNNING KARNOSKY-SINGER ATTRIBUTION ON AN UNHEDGED PORTFOLIO

The Karnosky-Singer framework can be applied to both hedged and unhedged portfolios. If no hedging is in place, the calculation reduces to the unhedged approach. There is, therefore, no theoretical penalty in implementing this model for routine attribution, although the Karnosky-Singer approach has extra data requirements (a cash return for each market) while the naive approach does not.

5

Smoothing algorithms

5.1 Why returns do not combine neatly over time

5.2 The importance of internally consistent return contributions

5.3 Path-independence

5.4 Carino smoothing

5.5 Geometric smoothing

5.6 Foreign exchange return and smoothing

5.7 Summary

5.1 WHY RETURNS DO NOT COMBINE NEATLY OVER TIME

Whether they arise from individual securities, sectors or portfolio risks, a fundamental property of return contributions is that they compound additively over markets, but geometrically over time. One outcome of this is that, for a portfolio where return is calculated over more than one time period, *cross terms* or *compounding* will distort the results and potentially obscure the true sources of return in a portfolio.

5.1.1 Cross terms

Suppose that a security has a return r_1 over day 1, and return r_2 over day 2. Then its overall return over the two days will be given by $(1 + r_1) \times (1 + r_2) - 1$, or $r_1 + r_2 + r_1 r_2$. In other words, its overall return is the arithmetic sum of the two daily returns, plus the cross term $r_1 r_2$.

Because of this cross term, it is not possible to decompose a return that has been compounded over more than one interval in terms of an arithmetic sum of individual returns. However, it is often highly desirable to adjust returns so that it *appears* possible.

This chapter explains why such an adjustment is not just aesthetically appealing but necessary, particularly for attribution analysis. To this end, I present several algorithms that allow individual return contributions to be adjusted and combined in a self-consistent way so that they combine to the portfolio's known, true performance.

Example 1

Consider a portfolio that holds two securities. The portfolio and security returns are the same over two successive months. (See Tables 5.1 and 5.2.)

Table 5.1 Weights and returns of sample 2-security portfolio over month 1

Security	w	r	c
Security 1	40%	20%	8%
Security 2	60%	10%	6%
TOTAL	100%		14%

Table 5.2 Weights and returns of sample 2-security portfolio over month 2

Security	w	r	c
Security 1	40%	20%	8%
Security 2	60%	10%	6%
TOTAL	100%		14%

Here, w is weight, r is return and $c = wr$ is performance contribution.

The portfolio's overall return over each single period is calculated by aggregating each security's performance contribution over the portfolio, and then aggregating these returns over time:

$$R = (1 + 14\%) \times (1 + 14\%) - 1 = 29.96\%$$

Can we arrive at the same result by aggregating security returns over time, and then over the portfolio? The weight of each security is unchanged over the two intervals, so at first glimpse this might seem possible.

The aggregated return of Security 1 is

$$r_1 = (1 + 20\%) \times (1 + 20\%) - 1 = 44.0\%$$

The aggregated return of Security 2 is

$$r_2 = (1 + 10\%) \times (1 + 10\%) - 1 = 21.0\%$$

The aggregate return over the whole interval is then $(40\% \times 44\%) + (60\% \times 21\%) = 30.2\%$, which is close, but not identical, to the correct result of 29.96%.

Example 2

Consider the attribution returns of the simple equity portfolio shown in Table 5.3. As before, the total return of the portfolio (32.50%) is not equal to the sum of the individual compounded returns from the benchmark, asset allocation and stock selection (18.80% + 14.40% – 1.30% = 31.90%).

Table 5.3 **Attribution returns of simple equity portfolio**

Period	R_B	r_{AA}	r_{SS}	*Total*
Period 1	10%	10%	5%	25%
Period 2	8%	4%	–6%	6%
TOTAL	18.80%	14.40%	–1.30%	32.50%

Another way to account for this discrepancy is to recognise that addition and multiplication are not commutative operations. Returns are combined additively across a portfolio, but multiplicatively over time. Since the return of each security aggregates at a quite different rate from that of the portfolio, there is no reason to expect that they should aggregate to anything like the portfolio's total return. The calculation must be carried out in one particular order to reach the correct overall return.[1]

[1] This also ignores the fact that the market weight of each security will probably vary over the calculation interval.

5.2 THE IMPORTANCE OF INTERNALLY CONSISTENT RETURN CONTRIBUTIONS

Given that we know the individual weights and returns of each security, we can calculate the overall return of the portfolio exactly. What do we lose by not being able to replicate this return by calculating returns in a different order?

From a pure performance measurement perspective, little useful information is lost. It may be useful to see which sectors or securities have contributed the most to the portfolio's performance, but it is seldom critical.

However, matters become different when one has a requirement to compare the returns made by different sources of *risk* in the portfolio – in other words, to run an attribution analysis. Example 2 showed that the sum of returns on individual risks need not aggregate to the overall outperformance when compounded over multiple periods.

To take an extreme example: suppose we are considering a set of returns that have been compounded multiple times. If the overall return due to asset allocation was 5 bp, and that from stock selection was 10 bp, but the portfolio's cumulative outperformance was 20 bp, how much did each risk contribute to the total? If the numbers do not match up, it is impossible to say, and this makes the value of the analysis moot.

For attribution analysis, where the active return of a portfolio is decomposed by source of risk, it is therefore highly desirable that the active return contributions from each source of risk be measured in ways that ensure they aggregate to the total outperformance. Ideally, one should be able to drill down to the individual security level and identify the contribution to return from individual sectors, securities or risks, knowing that return contributions at lower levels will combine to aggregate returns at higher levels.

What is needed is a way to adjust the return contributions of a portfolio so that its overall return can be calculated either by aggregating all security returns by sector and then by date, or by date and then by sector.

5.3 PATH-INDEPENDENCE

As long as the contributions from risk remain relatively unchanged, and their aggregated contributions combine to the overall return of the portfolio at each sample date, we have met the main requirements for attribution; a clear view of the sources of outperformance in terms of the underlying risk factors. It also makes reporting much more straightforward, but that is another issue.

In order to make these contributions act in this way, some sort of rescaling of performance contributions is required. Generally speaking, changing weights for reporting purposes is a bad idea, as this can distort the portfolio's exposures. Rescaling is therefore usually performed on returns or performance contributions, while ensuring that overall portfolio performance remains unchanged.

When smoothing, the first decision should be whether the adjusted returns of contributions r_1 and r_2 should combine *arithmetically* or *geometrically* to the total portfolio return R.

- Arithmetic: numbers add up, but compounding over time is lost:

$$R = r_1 + r_2 \tag{5.1}$$

- Geometric: compounding over time is retained, but additivity of returns over individual samples is lost:

$$R = (1 + r_1)(1 + r_2) - 1 \tag{5.2}$$

In both cases, we rescale all contributions so that they aggregate to the correct totals, irrespective of the order in which the return contributions were combined – whether by sector, by source of risk or by time. In other words, they become *path-independent*.

For the numbers in a performance or attribution report to act in a self-consistent manner, the values must be adjusted so that they combine to the correct totals. The trick is to ensure that the adjustment is not too obvious, and that it does not distort the results so badly that useful information is lost. In particular, security- or sector-level performance contributions should have the same sign as they did before the rescaling, and the relative magnitude of these contributions should stay as constant as possible. However, there is no right or wrong way to perform smoothing; it is a matter of preference (or prejudice).[2]

Many algorithms have been published to perform smoothing. In my view, it is more important to understand the reasons *why* smoothing is applied than the specific details of each technique. Bacon (2008) provides useful summaries of many widely used algorithms.

In the next two sections we will describe two of the most widely used smoothing algorithms, and demonstrate their use on the same data set. They are usually presented in terms of their impact on performance contribution rather than raw return, for the reasons outlined in Chapter 2.

[2] This may seem a rather blunt statement when applied to a rigorous, quantitative discipline as performance measurement. However, smoothing remains a critical requirement for useful and unambiguous attribution results, and it is better to understand why it is needed than to sweep its existence under the carpet.

5.4 CARINO SMOOTHING

Consider the following single-currency portfolio and benchmark, which have weights and returns supplied over four intervals Q1, Q2, Q3, Q4 (Tables 5.4–5.7).

Table 5.4

Weights and returns for Q1

Q1	*w*	*W*	*r*	*R*
Sector 1	30%	10%	–20%	0%
Sector 2	10%	20%	20%	20%
Sector 3	60%	70%	–20%	20%
TOTALS	100%	100%	–16%	18%

Table 5.5

Weights and returns for Q2

Q2	*w*	*W*	*r*	*R*
Sector 1	40%	10%	10%	30%
Sector 2	40%	40%	–30%	0%
Sector 3	20%	50%	20%	0%
TOTALS	100%	100%	–4%	3%

Table 5.6

Weights and returns for Q3

Q3	*w*	*W*	*r*	*R*
Sector 1	20%	30%	20%	–20%
Sector 2	10%	20%	–20%	–20%
Sector 3	70%	50%	30%	–20%
TOTALS	100%	100%	23%	–20%

Table 5.7

Weights and returns for Q4

Q4	*w*	*W*	*r*	*R*
Sector 1	20%	40%	20%	20%
Sector 2	20%	20%	30%	30%
Sector 3	60%	40%	10%	0%
TOTALS	100%	100%	16%	14%

For convenience, the performance contributions (product of weight and return for each sector) from portfolio and benchmark are given in Tables 5.8 and 5.9.

Table 5.8 **Performance contributions from portfolio**

c_P	Q1	Q2	Q3	Q4
Sector 1	–6%	4%	4%	4%
Sector 2	2%	–12%	–2%	6%
Sector 3	–12%	4%	21%	6%
TOTAL	–16%	–4%	23%	16%

Table 5.9 **Performance contributions from benchmark**

c_B	Q1	Q2	Q3	Q4
Sector 1	0%	3%	–6%	8%
Sector 2	4%	0%	–4%	6%
Sector 3	14%	0%	–10%	0%
TOTAL	18%	3%	–20%	14%

The aggregated performance of the portfolio over the four intervals is $(1 - 16\%) \times (1 - 4\%) \times (1 + 23\%) \times (1 + 16\%) - 1 = 15.0572\%$. The aggregated performance of the benchmark is $(1 + 18\%) \times (1 + 3\%) \times (1 + 14\%) \times (1 + 16\%) - 1 = 10.8445\%$. Net outperformance is therefore $15.0572\% - 10.8445\% = 4.2127\%$.

The Carino smoothing algorithm (Carino, 1999) is designed to work on a portfolio/benchmark pair, although it is easily adapted for use on a single portfolio, as I show below. Carino's approach introduces a period-dependent factor k, given by

$$k = \begin{cases} \dfrac{log_e(1 + r^P) - log_e(1 + r^B)}{r^P - r^B} & \text{if } r^P \neq r^B \\ 1 & \text{if } r^P = r^B \end{cases} \tag{5.3}$$

where r^P and r^B are the aggregated portfolio and benchmark returns over the entire interval, and a factor k_t for each interval t, given by

$$k_t = \begin{cases} \dfrac{log_e(1 + r_t^P) - log_e(1 + r_t^B)}{r_t^P - r_t^B} & \text{if } r_t^P \neq r_t^B \\ 1 & \text{if } r_t^P = r_t^B \end{cases} \tag{5.4}$$

where r_t^P and r_t^B are the portfolio and benchmark return over each interval t.[3] For instance, here

[3] If you are calculating these quantities in Excel, remember to use the *LN* (natural logarithm, or log to base*e*) function, rather than the *LOG* (log to base 10) function.

$$k = \frac{log_e(1 + 15.0572\%) - log_e(1 + 10.8445\%)}{15.0572\% - 10.8445\%} = 0.885444$$

and

$$k_1 = \frac{log_e(1 - 16\%) - log_e(1 + 18\%)}{16\% - 18\%} = 0.999611$$

To apply Carino smoothing, multiply all performance contributions at time t by k_t/k. The sum of all smoothed performance contributions over all intervals will then give the overall compounded portfolio return over the same period.

For instance, at interval Q1, $k_1/k = 0.999611/0.885444 = 1.128938$. Multiplying every entry in Table 5.8 by this quantity and adding the results together gives a smoothed return for this period of -18.0630% (Table 5.10):

Table 5.10

Carino smoothing applied to Q1

c_P	Q1
Sector 1	-6.7736%
Sector 2	2.2579%
Sector 3	-13.5473%
TOTAL	-18.0630%

The correction can be applied to per-period portfolio returns, as well as to individual performance contributions, to give the corrected returns (Table 5.11):

Table 5.11

Carino factors and smoothed returns

Interval	k	r^P	r^B
Q1	0.999611	-18.0630%	20.3209%
Q2	1.005440	-4.5421%	3.4066%
Q3	1.000367	25.9852%	-22.5958%
Q4	0.869587	15.7135%	13.7493%
TOTAL	0.885444	19.0936%	14.8809%

After applying the correction to the aggregated returns shown in Tables 5.4 to 5.7, we arrive at the figures shown in Table 5.11. Although they differ from the actual interval-specific returns, and their sum over the four intervals does not equal the actual aggregated return, the difference between the two corrected aggregated returns of 19.0936% − 14.8809% = 4.2127% does equal the true active return, as required.

If it is necessary to ensure that the aggregated smoothed portfolio return equals the unsmoothed portfolio return, use the following simpler expressions to smooth the portfolio and benchmark separately:

$$k = \begin{cases} \dfrac{log_e(1 + r)}{r} & \text{if } r \neq 0 \\ 1 & \text{if } r = 0 \end{cases} \tag{5.5}$$

where r is the aggregated portfolio return over the entire interval, and the factor k_t for each interval t is given by

$$k_t = \begin{cases} \dfrac{log_e(1 + r_t)}{r_t} & \text{if } r_t \neq 0 \\ 1 & \text{if } r_t = 0 \end{cases} \tag{5.6}$$

Note that the smoothing factors are dependent on the interval over which the return is measured. This means that smoothing must be recalculated if, for instance, an ad hoc report is required over an arbitrary time interval, which requires, in turn, that the unsmoothed data be stored.

Other arithmetic smoothing algorithms have been described by

- Menchero (2000)
- Groupe de Recherche en Attribution de Performance (1997)
- Davies and Laker (2001)
- Frongello (2002)

Each algorithm has specific advantages and disadvantages, and the reader is referred to Chapter 8 in Bacon (2008) or the papers cited above for a detailed analysis of each approach. However, one is so important that I treat it separately in the next section.

5.5 GEOMETRIC SMOOTHING

Geometric smoothing should be used when there is a requirement for performance contributions to compound multiplicatively, rather than arithmetically. In this approach, performance contributions are rescaled using the following expression:

$$1 + \hat{c_i} = (1 + c_i)\left[\frac{1 + r}{\prod_{i=1}^{i=n}(1 + c_i)}\right]^{\frac{|c_i|}{\sum_i |c_i|}} \tag{5.7}$$

where for an arbitrary time interval, and a portfolio with n securities:

- c_i is performance contribution from security i;

- r is overall performance;
- $\hat{c_i}$ is the smoothed performance contribution.

The result of applying this transformation is that

$$r = \left[\prod_i (1 + \hat{c_i})\right] - 1 \tag{5.8}$$

To illustrate the algorithm, consider the portfolio shown in Q1 in the previous example. Table 5.12 shows the various intermediate quantities.

Table 5.12

Geometrically smoothed performance contributions

Q1	*w*	*r*	*c*	*abs(c)*	*1+c*	*c*
Sector 1	40%	20%	8.00%	8.00%	1.0800	8.0036431%
Sector 2	30%	-5%	-1.50%	1.50%	0.9850	-1.4993770%
Sector 3	30%	6%	1.80%	1.80%	1.0180	1.8007726%
TOTALS	100%	8.30%				

The geometrically smoothed performance contributions in the right hand column are given by

$$c_1 = 1.080 \times \left[\frac{1.083}{(1.080 \times 0.985 \times 1.018)}\right]^{\frac{0.080}{0.113}} - 1 = 8.0036431\%$$

$$c_2 = 0.985 \times \left[\frac{1.083}{(1.080 \times 0.985 \times 1.018)}\right]^{\frac{0.015}{0.113}} - 1 = -1.4993770\%$$

$$c_3 = 1.018 \times \left[\frac{1.083}{(1.080 \times 0.985 \times 1.018)}\right]^{\frac{0.018}{0.113}} - 1 = 1.8007726\%$$

Aggregating these performance contributions geometrically gives

$$(1 + 8.0036431\%) \times (1 - 1.4993770\%) \times (1 + 1.8007726\%) - 1 = 8.3000\%$$

as required.

Repeating the calculation for the successive intervals give the following tables of smoothed contribution returns (Tables 5.13 and 5.14). The right-hand column is the aggregate return for each quarter, and the bottom row is the aggregate return for each sector.

Note that the overall return in the bottom right of each table can be calculated by:

- combining the aggregated returns over each quarter;
- combining the aggregated returns over each sector;
- combining individual performance contributions over sector *and* time.

Table 5.13

Geometrically smoothed return contributions for portfolio

c_P	Q1	Q2	Q3	Q4	Total
Sector 1	−6.1253%	4.1784%	3.9596%	3.8094%	5.5425%
Sector 2	1.9546%	−11.5463%	−2.0190%	5.7087%	−6.5939%
Sector 3	−12.2345%	4.1784%	20.7533%	5.7087%	16.7108%
TOTAL	−16.0000%	−4.0000%	23.0000%	16.0000%	15.0572%

Table 5.14

Geometrically smoothed return contributions for benchmark

c_B	Q1	Q2	Q3	Q4	Total
Sector 1	0.0000%	3.0000%	−6.4245%	7.7410%	3.8438%
Sector 2	3.8906%	0.0000%	−4.2892%	5.8093%	5.2110%
Sector 3	13.5810%	0.0000%	−10.6763%	0.0000%	1.4547%
TOTAL	18.0000%	3.0000%	−20.0000%	14.0000%	10.8445%

We have now adjusted the performance contributions so that they aggregate geometrically over market and over time to the known overall portfolio return. The aggregation is path-independent, as required.[4]

For relative, or active, returns, the geometric approach uses

$$r_{active} = \frac{1 + r_P}{1 + r_B} - 1$$

so in this case the active return is given by the geometric difference

$$r_{active} = \frac{1 + 15.0572\%}{1 + 10.8445\%} - 1 = 3.8005\%$$

rather than the arithmetic difference

$$r_{active} = 15.0572\% - 10.8445\% = 4.2127\%$$

Because return contributions now combine path-independently, active contributions can also be calculated in this way. For instance, the active return r^{S1} of Sector 1 over the four reporting quarters is given by

$$r^{S1} = \frac{1 + 5.5425\%}{1 + 3.8438\%} - 1 = 1.6358\%$$

The active returns for each sector may then be combined to give the total active return.

[4] To combine many return contributions c_i geometrically, it is often easier to calculate $S = \sum_i log_e(1 + c_i)$; then the summed aggregated return will be $e^S - 1$. This applies equally to spreadsheets and databases, where summation functions are usually built-in.

Unlike Carino smoothing, geometrical smoothing does not require that the original unsmoothed data be stored. Once security-level geometrically smoothed return contributions are calculated, they may be combined with previously calculated returns over any interval.

5.6 FOREIGN EXCHANGE RETURN AND SMOOTHING

The situation becomes more complex still when multi-currency portfolios are considered.

Recall that local currency return and currency return combine geometrically.

$$1 + r_{base} = (1 + r_{local})(1 + r_{FX})$$

or equivalently

$$1 + r_{FX} = \frac{(1 + r_{base})}{(1 + r_{local})}$$

In other words, the decomposition of base currency returns into local currency returns and foreign exchange returns is subject to the same difficulties as is compounding over time.

While it is possible to cast Brinson attribution in geometric terms to remove this problem (Bacon 2008, Chapter 5), the mathematics is complex, especially for cases where each security generates multiple sources of return. Given that the results will be adjusted anyway, it is often simpler to treat FX return additively, and set the local currency of a security as its base currency return, minus its local currency return.

$$r_{FX} = r_{base} - r_{local}$$

To apply smoothing, FX return may then be treated in the same way as any other source of return. The overall return of the portfolio will be unaffected, and it is arguable whether any significant detail will be lost after smoothing is applied. The benefit is a much simpler calculation.

5.7 SUMMARY

Pragmatically, the user should be able to present returns in a form that is acceptable by clients. Inevitably, some will comment that 'the numbers don't add up' when presented with an aggregated geometric report. Rather than trying to convey the concepts outlined in this chapter, it is often easier to present an arithmetically smoothed report.

For the same reason, you may also find different areas of your organisation requesting different smoothing algorithms for results on the same portfolio.

Unless your returns are particularly extreme, the choice of smoothing method will seldom make much difference to the overall conclusions of your attribution analysis. There is no 'best' way to perform smoothing, and a good software system will offer a range of options to allow the user to select and experiment with various smoothing algorithms.

Part 2

FIXED INCOME ATTRIBUTION

6. An overview of fixed income risks

7. Yield curves in attribution

8. Pricing, risk and the attribution equation

6

An overview of fixed income risks

6.1 Introduction
6.2 What is a bond?
6.3 Pricing conventions
6.4 Maturity
6.5 Coupons
6.6 Discounted cash flows and net present value
6.7 Pricing a bond from its discounted cash flows
6.8 Bond yield and carry return
6.9 Prices and yields
6.10 Return of a bond
6.11 Credit effects
6.12 The three Cs

6.1 INTRODUCTION

Our discussion of attribution starts with an overview of bonds, showing how they are priced, what risks drive their valuation and how the effects of these risks can be used to calculate attribution returns.

A bond is a very common type of fixed income security, and illustrates most of the effects that are measured by fixed income attribution. Understanding how to perform attribution on a bond is therefore the best route to understanding attribution on any other asset type.

6.2 WHAT IS A BOND?

Consider a government or a large multi-national company that needs to raise some cash. Although they could raise taxes or sell off some assets, these measures are seldom popular with the electorate or shareholders. So, very often, the solution is to borrow the money in the marketplace by issuing a *bond*.

A bond is simply an IOU with two defining features:

- a promise of constant interest payments, called *coupons*, to the bond's owner at regular, preset intervals;
- a promise that the amount borrowed will be repaid to the bond's owner at a known date in the future, called the *maturity date*.

The bond can be sold on by the original purchaser, in which case all subsequent payments are transferred to the bond's new owner. The amount raised when the bond is first issued is called the *face value* or the *principal*, and this is, roughly, the amount paid for the bond when it is issued, as well as the amount returned to the bond's owner at the maturity date.

Vast amounts of money have been raised by issuing bonds and similar securities. In early 2013 the total size of the global debt securities market was around $78 trillion, or about twice the size of the global equity market, or roughly five times the annual GDP of the United States, and issuance continues to grow.[1]

Coupons are paid at regular intervals, usually once or twice a year, up to the maturity date. The coupon is quoted as a percentage of the initial face value of the bond. The timing of the coupons is designed so that the last coupon payment date coincides with the maturity date.

---

[1] 'I used to think if there was reincarnation, I wanted to come back as the president or the pope or a .400 baseball hitter. But now I want to come back as the bond market. You can intimidate everybody', James Carville, adviser to the Clinton administration, quoted in the *Wall Street Journal*, 25 February 1993.

For instance, consider a bond with a face value of $1 million, paying a 5% coupon, maturing on 15 November 2020.

- If the bond pays annual coupons, it will make one annual payment to the bondholder of $50,000 on 15 November each year, up to and including the maturity date.
- If the bond pays semi-annual coupons, it will make two payments of $25,000 each year, one on 15 May and one on 15 November of each year.

Coupons are usually set to the market interest rate at the time when the bond was issued. This is why bond coupons vary so widely, with values on offer between 0.25% and 15%.

Unlike an equity, where the dividend can vary, a bond's coupon is always fixed. This is the origin of the term *fixed income*.

Both the maturity date and the coupon are set when the bond is issued.[2] An investor who buys the bond when it is issued and holds it to maturity knows the exact cost of the investment, the timing and amount of the bond's cash flows and the date at which the principal will be repaid – assuming that the bond's issuer keeps their side of the agreement. The terms and conditions of a bond, and its future cash flows, are set out in a prospectus prior to issue.

6.3 PRICING CONVENTIONS

The majority of bonds may be freely traded in the marketplace, but the price at which they change hands after they are issued will not necessarily be their face value. The future value of the bond's coupon payments and principal continually change as they depend on the current level of interest rates, and so the price of the bond will vary in turn according to the prevailing economic conditions.

The price at which the bond is traded is called the *market price*. For dollar bonds, the convention is to quote a market price in terms of $100 face value and to three decimal places. For example, a bond's price might be $105.554 per $100 face value. This means that every dollar of face value is worth $1.05554.

If the market price is less than the face value, we say the bond is *trading at a discount*. This occurs when interest rates are higher than the bond's coupon. The bond is worth less than when it was issued, since the investor can make

[2] Note that this only holds for plain, or *vanilla* bonds. A *callable bond* can repay its capital early under certain conditions. Conversely, a *debt restructuring agreement* may allow an issuer in financial difficulty to extend the bond's maturity date. Coupons can also vary, with their amount varying according to a predetermined schedule, or as a function of a reference market rate – a *floating rate note*. These cases are covered in later chapters.

a better annual return by investing funds at the prevailing interest rate than in the bond.

Conversely, if the market price is greater than the face value, the bond is *trading at a premium*. In this case, interest rates are lower than the bond's coupon, and the bond is worth more than its face value because it is paying more than the market rate.

If a bond's market price is equal to its face value, we say that it is *trading at par*. There are two points in a bond's lifetime when it always trades at or near par:

- *When it is issued.* As mentioned above, bonds are typically issued at par by setting their coupon to the current rate of interest for cash deposits. This means that the bond's market price roughly equals its face value when it is issued.
- *When it is repaid.* No matter how the bond's price varied during its lifetime, it is always worth par at maturity. If the bond is trading at a discount when it is bought, the owner will make a guaranteed capital gain if the bond is held to maturity. If the bond is trading at a premium, the same strategy will result in a capital loss, but this may be more than made up for by the bond's coupon payments over the same period.

6.4 MATURITY

It is common to talk about bonds in terms of their lifetime. For instance, a 10-year bond is a bond that matures in 10 years' time. Publications such as the *Wall Street Journal* carry quotes for 10- and 30-year bond yields for a range of countries. These are market yields for whichever heavily traded bond has its lifetime closest to these numbers.

Most bonds have lifetimes of up to 30 years, although some have even longer maturities. The Bank of England has issued 50-year bonds, and in recent years a 100-year gilt issue has been proposed to allow investors to hedge equally long-dated liabilities.

6.5 COUPONS

Before the days of computers, companies kept track of their bonds and interest payments by issuing paper certificates. The certificate was your claim to the principal, and also included paper coupons that you tore off and redeemed at the issuer's offices for cash when they became due. This is the origin of the term *coupon*.

6.6 DISCOUNTED CASH FLOWS AND NET PRESENT VALUE

To calculate the value of a bond requires an understanding of the value of a discounted cash flow.

Consider a dollar that is to be paid in a year's time, and assume that interest rates will stay constant over this period at a value r. What is that future payment worth at the present moment?

This is the same as asking how much would we have to invest now at an interest rate of r to receive a dollar in a year's time, which is given by

$$P = \frac{\$1}{(1 + rt)} \tag{6.1}$$

assuming annual compounding, or

$$P = \$1 \times e^{-rt} \tag{6.2}$$

assuming continuous compounding.

The expression $1/(1 + rt)$ or e^{-rt} is called the *discount factor*, and is always less than unity, indicating that a fixed cash flow to be paid in the future is worth less than the same cash flow paid immediately.[3]

6.7 PRICING A BOND FROM ITS DISCOUNTED CASH FLOWS

If a bond's maturity date is very close, so that it has only a single cash flow of principal repayment plus final coupon remaining, then the price of the bond is that cash flow's discount factor, times the final payment of principal plus coupon. However, most bonds have more than one cash flow in their future. A useful way to price such a bond is to regard it as a portfolio of cash flows, made up of its individual coupons and the final maturity payment. To price the bond, find the value of each individual cash flow by multiplying it by its discount factor, then add these values together to get the total price for the bond.

6.8 BOND YIELD AND CARRY RETURN

Investors talk about the yield, or rate of return, of cash or equities. The same concepts apply to bonds.

---

[3] There is a very rare exception to this case, which occurs when interest rates are *negative*. In this case the depositor is paying for the privilege of investing their money with a third party. Negative interest rates are usually used by central banks as an attempt to stimulate economic growth by encouraging lending.

The yield of a bond is the return it will make over time due to its internal cash flows, assuming that market conditions remain unchanged. This return is distinct from any additional return to be made from underlying changes in the marketplace, such as changes in interest rates.

The portion of a bond's return generated by yield is called its *carry return*, or its *carry* for short. Carry is given by the simple expression

$$r_{carry} = y\delta t \tag{6.3}$$

where y is the bond's yield and δt is the elapsed interval in years.

Carry return can be further decomposed into return generated by risk-free yields, capital gains and losses and security-specific features. This topic is covered in detail in Chapter 9.

6.9 PRICES AND YIELDS

Interest rates change over time, and this implies that the bond's price changes as well. If the yield of a bond falls, its price rises, and vice versa.

This behaviour may seem contradictory, since a high-yielding bond might appear to be worth more than a low-yielding one. However, recall that while the bond's yield (and hence discount factor) may change, its coupons always remain the same. As yield decreases, the discount factor increases, so its cash flows increase in value. Since a bond is simply a collection of future cash flows, a bond's price will rise as its yield decreases (and vice versa). So yields and prices always move in opposite directions – and, very conveniently, the relationship is more or less linear.

For historical reasons, the proportionality constant between price and yield is called the *modified duration* of the bond. It is defined as

$$\delta P = -P\ MD \times \delta y \tag{6.4}$$

where P is the bond's price, δP is the change in the bond's price, δy is the change in the bond's yield and MD is the modified duration. Modified duration is measured in units of years.

Modified duration is almost always positive, and the negative sign ensures that prices and yields move inversely as required.[4]

Modified duration is one of the most widely used sensitivity measures for a bond, and crops up in many contexts. For instance, we can talk about the modified duration of a portfolio, which is calculated from the weighted modified durations of its constituent bonds.

---

[4] The exception is when the bond contains embedded options, which can, under some circumstances, make the bond's price increase as interest rates increase, or vice versa. In this case, modified duration is negative.

6.10 RETURN OF A BOND

I have now covered the main sources of return for a bond. To summarise, a bond's return has two main drivers:

- the absolute level of its yield;
- changes in its yield.

The returns are called, respectively, *carry return* (or return due to the passage of time) and *market return* (or return due to movements in the market). Market return can be further decomposed into changes in risk-free interest rates, and movements in credit spreads.[5]

One way to calculate a bond's market (or curve) return is to reprice the bond twice, either using an explicit pricing formula, or by pricing the security from its individual cash flows. In either case the bond is priced using its market yields at the start and end of the interval, but at the same date. The difference between the prices generates return, which is attributed to the bond's change in yield.

However, this repricing can require substantial work, as it involves working out the timings and the amounts of every future cash flow paid by the bond, and repricing everything twice.

Sometimes this is the right thing to do. But you may be able to use a short cut. *If you know the bond's modified duration, you can skip pricing the bond entirely, and to go straight from the bond's change in yield to its return.*

To do this, start with the equation

$$\delta P = -P \times MD \times \delta y \qquad (6.5)$$

Dividing through by P and noting that $r = \delta p/P$ gives

$$r = -MD \times \delta y \qquad (6.6)$$

In other words, once we know the change in yield of the security and its modified duration, it is very straightforward to calculate its return due to a change in yield.

Combining this with the expression for carry return (6.3) gives the general expression for the return of a bond:

$$R = (y \times \delta t) - (MD \times \delta y) \qquad (6.7)$$

where:

- R is the bond's return;
- y is its yield to maturity;

[5] This discussion assumes implicitly that all discount factors use the same interest rate. This is not necessarily the case, as I show in Chapter 7.

- δy is change in yield to maturity over the calculation interval;
- δt is change in time, measured as the fraction of a year over which the calculation is performed;
- MD is modified duration (or just 'duration'), which measures the sensitivity of the bond's price (and hence its return) to changes in yield. Note the negative sign in front of the modified duration term. Since duration is positive, this means that returns go down if yields go up, just as I described earlier.

Equation (6.7) occurs so often in attribution analysis that we call it the *fundamental attribution equation*. Bear in mind that it is not applicable to all asset types, and may need to be modified or extended if the current security is not a bond. A formal derivation of this equation is supplied in Chapter 8, together with a numerical example.

6.11 CREDIT EFFECTS

Not all bonds are equal, and, for a range of reasons, some are less likely to repay their investors than others.

There is seldom any doubt of the ability of a sovereign issuer with a solid economy to pay their bondholders on schedule, and as a result sovereign debt is generally regarded as risk-free, with the yield of this debt defining a risk-free yield. However, an issuer in financial trouble may not be able to make the promised coupon payments on their bonds. If they declare bankruptcy, they may not pay back the bond's principal. Both events are called a *default*.

The markets are usually aware of an issuer's impending financial difficulties, so if there is a risk of a default, their bonds will trade at a lower price. Because of the inverse relationship between price and yield, this lower price translates to a higher yield that compensates the bondholder for the extra risk they are taking in holding the bond.

The extra yield paid out by such a bond, over and above the risk-free yield of an identical sovereign bond, is called the *credit spread*. If the credit spread increases, the price and return of the bond will fall as a result, even if the risk-free yield remains constant.

Changes in the credit spread therefore affect a bond's price, and hence its carry and market returns, in exactly the same way as changes in the underlying risk-free yield. In addition to carry and sovereign curve return, some bonds therefore also show a third source of return from *credit effects*.

Most bonds are assigned a credit rating by one or more of the major ratings agencies. A credit rating is a label that indicates the probability of a default, with AAA-rated bonds representing negligible risk to the owner.

6.12 THE THREE Cs

A convenient way to summarise the three main sources of return in a fixed income portfolio is as follows:

- *Carry* – return from carry.
- *Curve* – return from movements in the sovereign curve.
- *Credit* – return from movements in credit curves.

7

Yield curves in attribution

7.1 Introduction

7.2 Why interest rates vary by term

7.3 Interpolation

7.4 Par curves and zero curves

7.5 Credit spreads

7.1 INTRODUCTION

So far, I have talked about interest rates as if each bond's cash flows can be discounted at a single rate. In fact this is seldom the case, and the ramifications of interest rates varying by term (or borrowing period) form one of the core topics of fixed income attribution.

7.2 WHY INTEREST RATES VARY BY TERM

Suppose you run a bank, and have two clients who are identical in every way. One client wants to borrow £1 million from you for a period of a week. The other wants to borrow £1 million for 10 years. Does it make sense to charge them both the same rate of interest?

The loan to the 10-year borrower is substantially more risky. Many events can occur over a period of this length, all of which mean you will not get your money back. There is also the risk of inflation, which will erode the value of your capital.

For both reasons, interest rates on longer-term borrowings tend to be higher than those on short-term borrowings, with interest rates charged in the marketplace rising as the term of the debt becomes longer. Therefore, a plot of bond yields against term typically shows an upwards-sloping curve. The curve flattens out at longer maturities, since from the perspective of the present economic conditions 50- and 100-year yields are regarded as equivalent (Figure 7.1).

The same considerations apply to bonds, which repay their principal at maturity. A plot of the yields to maturity of a group of similar bonds against their times to maturity will usually produce a similarly-shaped graph.

Figure 7.1

GBP yield curve

Source: Compiled with data from Bank of England

A plot of yields to maturity against term to maturity is called a *par curve*. In general, a graph of interest rates plotted against applicable maturity is called a *yield curve* or a *term structure*.

Yield curves are not always positively sloped, however. Depending on prevailing economic conditions, yield curves can also be flat (short- and long-term rates the same), or inverted, in which case short-term interest rates are higher than long-term interest rates. This condition is generally seen as indicating a forthcoming recession, since the market is expecting future interest rates to fall in response to worsening economic conditions.

There is a considerable volume of research on the shape of yield curves, and they form a frequent topic for financial commentators. From the attribution analyst's perspective, it is usually enough to be aware that the level and shape of yield curves change continuously, and that this can have a major effect on the returns of fixed income portfolios.

The level of the curve at zero maturity is the cash rate, which is set by the central bank. Apart from this, the shape and level of the curve is determined entirely by the market.

Recall that in Chapter 6 we assumed that the same interest rate could be used to discount all future cash flows. As you now see, this is not the case. If the yield curve slopes upwards, then a lower yield should be used to discount near cash flows, and a higher yield to discount cash flows in the distant future. This can affect bond prices and returns quite substantially.

7.3 INTERPOLATION

Although yield curves are displayed as graphs, they are generally supplied as a range of sample points at predefined maturities, such as 2, 5, 10, 20, and 30 years. A 25-year yield can be calculated by fitting a curve between the 20- and 30-year points, using linear or cubic interpolation. Yields greater than the longest maturity point are typically set to the yield at that point, since yield curves flatten out at long maturities.

In general, a linearly interpolated yield y_t at maturity t over a set of n maturities m_i and yields y_i $\{(m_1,y_1),(m_2,y_2),\ldots,(m_n,y_n)\}$ is given by

$$y_t = \begin{cases} y_1 & (t < m_1) \\ y_n + \dfrac{(y_{n+1} - y_n)}{(m_{n+1} - m_n)}(t - t_n) & (m_1 \leq t < m_{n-1}) \\ y_n & (t \geq m_n) \end{cases} \tag{7.1}$$

7.4 PAR CURVES AND ZERO CURVES

A par curve shows interest rates for bonds at a range of maturities. However, these rates cannot be used directly to price future cash flows.

The reason is that the bonds whose yields make up the a par curve pay coupons as well as their final principal repayment. These coupons affect the bond's yield. To calculate a discount yield for the maturity payment, the effects of these coupons must be removed.

Bonds that pay no coupons can have their yields used directly for discounting other cash flows at the same maturity. Such yields are called *zero coupon yields*. Bank bills are structured in this way, so it is very easy to use them to get discount yields; just measure their quoted yields in the marketplace, and plot them against the relevant time to maturity.

Unfortunately, bank bills typically have maturities of less than a year, and a typical yield curve needs to be quoted out to maturities of 30 years or longer. How can we find discount yields from other securities?

A common method is to start with bond yields, and to remove the effects of their coupons by using an algorithm called *bootstrapping* (Choudhry, 1994). The result is another yield curve with roughly the same shape as the par curve, but that can be used for discounting.[1]

A yield curve constructed using this process is called a *zero curve* or a *spot curve*, as it is made up of what would be the yields of zero coupon bonds if they existed at all maturities. Zero curves offer the clearest possible view of future interest rates, as they are undistorted by any security-specific factors.

Attribution analysts typically work with at least two types of curve: *par curves* and *zero curves*. Which one you use for attribution depends on how you are pricing your securities.

- To price a bond using a single yield to maturity, interpolate the appropriate yield from the par curve and use this yield in a pricing formula supplied by the bond issuer. The yield, and hence the price, will be approximate but is usually good enough for attribution purposes.
- To price a bond by discounting its individual cash flows, read the appropriate discounting yields from the zero curve and use them to price each cash flow. Then add the discounted cash flows together to get the bond's price.

The zero curve gives the clearest view of current and future interest rates, so this is the ideal curve to use for attribution. However, par curves and zero curves have much the same shape and move in tandem, so a change in the par curve will usually be close to a change in the zero curve at the same maturity.

[1] In practice a full bootstrap will also use prices of futures and swaps, but the principle remains the same.

7.4.1 Parallel shift

In practice, the par curve typically moves up and down in a more or less parallel manner, and 70–80% of all changes in bond yields can be described in terms of this type of movement (Phoa, 1998). *Parallel movements in the yield curve are therefore among the most important drivers of portfolio performance.*

This is convenient, because the most widely used sensitivity measure for bonds is modified duration (see Chapter 6), which measures how the bond's price and return respond to parallel movements in rates. A bond's market return, which was generated by changes in yield, can therefore be decomposed into return generated by parallel movement in the curve, and return from non-parallel movements.

7.4.2 Measuring parallel shift

Despite its importance in attribution analysis, there is no market consensus on how to calculate parallel curve movements from one date to another. Widely used methods either measure the level of the curve at a predefined maturity, or take the average level of the curve. This topic is covered in detail in Chapter 10.

7.4.3 Measuring non-parallel shift

Remove the parallel movement from the curve, and what is left can be interpreted as mostly steepening and flattening; in other words, a *twist* in the curve. For instance, short rates might fall while long rates stay constant, in which case we say the curve has become steeper. Such twist movements account for around 10–15% of all changes in yields (Phoa, 1998).

Further, if you take out the parallel movements and twist movements, what is left over can be viewed as a *curvature* movement, where the motion around middling maturities is greater than those for long and short maturities (or vice versa). Curvature movements account for perhaps 5% of changes in yields (Phoa, 1998).

Anything left over that cannot be interpreted as shift, twist or curvature is either regarded as noise or bundled together with curvature effects.

Again, this is very convenient, because it reflects the language in which fixed income traders describe positions in the market.

For instance, suppose a trader puts on a *curve flattening trade*. In this case the trader is expecting the curve to twist and become flatter, so that rates at longer maturities become closer to rates at shorter maturities. An attribution report will then provide feedback on the return generated by this trade, as distinct to returns generated by parallel movements, a tightening in credit spreads or other effects. The attribution report is calculating returns made from types of risk, as distinct to returns from individual positions.

The ability to forecast these types of yield curve movements can be a critical skill in making money in the fixed income markets. If interest rates are about to make a parallel movement downwards, bond prices will rise. If your performance is being measured against a benchmark, one way to attempt to outperform that benchmark is to increase your portfolio's exposure to interest rate changes by increasing its modified duration.

The implicit assumption here is that rates move in a parallel manner, and that a portfolio can be approximated by a single cash flow. In fact, the returns of a portfolio are driven by a complex interplay between the timing and size of the various cash flows and the movement of the underlying curve. So an equally important skill is being able to forecast how rates will move across various maturities – and not just whether the curve will move up or down, but where and how it will flatten, steepen and become more or less curved, depending on current and future economic conditions.

A portfolio that has the same duration as its benchmark is said to be *immunised* against parallel shifts. Any parallel curve movements up or down will generate identical returns in the portfolio and benchmark, so the portfolio is hedged against parallel curve movements.

However, such immunisation does not apply to other types of curve movement. It is common to come across portfolios that have been hedged in this way, but still underperform against their benchmark because of adverse higher-order movements in the curve, such as twist or curvature. This is exactly the sort of outcome that fixed income attribution is designed to measure.

There are many ways to measure the effects of changes in the yield curve, and we cover these in more detail in Chapter 10.

7.5 CREDIT SPREADS

Many securities also have exposure to *sector* or *credit curves*. Movements in these additional curves can also have a major impact on the security's return. This topic is treated in more detail in Section 11.1.

8

Pricing, risk and the attribution equation

8.1 Introduction

8.2 Pricing securities from first principles

8.3 Calculating return using the perturbational equation

8.4 Residuals

8.5 Stand-alone portfolios

8.1 INTRODUCTION

A central requirement for fixed income attribution is the ability to translate changes in market risks into return.

Since the majority of securities can be priced using explicit formulae, one might think that this would be a straightforward task. In fact, the process can be fraught with difficulty. This chapter covers some of the more effective and widely used techniques for calculating attribution returns.

8.2 PRICING SECURITIES FROM FIRST PRINCIPLES

The fundamental way to price a security is to calculate its individual cash flows, to price them using the appropriate discount rate and to add them together. The security is priced with and without the current risk in place, and the return due to that risk is then given by the difference between the two prices, divided by the starting price.

Central banks and corporate issuers usually provide detailed documentation on the pricing of the bonds they issue. For instance, the pricing of a UK gilt bond is described in detail in UK DMO (2005).

8.3 CALCULATING RETURN USING THE PERTURBATIONAL EQUATION

Assuming that the price p of an arbitrary security is a function of time t and yield y, we can write δp in terms of a Taylor expansion to give

$$\delta p = \frac{\partial p}{\partial t}\delta t + \frac{\partial p}{\partial t}\delta y + \frac{1}{2}\frac{\partial^2 p}{\partial y^2}\delta y^2 + O(\delta t^2, \delta y^3) \tag{8.1}$$

We expand to one term in time but two in yield. This is because virtually all securities have small second-order dependence on time, but can have appreciable second-order yield dependence.

Dividing throughout by p and defining quantities r (return), y (yield to maturity), MD (modified duration), C (convexity) as

$$r = \frac{\delta p}{p} \tag{8.2}$$

$$y = \frac{\partial p}{\partial t} \tag{8.3}$$

$$MD = -\frac{1}{p}\frac{\partial p}{\partial y} \tag{8.4}$$

$$C = \frac{1}{p}\frac{\partial^2 p}{\partial y^2} \quad (8.5)$$

equation (8.1) then becomes

$$r \approx y\delta t - MD\delta y + \frac{1}{2}C\delta y^2 \quad (8.6)$$

This is the full version of the fundamental attribution equation, first introduced in equation (6.7) in Chapter 6. It is also called the *perturbational equation*.

The perturbational equation is essentially a proxy for any pricing function. Instead of requiring the details of how an arbitrary security is priced, it replicates the results of a returns calculation by using the security's *risk numbers*: yield to maturity, modified duration and convexity.

In Table 8.1:

- P is market price;
- AI is accrued interest;
- Y is yield to maturity;
- MD is modified duration;
- C is coupon;
- r_M is market return, calculated from market price and coupon payments;
- δy is change in yield over the current interval;
- r_C is calculated return, using the expression $r = y \times \delta t - MD \times \delta y$;
- δr is the difference between market and calculated return, also called the *residual* for the calculation.

Table 8.1 illustrates the use of the attribution equation by calculating the market return of a UK gilt-edged security and compared it to the return calculated from the perturbational equation, omitting the convexity term.

Note that a coupon was paid on 28 November.

This calculation illustrates several practical points for attribution on individual bonds:

- It is often difficult to work out exactly when a coupon payment took place, based solely on a knowledge of the bond's terms and conditions. However, in this case we have a value for the accrued interest. The coupon was paid at the date on which the accrued interest was reset.
- The value of the coupon is very close to the difference between the two values of the accrued interest before and after this reset. This is the value that is used for the coupon cash flow.

Table 8.1 **Attribution on a 4¼% Treasury Gilt 2049**

Date	$P(£)$	$AI(£)$	Y	MD	C	r_M	$y\delta t$	δy	$-MD\delta y$	r_C	δr
31-Oct-12	124.506967	1.706967	3.196189%								
01-Nov-12	123.678579	1.718579	3.229840%	20.07	0	–0.665%	0.000088	0.000337	–0.006754	–0.667%	0.001%
02-Nov-12	123.783415	1.753415	3.226925%	20.06	0	0.085%	0.000088	–0.000029	0.000585	0.067%	0.017%
05-Nov-12	124.425027	1.765027	3.201617%	20.1	0	0.518%	0.000265	–0.000253	0.005087	0.535%	–0.017%
06-Nov-12	124.076639	1.776639	3.216006%	20.08	0	–0.280%	0.000088	0.000144	–0.002889	–0.280%	0.000%
07-Nov-12	125.258251	1.788251	3.169320%	20.16	0	0.952%	0.000088	–0.000467	0.009412	0.950%	0.002%
08-Nov-12	125.599863	1.799863	3.156240%	20.18	0	0.273%	0.000087	–0.000131	0.002640	0.273%	0.000%
09-Nov-12	125.954699	1.834699	3.143533%	20.19	0	0.283%	0.000086	–0.000127	0.002566	0.265%	0.017%
12-Nov-12	125.576311	1.846311	3.158867%	20.16	0	–0.300%	0.000258	0.000153	–0.003091	–0.283%	–0.017%
13-Nov-12	125.777923	1.857923	3.151337%	20.17	0	0.161%	0.000087	–0.000075	0.001519	0.161%	0.000%
14-Nov-12	124.799536	1.869536	3.190545%	20.1	0	–0.778%	0.000086	0.000392	–0.007881	–0.779%	0.002%
15-Nov-12	125.761148	1.881148	3.152846%	20.16	0	0.771%	0.000087	–0.000377	0.007600	0.769%	0.002%
16-Nov-12	126.665984	1.915984	3.118603%	20.22	0	0.719%	0.000086	–0.000342	0.006924	0.701%	0.018%
19-Nov-12	125.707596	1.927596	3.156656%	20.15	0	–0.757%	0.000256	0.000381	–0.007668	–0.741%	–0.015%
20-Nov-12	124.059208	1.939208	3.222799%	20.03	0	–1.311%	0.000086	0.000661	–0.013248	–1.316%	0.005%
21-Nov-12	123.94082	1.95082	3.228005%	20.01	0	–0.095%	0.000088	0.000052	–0.001042	–0.095%	0.000%
22-Nov-12	124.732432	1.962432	3.196671%	20.07	0	0.639%	0.000088	–0.000313	0.006289	0.638%	0.001%
23-Nov-12	125.117268	1.997268	3.182619%	20.08	0	0.309%	0.000088	–0.000141	0.002822	0.291%	0.018%
26-Nov-12	125.03888	2.00888	3.186170%	20.08	0	–0.063%	0.000262	0.000036	–0.000713	–0.045%	–0.018%
27-Nov-12	124.650492	2.020492	3.202110%	20.04	0	–0.311%	0.000087	0.000159	–0.003194	–0.311%	0.000%
28-Nov-12	124.457104	–0.092896	3.126130%	20.52	2.113388	1.540%	0.000088	–0.000760	0.015591	1.568%	–0.028%
29-Nov-12	124.398716	–0.081284	3.128830%	20.51	0	–0.047%	0.000086	0.000027	–0.000554	–0.047%	0.000%
30-Nov-12	124.753552	–0.046448	3.116188%	20.53	0	0.285%	0.000086	–0.000126	0.002595	0.268%	0.017%

Source: Compiled with data from the UK Debt Management Office, http://www.dmo.gov.uk

- No convexity value was available, so I have used the simpler expression $r_C = y \times \delta t - MD \times \delta y$. This makes little difference to the overall results.
- Even for this gilt-edged security, there is appreciable day-to-day noise in the attribution calculation. However, over time the market and calculated returns follow each other closely. Useful ways to see this are either by constructing a scatter chart of true against calculated returns, or by graphing cumulative returns over time.

The use of expression (8.6) to perform attribution can be extremely appealing. If risk numbers for all the securities in a portfolio and benchmark are available, their use makes attribution:

- flexible;
- straightforward – the same expression can be used for all securities (but see comments below);
- simple – no pricing machinery is required;
- fast – the expression is simple to implement and calculate;
- futureproof – if new security types are introduced, then they can probably be modelled in this framework.

It is tempting to view (8.6) as a 'one size fits all' approach to attribution, and numerous commercial systems have been built on this basis. Unfortunately, this is not always a valid assumption:

- Some securities have other sources of return, such as inflation for TIPS (Treasury Inflation Protected Securities) and inflation-linked gilts.
- Many securities have multiple risk sensitivities. For instance, an FRN (floating rate note) has *two* duration measures: one for risk-free curve movements and one for credit spread movements.
- The model assumes a security with a single cashflow. For securities with large bullet payments, such as government and corporate bonds, the payment of coupons that are small relative to the final principal repayment does not affect this assumption too much. However, for sinking securities where the bond's principal is repaid in large tranches over its lifetime, the cash flow structure is much more complex and the accuracy of modelling the bond's return in terms of a single risk measure becomes questionable. In this case, many practitioners turn to the use of *key rate durations*, which increase the amounts of data needed by orders of magnitude.
- Some specialised types of securities, such as Australian and New Zealand bond futures, do not generate carry.

Any system that offers perturbational-based attribution should also offer the ability to customise the perturbational equation according to the type of security.[1]

8.3.1 When should you not use risk numbers for attribution?

Unfortunately, supplying daily risk numbers can be a surprisingly difficult (and expensive) problem. It can take many man-months to set up reliable, robust feeds for risk numbers. Further, risk numbers for some security types may not be available from commercial feeds at all, particularly for OTC derivatives, such as interest rate swaps, requiring in-house calculation.

Attribution systems are also *brittle*. This means that if one risk number is wrong, it can skew the entire analysis. This applies especially to bond futures, which often have substantial weights in managed portfolios.

Many millions of dollars have been wasted on attribution systems that assume that accurate, timely risk numbers are available. Be very careful before you commit to an attribution system that is designed on this principle.

The best attribution systems allow the use of both risk numbers and first-principles pricing, so are not subject to this risk.

8.3.2 Raw pricing functions or risk numbers: which are better?

It depends. For structurally simple, liquid securities, raw pricing functions are ideal. With a supply of daily yield curve files, all other analytics may be calculated internally.

For other security types, you may prefer to use risk numbers for some or all of your holdings, such as for securities requiring a complex pricing model, or specific yields.

Both models can be used concurrently in the same portfolio, if the attribution software supports this approach. In addition, there may be tradeoffs between implementation time and analytical complexity. For instance, there is little point in building a complex pricing model for a very particular type of swap if its performance contribution is minimal.

8.4 RESIDUALS

No matter how good your attribution model may be, it is unlikely to account exactly for all the market return generated by a security. The reason

[1] I have seen attribution systems that are built in exactly this way and that are used on portfolios of corporate bonds. The difficulty is that portfolio managers often like to invest in new types of security, and the attribution system may not be able to keep up with the new analytical requirements.

is that the market price of a security usually differs slightly from the theoretical price.

The difference between the true return and the theoretical return is called the *residual*.[2] Generally, a low residual is desirable and expected, both at the security and the portfolio level, but there are cases in which higher residuals are expected. For instance, pricing a corporate bond using a sovereign curve ignores all the return generated except for changes in the credit curve, and this will generate a substantial residual that is actually equivalent to credit return.

8.5 STAND-ALONE PORTFOLIOS

An important difference between top-down attribution and bottom-up attribution at the security level is that bottom-up attribution does not require a benchmark.

The Brinson attribution algorithms are expressed in terms of differences between the sector weights and returns for a portfolio and a benchmark. In contrast, bottom-up fixed income attribution may be run on a portfolio without any benchmark being present, or vice versa.

If a benchmark is available, the active returns from each source of risk may be derived in the same way. For instance, if the performance contributions to active return from each source of risk are as shown in the C_P and C_B columns in Table 8.2, the active performance contribution from each is the difference in the third column δC. The portfolio and benchmark analyses could have been run separately and only combined for this report.

Table 8.2 **Absolute and relative performance contributions for simple fixed income portfolio and benchmark**

Risk	C_P	C_B	δC
Carry	6 bp	4 bp	2 bp
Curve	10 bp	7 bp	3 bp
Credit	2 bp	4 bp	−2 bp
Total	18 bp	15 bp	3 bp

Note that the requirement for a benchmark still applies if any part of the calculation is top-down. For instance, balanced attribution (Chapter 13) combines elements of both Brinson and bottom-up attribution, and so requires benchmark data.

[2] Usage of the term *residual* is not consistent between practitioners. Fixed income attribution analysis uses *residual* in the above sense, but *residual* is also used to describe the total return of a portfolio not equalling the sum of its parts.

Part 3

SOURCES OF FIXED INCOME RETURN

9. Carry return

10. Sovereign curve attribution

11. Sector and credit return

12. Other security-specific sources of return

13. Balanced attribution

14. Duration allocation attribution

9

Carry return

9.1 Introduction

9.2 Carry-based investment strategies

9.3 Types of yield

9.4 Calculating carry return

9.5 Pros and cons of YTM

9.6 Decomposing carry

9.7 Which yield to use?

9.8 Decomposing carry return

9.9 Yield for non-bond securities

9.10 Using yield to maturity in attribution reports

9.1 INTRODUCTION

What is the return of a portfolio when the markets are closed?

For equity markets, the answer is straightforward. The reference prices at which the markets last closed should be used for revaluation. Since prices do not change and no dividends are announced, the portfolio's return will always be zero.

Matters are slightly more complex in the fixed income markets. Here, most securities offer regular, known cash flows to their owners, even if underlying interest rates fluctuate wildly. A bond's value will therefore increase over time as the next coupon draws closer, and this *accrued interest* is generated whether or not the markets are open. In other words, bonds are designed to generate a trickle of return every day of the week, including weekends and holidays.

The measurement of this *carry return*,[1] as distinct to return due to changes in other market conditions, is the subject of the present chapter.

9.2 CARRY-BASED INVESTMENT STRATEGIES

A common investment strategy is to structure a portfolio so that it generates higher carry return than its benchmark, while remaining hedged against other fixed income risks. The carry generated by a security is proportional to its yield, so this outperformance arises from investing in securities with higher yields than their counterparts in the benchmark. Such portfolios are often labelled *high-yield*.

A hedged high-yield portfolio should outperform its benchmark regardless of how underlying interest rates change. However, this outperformance will come with greater exposure to credit events and the risk of more frequent adverse events such as missed coupons, default, early redemption of callable bonds and market illiquidity, all of which can drive the portfolio's return down. A trader who manages such a portfolio must be skilled at assessing the risks involved in investing in these higher-yielding securities, and deciding where the market is wrong.

An attribution report will confirm that a high-yield strategy has actually worked, and that the portfolio is genuinely generating more yield-driven return than the benchmark. In addition, it will isolate market sectors where the strategy may not be working. Equally importantly, the report will confirm that the manager is not making or losing return because of

[1] Carry return is also referred to as *yield return, time return* or *coupon return*. A security or portfolio that has a high yield will generate a high carry return, so the two terms are often used interchangeably in attribution analyses.

other sources of risk, such as movements in the yield curve or changes in the credit spread.

9.3 TYPES OF YIELD

Several measures for a yield are used in the markets, according to the investment horizon and future intentions of the security's owner.

Some of these yield measurements are only applicable to coupon-paying securities, but the concept of yield applies to all fixed income instruments, including those that pay no coupons, and derivative securities.

9.3.1 Nominal yield

Consider a bond with a face (or par) value of $100 and a 5% annual coupon that matures in five years.

If this bond was purchased at par when it was first issued, and held to maturity when it is again priced at par, the annual rate of return made by holding the bond will be $5/$100 = 5%. This is called the nominal (or flat) yield, and is equal to the annual income of the bond, divided by its par value.

In practice, you would only use this measure of yield if you never expected to trade the bond. Even if this were the case, you might still need to mark-to-market the investment, since the market price of the bond is likely to vary away from par over its lifetime.

9.3.2 Simple yield

Suppose the same bond only has a year to run until maturity. For each $100 invested, the owner will receive a coupon payment of $5 and a profit of $5 due to the increase of the bond's price from $95 now to $100 at maturity. The return over the twelve months to maturity is therefore $10/$95 = 10.52%. This return is called the *simple yield.*

9.3.3 Running yield

The current, or running, yield is the annual coupon of the bond divided by its current clean price, which is the market price excluding accrued interest. If the clean price of this $100 par value bond is $95, then its running yield is $5/$95 = 5.36%. This is the bond's yield under the assumption that it can later be sold for the same price.

Running yield is most useful when one needs to compare the relative returns of various investment options over a short horizon compared to the lifetime of the investments.

9.3.4 Yield to maturity

The most widely used measure of yield is redemption yield, or *yield to maturity* (YTM). YTM is the single yield y at which future cash flows must be discounted to equal the current market price of the bond P:

$$P = \sum_{i=1}^{n} \frac{C_i}{(1 + y)^{t_i}} \tag{9.1}$$

where C_i and t_i are the value and time from the present (in years) of cash flow i.

This equation may be solved for y either numerically or by trial and error.

Yield to maturity measures the return generated by the bond if the security is purchased now and held to maturity. It represents a single-valued proxy for the bond's cash flows and the current levels of the yield curve.

Yield to maturity differs from running yield in one crucial respect. To use a phrase from game theory, fixed income securities are subject to 'the shadow of the future' (Dawkins, 1976), in that almost all have a known maturity date at which they will be worth par, irrespective of their current value. The effect of this known price point in the future can and does affect the current price. Yield to maturity takes these resulting capital gains or losses into account, while running yield does not. This *pull-to-par* effect is covered in more detail in Section 9.8.1.

9.4 CALCULATING CARRY RETURN

There exist at least two ways to calculate carry return:

- The first is to reprice the security from first principles at different times, under the assumption that the security's yield remains unchanged, so that the only cause of a change in the price is the passage of time. The return implied by the change in price is the carry.

  While conceptually straightforward, this method is not recommended. To calculate carry return using direct pricing over a period when a coupon is paid requires that you know the exact dates on which payment occurred, and this can be difficult because of weekends, bank holidays and country-specific settlement conventions.

- The second, far easier method is to use the security's yield to maturity. The carry return of the bond over an interval is simply given by

$$r_{carry} = y\delta t \tag{9.2}$$

  where y is the bond's yield to maturity, and δt is the elapsed time over the interval.

It is just as accurate to calculate carry return using yield to maturity as it is to use a first principles approach, and much less work, especially if you already have market values of YTM available.

Example

Over a week, a bond with a YTM of 5.5% generates carry return of

$$r_{carry} = 5.5\% \times \frac{7}{365} = 0.1055\% = 10.55 \text{ bp}$$

9.5 PROS AND CONS OF YTM

Despite being complex to calculate, yield to maturity is probably the most useful of all the yield measures shown here, as it makes calculation of carry return straightforward.

However, YTM does have some shortfalls. An important underlying assumption is that the coupons can be reinvested at the initial YTM of the bond, which may not be the case.

9.6 DECOMPOSING CARRY

Carry return can be decomposed in at least two ways:

- Into pull-to-par and running yield returns.
- Into risk-free carry and credit carry, by decomposing the YTM of a security into a portion due to risk-free yield, and a credit spread component.

9.7 WHICH YIELD TO USE?

Which is the most useful yield measure for attribution? It depends on the time-scale over which you hold the bond:

- If you buy the bond at issue and hold it to maturity, you will be unaffected by any fluctuations in the market price of the bond. In this case, the nominal yield may be appropriate for measuring the return on your investment.

- If you are trading bonds over the short term, then the running yield may be most useful, since this is a day-to-day measure of yield and takes no account of the pull-to-parity effect.
- If you are buying a bond now to hold to maturity, the yield to maturity will probably give you the clearest picture of the bond's value relative to others.

In practice, YTM is most widely used in the marketplace, since it provides a fairly realistic measure of the relative returns of securities that may have completely different characteristics.

9.8 DECOMPOSING CARRY RETURN

Carry return may be decomposed in several ways that reflect different investment strategies.

9.8.1 Pull to par and running yield

Yield to maturity is a more general measure of return than running yield because it includes both the interest payments the bondholder receives, and the capital gain (or loss) made when the bond matures. If a security's price is substantially different from par as it approaches maturity, this may have a noticeable effect on the security's return because its value has to converge to par. Even if interest rates are substantially higher than when the bond was issued, so that it is priced at a discount, the price will still be pulled upwards by this effect, which will drive the bond's yield downwards as maturity approaches.[2]

This effect is known as *pull to par* (or *reduction of maturity*), and can have a pronounced effect on the returns of bonds that are nearing maturity.[3]

Consider the 5% bond described earlier. The income portion of the yield to maturity is the running yield of the bond, as calculated above.

One way to measure the capital gain portion is to take the difference between the current clean price and the par value of the bond (100 − 95 = 5), divided by the number of years to maturity (5/5 = 1), divided by the current clean price of the bond (1/0.95 = 1.05%). We can therefore expect an extra 105 basis points from pull-to-par effects over the next five years.

Most attribution calculations are run over a shorter interval, in which case one can use the expression

$$y_{YTM} = y_{running\ yield} + y_{pull\ to\ par} \quad (9.3)$$

[2] Bonds priced at a premium will be subject to the opposite effect.

[3] The exception is for perpetual bonds, or consols, which have no set maturity date, and some types of constant maturity futures on bonds.

The YTM and the running yield will typically be available for reporting, so it is straightforward to calculate the portion of the bond's yield due to pull to par, and hence the resulting carry return.

9.8.2 Risk-free carry and credit carry

Everything else being equal, a bond with a lower credit rating will trade at a higher YTM than a treasury equivalent. This reflects the higher risk taken by the bond owner, for which higher returns are required.

For portfolios with large number of high-yielding securities (equivalently, those with lower credit ratings), it may be useful to decompose yield return into risk-free return and risk return.

To take a relatively extreme example, in 2012 Greek government bonds were yielding 16% with a credit rating of CCC, indicating that the market had factored in a 50% probability of default. German bonds with the same maturity and coupon had a yield to maturity of around 3% and a credit rating of AAA, reflecting the market's consensus that these bonds carried a virtually zero percent chance of default. The risk-free yield of the Greek bond was 3%, and the risk-driven yield was 16% − 3% = 13%. These yields may then be used to calculate the risk-free carry and the credit carry for the bond.

In general,

$$y_{YTM} = y_{risk\text{-}free\ yield} + y_{credit\ yield} \tag{9.4}$$

9.8.3 Risk-free carry, sector carry and security-specific carry

A corporate security's yield may be a combination of yield due to its underlying risk-free curve, yield due to its sector curve and security-specific yield according to its position relative to its sector curve.

An attribution analysis will measure the return generated by changes in all these quantities, but their absolute levels also generate carry return. These levels may be determined using the techniques described in Chapter 11. In general,

$$y_{YTM} = y_{risk\text{-}free\ yield} + y_{sector\ yield} + y_{security\text{-}specific\ yield} \tag{9.5}$$

9.8.4 Carry due to optionality

A bond with an embedded call allows the issuer to withdraw the bond at certain predefined times and return the principal, plus any accrued interest, to the purchaser. For the bondholder, this means that their funds will have to be reinvested elsewhere.

The bond issuer usually only does this if (1) they no longer need the funds, or (2) prevailing rates are lower than when the bond was issued, so that they can cancel the bond and raise more money at a lower rate. This is seldom a welcome event for the bondholder. Since interest rates have fallen, the funds now have to be reinvested at lower rate.

This *reinvestment risk* adds extra uncertainty for the bondholder. To compensate for the possibility of lower future income, a bond with a call option trades at a higher yield than a similar security with no optionality. The extra carry return generated by this higher yield may be displayed in a separate category in an attribution report.

Conversely, a bond with an embedded put allows the bondholder to exchange the bond for cash at any time and to reinvest it at a higher rate if market conditions allow. In this case the bond issuer pays a lower yield, because the reinvestment risk is taken by the bond issuer.

Depending on the bond's option features, alternative measures of yield may be appropriate for an attribution report, such as *yield-to-call* and *yield-to-worst*.

The topic of return generated by optionality on bonds is covered in more detail in Chapter 21.

9.8.5 Inflation carry

The return on all security types discussed so far can be regarded as the sum of their real return and some compensation for the reduction in value from inflation. An inflation-linked bond removes the uncertainly due to inflation by indexing its value to some price index, to ensure that its real value does not fall.

The YTM of an inflation-linked bond is the current inflation rate, plus the real yield to maturity. The carry of an inflation-linked bond therefore requires both these quantities. For more information, refer to Chapter 17.

9.8.6 Other sources of carry

Even when all other effects are removed, bonds with the same maturity, coupon and credit rate can still show different yields. Reasons include:

- *Liquidity*. A bond from an obscure issuer, or one that is not heavily traded, may trade at a higher yield than one that is more liquid but otherwise identical, to compensate the buyer for the difficulties in selling the bond at a later date.
- *Cheap/dear effects*, or whether the bond is on or off the run; that is, a heavily traded reference issue.
- *Tax effects* – whether a bond is bid by the marketplace because of preferential tax treatment.

- *Repo effects* – whether the security is bid in the repo market.
- *Convexity effects* – whether a bond is more or less desirable because of high levels of convexity, leading to changes in its price and hence its yield. Higher convexity will lead to measurable outperformance when the term structure moves, but affects yield to a much lower degree.
- *Market noise* – change in yield that cannot be allocated to any other effect.

I am not aware of any sensible ways to split these effects apart without extensive further analysis. Fortunately, they tend to be minor.

9.9 YIELD FOR NON-BOND SECURITIES

Many fixed income securities pay coupons over a fixed term, but there are some exceptions. For instance, bank bills generate no running yield return, while perpetual bonds produce no pull-to-par return. The treatment of carry for particular security types is covered in Part 4.

9.10 USING YIELD TO MATURITY IN ATTRIBUTION REPORTS

The market convention is to use yield to maturity for reporting time return on attribution reports. Even if you do not actually need YTM to calculate carry return, it is still preferable to cast the attribution report in terms of YTM and to use equation (9.2) for reporting purposes. This follows market convention and is straightforward to explain to traders and investors.

10

Sovereign curve attribution

10.1 Introduction

10.2 Yield curve models

10.3 Parallel shift and modified duration, and why they matter

10.4 Measuring twist

10.5 Taxonomy of curve shifts

10.6 Sources of yield curve data

10.1 INTRODUCTION

This chapter describes some of the more common ways in which movements in risk-free curves are described and measured.

Virtually every fixed income security traded in the marketplace has its price affected to varying degrees by its associated risk-free curve, so changes in the level and shape of this curve form an important source of return for fixed income portfolios. Many investment strategies are framed entirely in terms of such movements.

The previous chapter described how changes in a security's yield may be converted into return. Coupled with the mathematical machinery described in Chapter 8, this chapter shows ways in which the change in yield arising from movements in the sovereign curve can be decomposed to reflect various investment strategies.

10.2 YIELD CURVE MODELS

A yield curve is generally defined by a set of yields at various tenor points, and this data then defines a yield at any arbitrary maturity. A sample yield curve is shown in Table 10.1.

Table 10.1

USD yield curve on 16 October 2014

Maturity	Yield
0.25	0.05%
0.5	0.10%
1	0.35%
2	0.75%
5	1.82%
7	2.17%
10	2.66%
20	2.94%

There are two approaches to using this data:

- the *parametric* approach, where the curve is modelled using a parametric function with a small number of parameters that has been fitted to this data;
- the *spline* approach, using non-parametric polynomial interpolation on raw curve data.

Both approaches are often encountered, but in practice the most widely used way to calculate a yield at an arbitrary maturity is simple linear interpolation between existing yield points.

Parametric and spline modelling is described in Appendix D.

10.3 PARALLEL SHIFT AND MODIFIED DURATION, AND WHY THEY MATTER

For the following reasons, parallel shift is generally regarded as one of the most important drivers of portfolio performance:

- Principal component analysis shows the bulk of yield curve movements can be modelled as parallel shifts (Phoa, 1998).
- One of the most common hedging measurements, modified duration, is a measure of a security's sensitivity to parallel shifts.

For both reasons, parallel shift is a useful measure of how markets have moved. However, it should always be used with caution. Not all market shifts are parallel, and not all security returns are driven by duration.

10.3.1 Measuring parallel shift

Despite its importance in fixed income attribution, there is no standard, agreed way to calculate the parallel shift of a yield curve. Commonly used techniques include:

1. measurement of the movement in the curve at a given maturity, such as the 5- or 10-year point, the benchmark's maturity or its modified duration, and setting that change to be the parallel movement;
2. forming an average of the curve's level at each sample point, and taking the difference over time;
3. calculating the area under the curve, dividing by the longest maturity, then taking the difference over time.

Each method carries its own advantages and disadvantages.

In general, if one is attempting to compare the duration return generated by different investors, then some standardisation of how they measure duration shifts is required. This is not widely appreciated, and at least one commercial system measures parallel shift as a function of the benchmark's composition, which has the unfortunate effect of generating different parallel return for identical portfolios, according to which benchmark is currently in use.

Option (1) designates the yield at a particular maturity M as the most representative yield on the curve. To measure the parallel shift of the curve as a whole, simply measure changes in this level:

$$\delta y_P = y_M^{t+1} - y_M^t \tag{10.1}$$

where y_M^t is the yield on the curve at maturity M at time t.

The difficulty here is in deciding what maturity best fits this criterion. If it changes over time, or if sample maturity differs between investors, then comparability between different analyses is lost.

Option (2) requires calculating the difference between the averages δy_P of all the curve's sample points at the start and end of an interval:

$$\delta y_P = \frac{1}{n}\left[\sum_{i=1}^{n}(y_i^{t+1} - y_i^t)\right] \tag{10.2}$$

where y_i^t is the yield of sample point i at time t. This might seem the obvious way of measuring changes in the overall level of the curve, but in practice yield curves tend to be more heavily sampled at lower maturities, and so this method overweights shorter maturities at the expense of longer maturities.

Option (3) is arguably the most accurate means of measuring parallel shift. By calculating the area under the curve and dividing by the longest maturity, it removes any sampling bias. It is also straightforward to calculate, which cannot be said of a principal component analysis. In this case, δy_P is given by

$$\delta y_P = \frac{1}{m_1 - m_0}\left[\int_{m_0}^{m_1} y^{t+1}(m)dm - \int_{m_0}^{m_1} y^t(m)dm\right] \tag{10.3}$$

where y^t and y^{t+1} are the yield curves at times t and $t + 1$, respectively. Numerically, this expression may be approximated by

$$\delta y_P = \sum_{i=0}^{m-1} \frac{y_{i+1}^T + y_i^T}{2(m_{i+1} - m_i)} - \sum_{i=0}^{m-1} \frac{y_{i+1}^{T+1} + y_i^{T+1}}{2(m_{i+1} - m_i)} \tag{10.4}$$

where each summand is the area under the yield curve between maturities T and $T + 1$.

Example

The level of the USD yield curve over the final quarter of 2008, a time of high market volatility, is shown in Table 10.2. Here I show each of the above techniques applied to this data.

Table 10.2

USD yield curve over Q4 2008

Maturity	30-Sep-08	30-Dec-08
0.25	1.60%	0.26%
0.5	1.78%	0.34%
1	2.00%	0.75%
2	2.28%	0.94%
5	3.38%	1.76%
7	3.85%	2.11%
10	4.43%	2.88%
20	4.31%	2.58%

Option 1: The parallel curve movement was the change in yield at the 7-year point, which is 2.11% − 3.85% = −1.74%.

Option 2: The average yield on 30-Sep-08 was 2.95%, and the average yield on 31-Dec-08 was 1.45%. The parallel curve change was therefore −1.50%.

Option 3: The areas under the USD curve, calculated using trapezoidal integration, are shown in the columns labelled 'Area' in Table 10.3.

Table 10.3

Areas under the USD yield curve

Maturity	30-Sep-08	Area	30-Dec-08	Area
0.25	1.60%		0.26%	
0.5	1.78%	0.42%	0.34%	0.08%
1	2.00%	0.95%	0.75%	0.27%
2	2.28%	2.14%	0.94%	0.85%
5	3.38%	8.49%	1.76%	4.05%
7	3.85%	7.23%	2.11%	3.87%
10	4.43%	12.42%	2.88%	7.49%
20	4.31%	43.70%	2.58%	27.30%
TOTAL		75.35%		43.90%

To see how these quantities are calculated, consider the part of the yield curve between 0.25 and 0.5 years. The area under the curve is approximated by a trapezoid with width $0.5 - 0.25 = 0.25$ years and sides with height 1.60% and 1.78%. Its area is therefore

$$0.5 \times (1.60\% + 1.78\%) \div 2 = 0.42\%$$

The average height of the curve is this area divided by the width of the measurement area ($20 - 0.25 = 19.75$ years), giving average curve levels of 3.83% and 2.22% at the start and end of the sample period, with an overall parallel curve change of −1.59%.

Other points to be considered include the longest and shortest maturities to be included in the calculation of the curve movement. Should money market rates contribute to a measure of yields that can go out to 50 years? Conversely, should 50-year rates be allowed to affect shifts in the cash market curve? These questions must be settled before calculation occurs.

It is important that the consumers of attribution reports understand what assumptions are being used when parallel shifts are calculated. Whatever measure you choose, make sure it is applied consistently.

10.4 MEASURING TWIST

A straightforward way to measure curve twist is to fit a straight line between the curve points at two given maturities, such as the 2- and 10-year points. The process is carried out at the start and the end of each attribution interval.

To find the twist at a given maturity, the level of this fitted curve at that maturity is measured and the difference taken.

This change in yield includes both shift (parallel) and twist movements in the curve. To isolate the twist, the change due to parallel movements should be subtracted from this value.

Example

We use the data in Table 10.2 to calculate the shift and twist movements in the curve at the 5-year point.

The slopes m_0 and m_1 of a straight line between the 2- and 10-year points at times t_0 (30-Sep-08) and t_1 (31-Dec-08) are

$$m_0 = \frac{4.43\% - 2.28\%}{10 - 2} = 0.2688\%$$

and

$$m_0 = \frac{2.88\% - 0.94\%}{10 - 2} = 0.2425\%$$

The equations of the straight lines $y(m)$ between these points at times t_0 and t_1 are therefore

$$y - 2.28\% = 0.2688\% \times (m - 2)$$

and

$$y - 0.94\% = 0.2425\% \times (m - 2)$$

respectively. The values of these expressions at maturity $m = 5$ are 3.09% and 1.67% respectively, so the total change in yield from shift and twist combined was −1.42%.

Assuming we used option 3 to calculate the parallel shift in the curve, the change in the curve due to twist at this maturity was therefore −1.42% −1.59% = 0.17%.

Curvature can now be measured as the change in the curve at the given maturity, minus the change due to shift and twist. At the 5-year point the level has dropped from 3.38% to 1.76%, or −1.62%. Since −1.42% of this is accounted for by shift and twist, the curvature component is therefore −1.62% + 1.42% = −0.20%.

To summarise, the yield change at the 5-year point is decomposed as shown in Table 10.4:

Table 10.4

Change in 5-year USD yields over Q4 2008

Movement	Change
Shift	−1.59%
Twist	0.17%
Curvature	−0.20%
TOTAL	−1.62%

Other ways to measure twist include fitting the yield curves to a Nelson-Siegel function and measuring the value of β_1, or fitting a first order polynomial to the entire curve using a least-squares approach and measuring its slope (see Section 10.5.9). At present there is no standard market approach to measuring curve twist.

It is also possible to define twist in terms of curve rotations about a given maturity point. Although appealing, such an approach should be applied very carefully. Colin (2005) gives an example of how this technique can be abused by allowing the twist point to vary over time.

10.5 TAXONOMY OF CURVE SHIFTS

An important part of attribution is ensuring that the curve decomposition matches the investment process. The techniques presented here range from the trivial to the complex.

In most cases, simpler is better. For instance, consider a global investor who holds sovereign debt issued by many countries. Their views on allocation to each market are likely driven by a macro-economic view of the overall direction of interest rates.

This manager is unlikely to hold a detailed view on the curvature of each market curve, and to provide attribution information at this level will probably only act as a distraction.

This section presents some of the most commonly used ways to decompose sovereign curve movements.

10.5.1 No sovereign curve effects

This approach ignores the effects of movements in the risk-free curve. If any return does occur from this source of risk, it is treated as residual.

The approach is appropriate for portfolios that are purely credit driven and have no exposure to changes in the sovereign curve.

However, interest-rate risk exposure is extremely common in fixed income portfolios, so explicitly ignoring any risk-free returns is seldom a good idea.

The exception is if you are absolutely certain that this is not the case, as with an equity portfolio.

10.5.2 Undecomposed curve return

Each security is repriced using the yield curve at the start and end of each calculation interval. From these prices, a single security interval return is calculated.

This type of decomposition is the simplest possible attribution, and can be shown together with carry and credit returns.

A portfolio manager might wish to see this return to verify that no interest rate exposure was taken, or that interest rate hedging worked.

10.5.3 Duration and curvature

In this model, curve shifts are regarded as a combination of a parallel component and a non-parallel component. The sum of the two movements is the overall curve change.

To implement this model, the parallel curve change is calculated using one of the techniques shown earlier. Curvature is then given by overall curve change, minus parallel shift.

For instance, suppose the curve showed a parallel movement of 10 bp upwards over a month. The yield of a bond with a 5-year maturity moved up by 15 bp. In this case, we would assign 10 bp of the bond's yield change to parallel shift, and 15 bp − 10 bp = 5 bp to non-parallel, or curvature, shift.

For simple duration attribution, three prices p_0, p_1, p_2 are required:

- p_0 uses the curve at the start of the interval;
- p_1 uses the starting curve plus the parallel change in the curve;

- p_2 uses the starting curve, plus parallel changes, plus non-parallel changes, which is equivalent to the curve at the end of interval.

Return due to parallel shift is then given by

$$r_{parallel} = \frac{p_1 - p_0}{p_0}$$

and the return due to non-parallel shift by

$$r_{non\text{-}parallel} = \frac{p_2 - p_1}{p_0}$$

The sum of the two terms is

$$r_{total} = \frac{p_2 - p_0}{p_0}$$

which is the overall return of the security over the interval due to movements in the curve.

10.5.4 Shift, twist and curvature

In this model, shift and twist are calculated as defined previously. Curvature is then set to be the change in the actual curve, minus the change due to shift and twist movements.

An attribution model that uses this approach will calculate *four* yield curves:

- the curve at the start of the interval;
- the starting curve, plus the parallel change in the curve;
- the starting curve, plus parallel changes, plus twist changes;
- the starting curve, plus parallel changes, plus twist changes, plus other higher-order changes. This curve is equivalent to the curve at the end of the interval.

Each security is priced on each curve to generate four prices p_0, p_1, p_2, p_3.

Return due to parallel shift is then calculated by

$$r_{parallel} = \frac{p_1 - p_0}{p_0}$$

return due to twist shift by

$$r_{twist} = \frac{p_2 - p_1}{p_0}$$

and return due to curvature by

$$r_{curvature} = \frac{p_3 - p_2}{p_0}$$

As before, the sum of the three terms is the overall return of the security due to curve movements.

Curvature movement is sometimes referred to as *butterfly*, and attribution analysis that includes these three effects may be labelled *shift-twist-butterfly* attribution. The origin of the term is obscure.

10.5.5 Principal component analysis

Principal component analysis (PCA) is a relatively recently developed statistical technique to perform dimensionality reduction. Given a system with a large number of dimensions, PCA identifies functions that characterise the changes seen as lower-dimensional systems (Colin, 2007).

Principal component analysis uses a suitably large number of historical yield curve changes to determine a small set of basis functions that can be linearly combined to represent these curve movements in the most economical way.

This is accomplished by forming the variance-covariance matrix V from the sample of spot rate changes at N selected maturities. By calculating the N orthogonal eigenvectors of V and ranking by eigenvalue size, the highest ranked eigenvector forms a basis function that explains as much as possible of the observed curve motion in terms of a single vector. By using a combination of this vector and lower ranked eigenvectors, the underlying data can be approximated to any degree of accuracy required.

The variances of the principal components are given by the magnitudes of the eigenvalues, so that the eigenvector with the highest value has the most explanatory power on the underlying data. If the values of the majority of eigenvalues are low, then this indicates that the underlying data can be closely modelled by a small number of functions, which represent some underlying structure in the data. Therefore, PCA is a useful technique for reducing the dimensionality of a modelling problem. In particular, PCA has been found to work well on yield curve changes (Phoa, 1998; Barber and Copper, 1996), since in practice practically all yield curve changes can be closely approximated using linear combinations of the first three eigenfunctions from a PCA.

Principal component analysis on historical yield curve data shows that curve movements fall into a number of fairly clearly defined types. Typically, the first eigenfunction is close to a flat line, the second rises monotonically but is seldom a straight line and the third imposes some curvature motion. These functions are usually interpreted as shift, twist and curvature.

Principal component analysis has the very desirable feature of allocating as much of a yield curve's movement to lower order movements as possible; however, there are disadvantages:

- Investment managers do not make decisions in terms of a PCA market view.
- PCA can require a substantial curve history.

- The results are dependent on the data set used to construct the basis functions and the interval over which they were constructed, so results calculated over different intervals may not be comparable.

If a shift/twist/butterfly (STB) analysis shows a small twist return but a large curvature return, it may be useful to repeat the analysis with a PCA decomposition. If the third-order PCA component is large, then the curvature effect is probably genuine.

However, these movements are typically slightly different from more conventional interpretations of these terms. The shift movement from PCA is usually close, but not identical to, a parallel curve shift, and the twist movement is not uniform across all maturities. For these reasons, PCA may not directly represent investment outcomes in terms of the decisions that were taken by the trader.

10.5.6 Key rate durations

Mortgage-backed bonds and other amortising securities typically have their cash flows spread across a range of maturities, rather than being concentrated at a single maturity payment. As a result, they have a much more complex exposure to yield curve movements than a simple bullet security such as a treasury bond.

The key rate duration (KRD) approach ignores global curve movements, and instead calculates the effect of changes in the yield curve at predefined maturity points. The rates at these points are then labelled *key rates*. KRD analysis measures the effects of changes at these key rate points, rather than different types of global curve movements.

KRD returns may be calculated from first principles or perturbationally. In practice, perturbational KRD models often require unfeasible amounts of data, which can lead to operational difficulties.

10.5.7 KRD from first principles

A KRD analysis uses a zero coupon yield curve at the start and end of an interval, and a set of reference maturities:

- First, the security is first priced off the start curve.
- Next, the start curve is modified so that its level at the first reference maturity is changed to the corresponding level at the end curve. Yields that lie at or beyond neighbouring reference maturities are left unchanged, while yields that lie in the interval adjoining the current reference

maturity are linearly scaled. The security is then priced off this intermediate curve.

- The start curve is then successively modified so that its value at the *n*th reference maturity is changed to the value from the end curve, as described earlier. At each change, the security is priced using the new curve.
- At the end of the process, the intermediate curve is identical to the end curve.

The return due to the changes in the prices is now calculated. The sum of the returns will equal the overall return for the security over the interval, and the individual sub-returns are generated by changes at the given reference maturities.

10.5.8 Perturbational KRD

The sensitivity of a security's price to changes at a particular maturity is measured by the key rate duration, just as its sensitivity to parallel curve shifts of a security's overall price is measured by the modified duration.

If the values of these key rate durations are available, the overall security return from curve movements is then given by

$$r_{risk\text{-}free\ curve} = -\sum_{i=1}^{n} KRD_i \times \delta y_i \tag{10.5}$$

where n is the number of key rates, KRD_i is the key rate duration at maturity i and δy_i is the change in the zero curve at that maturity.

For perturbational attribution, the KRD approach requires knowledge of each security's sensitivity to changes in the sovereign curve at each key rate. These key rate durations must be sourced externally. A perturbational KRD approach therefore requires substantially more data than a conventional perturbational approach.

10.5.9 CCB attribution

CCB attribution uses the Colin-Cubilié-Bardoux algorithm (Colin et al., 2006) to calculate the twist and curvature movements of a yield curve. The technique takes a conventional approach to calculating the parallel shift of a yield curve, but performs a least-squares fit of a first-order polynomial to calculate the twist of the curve. This removes many of the inherent problems involved when fixed twist points are defined.

10.6 SOURCES OF YIELD CURVE DATA

The definition and calculation of yield curves for attribution is something of a black art, and can be comparable in difficulty to maintaining a benchmark from scratch, particularly where custom curves are to be set up. The three main sources of sovereign curve data are:

- *Existing portfolios*: One convenient source of yield curve data can be your existing portfolios and benchmarks. However, yields from this source should be treated with care. None of the data will have been filtered or selected, and its use can present many difficulties.

  For sovereign curves, it may be preferable to select a subset of liquid reference issues and to use these to define the curve. These securities might be on-the-run bonds in the US, deliverable bonds for futures contracts or securities that are otherwise known to be highly liquid.

  It is critically important that curves used for attribution (i) model the markets accurately; (ii) are smooth and (iii) do not show unrealistic levels of noise and variation from day to day. This can cause difficulties for countries with a limited number of government bond issues, such as New Zealand or Singapore. Data on reference bonds may only be provided as par yields, requiring the use of a bootstrap to construct a zero curve.
- *Central banks*: Many central banks publish machine-readable sovereign curve data, which is often ideal for running basic attribution analyses. For instance, the Bank of England publishes both zero sovereign curve and real yield curves on a daily basis. However, sovereign curves are not available for some currencies, or in limited form for others, and credit curves are not available from this source. Data is usually available in the form of CSV or XML files, or Excel spreadsheets.

  Appendix H provides a list of central banks that publish sovereign curve data.
- *Data vendors*: A data vendor may be the only realistic source of yield curves for smaller countries.

11

Sector and credit return

11.1 Credit spreads

11.2 Sectors and credit ratings

11.3 Building sector curves

11.4 Attribution using sector curves

11.5 Attribution on Euro bond portfolios

11.6 Attribution on credit portfolios

11.7 Credit attribution without a credit curve

11.1 CREDIT SPREADS

A major source of return in many fixed income portfolios is *credit* or *sector spread.*

Securities such as UK gilts and US treasury bonds are conventionally regarded as risk-free. Although their prices may vary as market conditions change, default on a coupon or a repayment of principal is never expected to occur because of the issuer's ability to levy taxes. Such securities are referred to as *government* or *sovereign* debt.

However, government bonds only form a part of the debt on issue in the capital markets. Bonds are also issued by other non-sovereign entities, such companies (corporate bonds) or local governments (muni bonds). Often, these instruments carry additional risk due to the possibility of default and a resulting capital loss for the purchaser.

A corporate bond may have exactly the same terms and conditions as a government bond. However, because it is a riskier investment, it will trade at a lower price than its risk-free counterpart. If its coupons are fixed, it will then generate a higher yield over time, thus compensating the owner for the additional risks incurred in holding the instrument.

The difference in yield between a corporate bond and a government bond with the same maturity, coupon and payment frequency is called the *credit spread.* If the bond is one of a number that fall into a particular sector, their yields define a yield curve, and this is called a *sector curve.* A typical sector might be all securities in a particular industry with the same credit rating and currency.

A credit spread can refer to an individual bond, but just as frequently it will refer to the difference in levels between a sector curve and a risk-free curve. Generally this spread is not constant, but increases at longer maturities. This effect is illustrated in Figure 11.1.

Figure 11.1

CAD credit curves

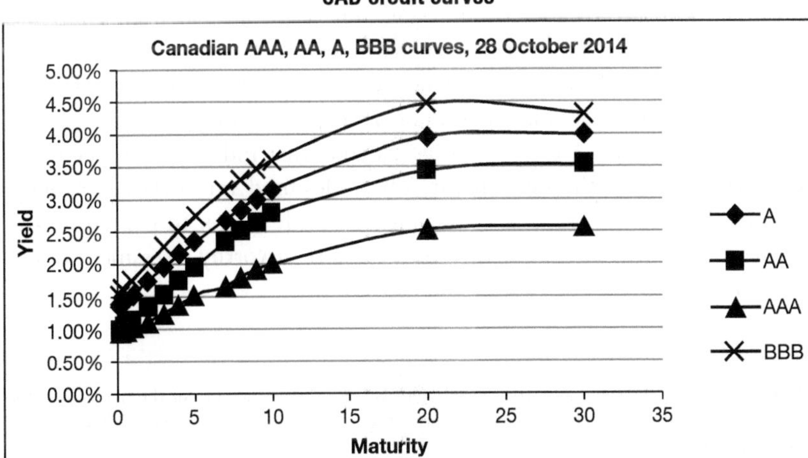

Credit spreads move independently from the underlying risk-free yield curve depending on the perceived creditworthiness of the bond's issuer. The result is that they generate an additional source of return for corporate bonds, in addition to the conventional sources of carry and market return.

Example

The yield to maturity (YTM) of a 10-year corporate bond was 5.2% at the start of a month and 4.7% at its end. The yield to maturity of a 10-year government bond with the same maturity date, coupon and payment frequency was 3.3% at the start of the same month and 3.1% at its end. The modified duration of the bond was seven years. What was the return from carry, sovereign curve return and credit spread?

- The carry return was $5.2\%/12 = 0.43\%$.[1]
- The sovereign yield changed from 3.3% to 3.1%, so the return due to changes in the sovereign curve was $-7 \times (0.031 - 0.033) = 1.4\%$.
- The credit spread changed from 5.2% to 4.7%, so the return due to changes in the credit curve was $-7 \times (0.047 - 0.052) - (0.031 - 0.033) = 2.1\%$.

Note that changes in the sovereign curve are subtracted from the overall yield, since this includes the changes due to both the level of the sovereign curve and the credit spread.

11.2 SECTORS AND CREDIT RATINGS

Corporate bonds vary widely in creditworthiness. The best are those with the highest possible AAA rating, typically issued by well-established companies with strong financial balance sheets. The worst are highly speculative investments. These are sometimes called *junk bonds*, and pay highly inflated yields to compensate the investor for their risks.

To allow risks to be assessed, one or more of the three credit ratings agencies (Moody's, Fitch, Standard and Poor's) assign a *credit rating* to most bonds at the time of issue. A credit rating is a code that indicates the perceived creditworthiness of the instrument. The codes used vary between agency, but give largely the same information (see Table 11.1). In principle, the purchaser or holder of the security then has a trustworthy assessment of the bond's risks.

---

[1] Strictly speaking, to calculate carry one should use an average measure of the YTM over the interval. Since most calculations are over short intervals, the effect of variation in YTM on carry is negligible.

Table 11.1

Equivalent credit ratings by issuer

Standard and Poor's	Moody's	Fitch
AAA	Aaa	AAA
AA+	Aa1	AA+
AA	Aa2	AA
AA–	Aa3	AA–
A+	A1	A+
A	A2	A
A–	A3	A–
BBB+	Baa1	BBB+
BBB	Baa2	BBB
BBB–	Baa3	BBB–
BB+	Ba1	BB+
BB	Ba2	BB
BB–	Ba3	BB–
B+	B1	B+
B	B2	B
B–	B3	B–
CCC+	Caa1	CCC
CCC	Caa2	CCC
CCC–	Caa3	CCC
CC	D	CCC
D	D	DDD
D	D	DD
D	D	D

Credit ratings are fairly well correlated with probability of default (see Table 11.2), and it is quite common for a bond's credit rating to change during its lifetime in response to changing conditions and the economic prospects of the bond-issuer. For instance, in August 2012 Standard and Poor's downgraded the US debt rating from AAA to AA+, citing concerns about the US budget deficit and political brinkmanship in Congress.

A downgrade is an important and news-worthy event, as it raises the costs of borrowing in the capital markets, whether the issuer be a corporation or a sovereign government.

Corporate bonds are often categorised by the type of issuer. The financial outlook for companies in the same market sector tends to be similar, so it can be useful to know the industrial sector for a given bond in order to compare it to its peers.

Table 11.2 **Cumulative historical default rates for US corporate bonds, compiled using data from the Municipal Bond Fairness Act 2008**

	Moody's		S&P	
Rating category	Muni	Corp	Muni	Corp
Aaa/AAA	0.00%	0.52%	0.00%	0.60%
Aa/AA	0.06%	0.52%	0.00%	1.50%
A/A	0.03%	1.29%	0.23%	2.91%
Baa/BBB	0.13%	4.64%	0.32%	10.29%
Ba/BB	2.65%	19.12%	1.74%	29.93%
B/B	11.86%	43.34%	8.48%	53.72%
Caa-C/CCC-C	16.58%	69.18%	44.81%	69.19%

11.3 BUILDING SECTOR CURVES

Sector groupings may include:

- bonds with a particular credit rating, eg AA, A, BBB+ in a given currency. These are called *credit curves*;
- bonds issued by a particular industry sector in a given currency. These are called *sector curves*;
- amount on issue;
- seniority of tranche.

Care should be taken in selecting bonds for inclusion in a particular sector curve. For instance, choosing all A-rated bonds for the Euro would lead to a very noisy curve, because the range of issuers varies widely, both by industry and by country. In this case the level and shape of the curve will not be obvious.

In general, it can be extremely difficult to construct usable sector curves for the following reasons:

- there may be too few bonds in a particular sector to define an accurate curve at an adequate fine level of detail;
- illiquidity of securities can lead to poorly defined and noise yield curves, particularly for emerging market debt;
- some bond classes may not exist at long maturities, so it may not be possible to define, say, a 30-year sector curve when the longest bond on issue matures in eight years.

Figure 11.2 illustrates some of these issues.[2] The sector curve lies along the lower boundary of the region defined by the cluster of yields. While

[2] Weighted average life (WAL) is used here instead of time to maturity, as the former measure includes the effects of embedded options on each bond's expected lifetime.

Figure 11.2

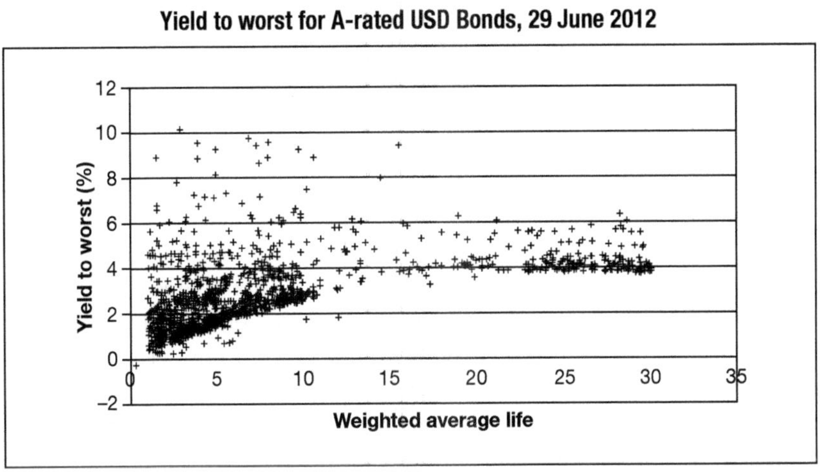

one could fit a curve to this boundary, it would not be straightforward: one would probably use a parameterised curve representation and a fitting routine to make the curve lie as closely to the edge of the area as possible. In addition, day-to-day fluctuations would run the risk of making the curve jump around, generating noisy returns.

Even with a large benchmark, some curve data may be missing or incomplete. For instance, the number of BBB-rated Norwegian bonds is very low, and to define a corresponding curve may be difficult.

11.3.1 Constraints on the shape of curves

In principle, an attribution analyst may have to monitor and work with thousands of different sector curves. It is therefore useful to be aware of some basic properties that all such curves must follow:

- All curves should equal the cash rate at zero maturity.
- Zero curves at different credit ratings for the same market should never cross. At any given maturity, the zero-coupon yield for a lower credit rating should always lie above the corresponding yield at a higher credit rating.
- Zero-coupon sector curves at the same maturity can cross because they may be affected by unrelated market conditions.

Be aware of movements in the curve beyond the longest maturity, and do not assume that the curve is flat at and beyond the longest points. There may be additional curve movements beyond this point.

For sector or credit curves that are defined by very low numbers of data points, more accurate results may be gained by looking at their spread to a known accurate curve and describing the curve as the risk-free curve plus this spread. This will ensure that the shape of the curve is broadly correct.

The generation of accurate sector and credit curves is a complex constrained optimisation problem. In addition to modelling existing sample points, sector curves must also conform to observed levels of other related curves and not show unrealistically high volatilities from day to day.

The selection of suitable securities to define market curves is comparable in most ways to running a large bond index, and is not for the faint-hearted. Unless you have substantial resources available, I strongly recommend that you use pre-calculated sector curves for your attribution analysis rather than trying to construct your own curves from raw yields. Consider whether you really need sector or credit curves for your analysis, bearing in mind that most of the return on your attribution report will come from carry, movements in the risk-free curve, and changes in the credit spread.

11.3.2 Option-adjusted spread

The spread of a security over its risk-free curve is sometimes referred to as the *option-adjusted spread* (OAS), rather than its spread.

OAS is a measure of the extra yield generated by embedded options in a callable or puttable bond. It is often used interchangeably with credit spread, even for bonds that do not have any embedded options.

11.4 ATTRIBUTION USING SECTOR CURVES

Sector spreads can be used in several ways to calculate attribution returns.

11.4.1 Credit return

The most direct way is to calculate the return generated by changes in credit spreads, and to aggregate this return by sector. Any changes in yield that are not accounted for by movements in the risk-free curve or movements in the sector curve (liquidity, market noise, residuals) are bundled together into an 'Other' category.

11.4.2 Sector and security spread

In this approach, one measures the change between the risk-free and the sector curve at each security's maturity, and the change between the sector curve and the actual yield of the security at its maturity. Return from the first change is called *sector spread*, and return from the second is called *security spread*.[3]

Spread change allocation allows the user to monitor the investor's skill in:

- picking industry sectors that outperformed;
- picking securities within these sectors that performed better than their peers.

Both sets of returns can be calculated for a portfolio in isolation, without referring to a benchmark. However, if a benchmark is available, a further analysis is possible based on relative weights by sector. In this case a Brinson-style analysis is also possible.

11.4.3 Sector curve allocation and selection

This type of analysis has similarities to the Brinson approach in that it measures whether given sectors are over- or underweighted relative to the benchmark, and whether those sectors over- or underperform. This type of analysis requires both benchmark data and sector curves, and is appropriate for the portfolio manager who concentrates on investment in particular bond sectors, rather than on a per-security basis.

For instance, a manager might hold a view that automotive bonds will outperform the rest of the market due to contracting credit spreads for this asset class. An attribution report that includes returns from sector curve allocation will show whether any returns were generated from this source of risk.

11.5 ATTRIBUTION ON EURO BOND PORTFOLIOS

Although government bonds issued by countries in the Eurozone are denominated in Euros, economic conditions currently vary widely from country to country across the Eurozone. In the absence of a bond backed by all countries, Euro bonds issued by different countries will trade at varying spreads to each other, reflecting their relative risks of default. For instance, Greek Euro bonds traded at spreads of 70% over German bonds during the European financial crisis of 2012, reflecting the market's assumption of an impending Greek default.

The reference curve for Euro bonds is usually taken to be the German curve, reflecting Germany's strong financial position and creditworthiness.

3 Confusingly, these terms are also sometimes labelled *spread return* and *selection return*, inviting confusion with the Brinson model.

Many fund managers will hold varying amounts of European government debt issued by other countries with the aim of profiting from contractions in credit spreads. The curves for these other countries are called *country curves* (see Figure 11.3).

Figure 11.3 **Euro par curves, 30 September 2014**

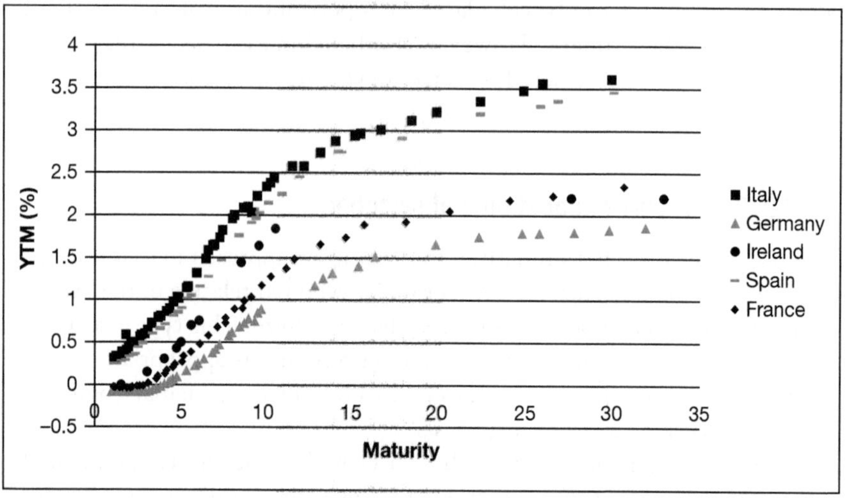

The returns made from such a strategy can be measured in two ways.

11.5.1 Attribution without country curves

Here, one measures the change in credit spread for each issue at the start and end of each measurement interval to calculate the return thus generated.

While straightforward, this approach aggregates country curve effects with security-specific effects. For countries that are only represented by a few securities, or for securities that have a volatile price, this can give misleading results.

11.5.2 Attribution with country curves

In this case one measures the change in the spread between the reference curve and the appropriate country curve at each bond's maturity, and the change in the spread between the country curve and the security's yield to maturity. The sum of the two is the overall credit spread change.

Country curves are perhaps the most straightforward sector curves to source, as they are relatively widely available.

11.6 ATTRIBUTION ON CREDIT PORTFOLIOS

A credit-based strategy can be run in at least two ways:

1. by investing in higher-yielding securities for which the market has overestimated risk;
2. by looking for undervalued securities with a price that will rise as their credit outlook improves.

Fixed income attribution can measure the return generated by either or both types of strategy.

For the most detailed possible credit attribution, one could supply all credit curves applicable for a given market, and measure the changes in spread between each curve for each security; one could then aggregate and measure the return generated by changes in the AAA-AA spread, the AA-A spread, the A-BBB spread and so on.[4]

11.7 CREDIT ATTRIBUTION WITHOUT A CREDIT CURVE

Occasionally you may be asked to provide a sector-curve analysis without having a sector curve available. For instance, you might have a portfolio of Euro bonds to analyse in which spreads vary widely by issuing country, but you may only have a risk-free German curve to hand.

The simplest way to do this is to look at the securities against which the report will be run, and use these to define a sector spread. For instance, looking at all the Italian bonds in the sample, one could calculate their credit spreads above the German curve, and from them calculate an average value, which will be the Italian spread.

This spread will then generate a sector curve return for all Italian bonds, and the difference in each bond's spread from the sector spread will generate a security-specific return.

For consistency you may prefer to select only bonds from the benchmark. However, this algorithm also works for a portfolio in isolation, or where a benchmark is not available.

---

[4] In practice, I have yet to be asked to provide such an analysis; credit analyses are usually restricted to much broader credit bands.

12

Other security-specific sources of return

12.1 Paydown

12.2 Convexity

12.3 Rolldown

12.4 Liquidity return

12.1 PAYDOWN

Amortising securities are structured so that their principal is repaid over the lifetime of the security, rather than as a single lump sum at maturity. Typically, the ratio of interest to principal is designed to change over time so that the borrower can make equal payments throughout the security's lifetime.

Some types of amortising bonds, such as mortgage-backed securities (MBSs), passthroughs and collateralised mortgage obligations (CMOs), have the additional feature that the borrower can pay the principal back to the lender faster than scheduled. When early repayments of principal are made, such securities can generate *paydown* return in addition to return from carry, curve and credit shifts:

- If the security is trading at a premium (price > \$100 per \$100 face value), any paydown of principal generates a loss.
- If the security is trading at a discount (price < \$100 per \$100 face value), any paydown of principal generates a profit.

To see why, suppose that a security is purchased at \$90 per \$100 face value. The owner is guaranteed to make a profit, irrespective of what happens in the marketplace. All they have to do is to hold it to maturity, wait for the price to converge to its par value, and bank a capital gain. This *pull to par* effect is described in Chapter 9.

However, this assumption holds only if the face value of the investment stays unchanged at \$100, which is precisely what sinking securities do not do. Suppose that the security had half of its face value returned to the purchaser just after it had been bought at \$90. The effect of this paydown is to halve the rate of return, because only 5% of the nominal face value will be generated by pull to par, not 10% as previously.

Paydown return is therefore closely related to pull-to-par return, but should be displayed separately as it is not a function of yield. In general, paydown return r_p is given by

$$r_p = \frac{100 - P}{P} \times \delta f \qquad (12.1)$$

where:

- P is the security's market price;
- δf is the change in the amount paid down over the calculation interval. f starts at 0.0 when the security is issued and increases over the security's lifetime to a value of 1.0 when all capital is repaid. A non-amortising security's f value is 0.0 for its entire lifetime.

Example

The following example is from Fabozzi (2012, p. 1675):

- An MBS has a market price of 105.
- Prepayment of capital over the next month will be 2.4%.

Return due to paydown is then

$$r_p = \frac{(100 - 105)}{105} \times 2.4\% = -11.4 \text{ bp}$$

The security was trading at a premium, so its paydown return was negative over the interval.

In general, paydown return should be calculated and displayed for all sinking securities, in addition to carry and market returns, when they allow early repayment of principal. Vanilla bonds such as US Treasuries do not show any paydown return, because their principal remains unchanged throughout their lifetime.

12.2 CONVEXITY

Equation (8.6) shows that the relationship between yield and price is roughly linear, with nonlinearity depending on the security's convexity.

12.2.1 Convexity and price

Convexity is a very desirable property in a bond. If bond yields fall, the price of a bond with high convexity will rise faster than a bond with low convexity. Conversely, if bond yields rise, a high convexity bond's price will not fall as much as a low convexity bond.

Roughly speaking, convexity varies as the square of the maturity of the bond, so long-dated bonds tend to show the highest convexity. In some cases this extra convexity makes long-dated issues so attractive that bonds at the end of the yield curve may see their price bid up in the marketplace. For this reason, some yield curves occasionally show a modest degree of inversion, or downwards slope, at the long end that is entirely due to convexity effects.

12.2.2 Trading convexity

In some cases it can be useful to separate a bond's convexity return from its duration return. Suppose that a trader owns a bond with the following characteristics (see Table 12.1):

Table 12.1

Barbell strategy before restructuring

Bond	Weight	YTM	MD	C
15-Jan-2020	100%	5.62%	4.64	27.15

The trader believes there will be significant volatility in the marketplace, but does not know which way the markets will move. Their strategy is to sell the bond and buy two other bonds as follows (see Table 12.2):

Table 12.2

Barbell strategy after restructuring

Bond	Weight	YTM	MD	C
15-Jan-2015	36.2%	5.87%	11.99	201.64
15-Jan-2025	63.8%	5.29	0.44	0.60
TOTAL	100.0%	5.50%	4.62	73.38

The purpose of this restructure is to construct a new portfolio with the same modified duration as the original, but with much higher convexity. This has increased the trader's portfolio's second-order sensitivity to yield changes. As long as there is a substantial change in yields, the new portfolio will outperform the old one, and this will occur whether the market moves up or down.

The strategy is based on two assumptions:

- That the market will move in a parallel manner. If non-parallel movements occur, the trader is only hedged against parallel curve movements, and the more complex cash flow structure of their new portfolio may generate losses if, for instance, the yield curve twists or flattens.
- That there will be any movement in the curve. In general, the yield of the new portfolio will be lower than that of the old. If there is no market movement, no returns will be made by the convexity position, but the lower yield will result in lower carry return than the older portfolio would otherwise have generated.

This is known as a *barbell* strategy, as it moves the main cashflows of a portfolio outwards so that they lie at opposite ends of the term structure, with the graph of exposures against maturity resembling a barbell.

To assess whether this strategy worked, one needs to know the portfolio's return from convexity, as distinct from modified duration. A first-principles approach to pricing will not generate a value for modified duration, in which case it will be necessary to calculate this quantity separately as follows.

Suppose that the current YTM is given by y. Given a pricing function $p = p(y,t)$, its numerical derivative may be substituted into equations (8.4) and (8.5) to give the effective duration and convexity:[1]

$$MD = -\frac{p(y + \delta y,t) - p(y,t)}{2\delta p(y,t)} \qquad (12.2)$$

$$C = \frac{p(y + \delta,t) - 2p(y,t) + p(y - \delta y,t)}{\delta^2 p(y,t)} \qquad (12.3)$$

where $\delta \ll 1$.

The modified duration and convexity returns are then given by the second and third terms in equation (8.6), respectively.

12.3 ROLLDOWN

Consider a security that has a single cash flow one year in the future. The yield curve is steeply sloped at the 1-year point, but flattens out at longer maturities.

Suppose further that market conditions do not change for a month, so that the level and shape of the yield curve remains unchanged over this interval.

At the end of the month, this one-year bond will have become an 11-month bond, and the yield used to price this security will now be read from the 11-month point rather than the 12-month point on the yield curve.

Since the yield curve is downwards sloping, the 11-month yield will be lower. Since the yield of the security is lower, the price will be higher, and a positive return will have been generated.

This effect is sometimes called *riding the yield curve*, as it is most effective when a security's cash flows are positioned at maturities where the curve is most steeply sloped.

Note that this return has not been generated by movements in the market, since we explicitly assumed that market conditions were unchanged. Nor has it been generated by elapsed time because the return is generated entirely by a change in yield. Rolldown is distinct from either source of return, and should be measured separately.

Everything else being equal, it can be worth positioning one's securities so that the bulk of their cash flows are positioned at the most steeply sloped parts of the curve. However, rolldown return is seldom substantial, and will be overwhelmed by even quite small changes in the level or shape of the curve.

---

[1] Effective duration measures yield sensitivity when optionality is present. If a bond has no options, its effective duration is equal to its modified duration, and similarly for convexity.

A bond's change in yield due to rolldown is given by

$$\delta y = Y^t(m_1) - Y^t(m_2) \tag{12.4}$$

where Y^t is the yield curve at time t, $Y^t(m_1)$ its value at maturity m_1 and $Y^t(m_2)$ its value at maturity m_2 where $m_2 < m_1$.

Return generated by rolldown may then be calculated in the same way as carry:

$$r_{rolldown} = MD \times \delta y_{rolldown} \tag{12.5}$$

Pull-to-par return is generated even if the yield curve is flat, as it is driven by differences between the price of the bond and its eventual par price. In contrast, rolldown return is driven entirely by the shape of the yield curve.

12.4 LIQUIDITY RETURN

A security's price may be affected by liquidity, which is a measure of the ease with which it may be bought or sold without affecting its price. For instance, a US bond that is *on-the-run* (a reference issue) will be traded in significantly larger volumes than one that is *off-the-run*, despite being identical in all other respects. The off-the-run bond may trade at a lower price, or a higher yield, because of perceived difficulties in unwinding the position.

Issue size can also affect liquidity, and hence the bond's yield. For instance, a corporate issue that has identical cash flows and creditworthiness to a highly liquid sovereign issue can trade at a substantially higher yield, because of perceived difficulties in unwinding a position in that security. The effect may be especially pronounced if the amount on issue of the corporate bond is small.

Liquidity considerations can generate returns in two ways:

- *By generating higher yields.* A security that is structurally identical to a liquid bond but has a smaller amount on issue will probably trade at a higher yield, because of perceived difficulties in buying or selling. This higher yield will generate a higher carry return to compensate.
- *By generating additional changes in yield.* A bond that was on-the-run a year ago but is now off-the-run will trade at a slightly higher yield, because of its lower price. This increase in yield will generate a negative return, although its magnitude may be so small as to make no appreciable difference to the bond's overall return over this interval.

13

Balanced attribution

13.1 Introduction

13.2 Calculating balanced attribution

13.1 INTRODUCTION

Consider a multi-currency portfolio with holdings in equity and fixed income investments from several different countries. The portfolio is managed as follows:

- First, an international asset allocation committee meets and decides the relative amounts to invest in different countries.
- For each country, a cash/equity/fixed income allocation decision is made.
- For the fixed income portions of the portfolio, the fund's assets are invested in appropriate assets within each country and managed using fixed income strategies (carry, curve, credit).

Hopefully, value is being added at all three levels. However, assessing the value generated by each decision is very difficult without a full, multi-level attribution report.

The analysis for this type of portfolio is called balanced (or mixed) attribution, as it is used on a balanced portfolio, which is a portfolio containing two or more asset classes.

There are two contexts in which balanced attribution is required:

- A portfolio containing a mixture of fixed income and non–fixed income assets.
- A portfolio containing only fixed income assets, if they have been managed at least in part using asset allocation decisions.

13.2 CALCULATING BALANCED ATTRIBUTION

Balanced attribution requires a mixture of top-down Brinson attribution and bottom-up fixed income attribution tools. From Chapter 3, equations (3.1) and (3.17), the active return of a sector S against benchmark is given by the sum of the asset allocation return

$$r_S^{AA} = (w_S^P - w_S^B)(r_S^B - r^B) \quad (13.1)$$

and the stock selection return by

$$r_S^{SS} = (r_S^P - r_S^B)w_S^P \quad (13.2)$$

Asset allocation returns are calculated using sector-level weights and returns as usual. However, balanced attribution requires that stock selection returns be decomposed by fixed income risk.

Suppose that the portfolio and benchmark returns r_S^P and r_S^B of a sector are each given by the sum of carry and curve returns:

$$\begin{aligned} r_S^P &= r_{S,carry}^P + r_{S,curve}^P \\ r_S^B &= r_{S,carry}^B + r_{S,curve}^B \end{aligned} \quad (13.3)$$

The stock selection return (13.2) can now be written

$$r_S^{SS} = (r_{S,carry}^P - r_{S,carry}^B)w_S^P + (r_{S,curve}^P - r_{S,curve}^B)w_S^P \quad (13.4)$$

In general, the stock selection term becomes a sum of terms over each fixed income risk i:

$$r_S^{SS} = \sum_i (r_{S,i}^P - r_{S,i}^B)w_S^P \quad (13.5)$$

Example

Consider the following portfolio (Table 13.1) and benchmark (Table 13.2). Fixed income returns have been decomposed into carry and curve returns with no residual.

Table 13.1 **Portfolio weight and returns for balanced attribution**

Sector	Weight	r_{carry}	r_{curve}	r_{total}
Germany	70%	5%	–1%	4%
Italy	30%	7%	–5%	2%

Table 13.2 **Benchmark weight and returns for balanced attribution**

Sector	Weight	r_{carry}	r_{curve}	r_{total}
Germany	50%	4%	–2%	2%
Italy	50%	5%	–6%	–1%

Table 13.3 **Portfolio performance contributions for balanced attribution**

Sector	c_{carry}	c_{curve}	c_{total}
Germany	3.5%	–0.7%	2.8%
Italy	2.1%	–1.5%	0.6%
TOTAL	5.6%	–2.2%	**3.4%**

Table 13.4 **Benchmark performance contributions for balanced attribution**

Sector	c_{carry}	c_{curve}	c_{total}
Germany	2.0%	–1.0%	1.0%
Italy	2.5%	–3.0%	–0.5%
TOTAL	4.5%	–4.0%	**0.5%**

From Tables 13.3 and 13.4, the active return of this portfolio over its benchmark is $3.4\% - 0.5\% = 2.9\%$.

This active return can be calculated using either Brinson attribution or mixed attribution. In the former case, the asset allocation and stock selection returns are given by (Table 13.5):

Table 13.5

Brinson attribution

Sector	c_{AA}	c_{SS}	c_{total}
Germany	0.3%	1.4%	1.7%
Italy	0.3%	0.9%	1.2%
TOTAL	0.6%	2.3%	**2.9%**

In the latter case, the stock selection contribution returns are decomposed into return contributions generated by each source of fixed income return, shown in Table 13.6:

Table 13.6

Balanced attribution

Sector	c_{AA}	c_{carry}	c_{curve}	c_{total}
Germany	0.3%	0.7%	0.7%	1.7%
Italy	0.3%	0.6%	0.3%	1.2%
TOTAL	0.6%	1.3%	1.0%	**2.9%**

In both cases the sum of the attribution contributions equals the overall active return, as expected.

14

Duration allocation attribution

14.1 Introduction

14.2 Return of a single fixed income security

14.3 Calculating duration returns

14.4 Discussion

14.1 INTRODUCTION

A manager who makes macro-level investment decisions on their portfolio's interest rate risk exposures against benchmark is following a *duration allocation* strategy. Duration allocation strategies are often run in parallel with security-level strategies involving exposure to active carry, movements in the risk-free curve and credit spread changes.

Duration allocation techniques are becoming increasingly widely used in fixed income investment, and are frequently combined with other bottom-up techniques to form *hybrid* investment strategies, with a return that must be measured using an appropriate hybrid attribution model.

This chapter describes a group of attribution algorithms that measure the return generated by duration allocation decisions, including cases in which investment follows a hierarchical process at several levels. I also cover the simultaneous measurement of returns from duration allocation, market allocation and micro-level fixed income–specific effects.

14.1.1 Bottom-up and equity attribution models

Duration allocation requires different attribution tools from those used for equity portfolios and for fixed income portfolios that are managed on a bottom-up basis:

- Interest rate risks are ignored by a market allocation attribution scheme. For instance, a classification of securities into 'equity' and 'fixed income' regards holdings in 90-day Treasury bills and 30-year Treasury bonds as equally risky, despite their substantially different interest rate exposures and the different returns that each type will generate in similar market conditions. In this case, a Brinson-style attribution model based purely on market exposures will give misleading results.
- A bottom-up attribution scheme attributes return to micro-level effects only, such as return from carry, curve movements and credit spread, which are then aggregated over sector or portfolio. While many portfolios are managed in this way, any value added by taking global views at the sector or portfolio level will be wrongly assigned to these micro-level returns.

  For instance, if the overall duration risk of portfolio and benchmark is the same, a bottom-up scheme will indicate that no overall duration return was made. However, substantial active duration allocation risk may still be present at the sector and sub-sector levels, which will result in different results to those calculated from a bottom-up analysis.

14.1.2 Duration allocation risk

Consider the portfolio and benchmark shown in Table 14.1, where w_i^P and w_i^B are the weights of sector i and MD_i^P and MD_i^B are the modified durations of sector i. The contribution to modified duration by portfolio sector i is given by $w_i^P MD_i^P$ and the overall modified duration of the portfolio is the sum of the duration contributions:

$$MD_P = \sum_{i \in P} w_i^P MD_i^P \tag{14.1}$$

The rightmost column shows the active duration contribution from each sector. Overall, the portfolio is 1.46 years long against its benchmark.

Table 14.1 **Sector weights and durations**

Sector	w^P	w^B	MD^P	MD^B	$w^P MD^P - w^B MD^B$
S1	40.0%	30.0%	3.4	2.4	0.64
S2	30.0%	10.0%	5.3	1.4	1.45
S3	10.0%	50.0%	1.2	0.5	–0.13
S4	20.0%	10.0%	0.5	6.0	–0.50
TOTAL	100.0%	100.0%	3.17	1.71	1.46

Active duration allocation positions were taken across all sectors. The largest position is generated by sector S2, which contributed 1.45 years to the overall long duration position.

14.1.3 Duration-based asset allocation

Any portfolio with significant interest rate exposure will show return driven at least in part by the duration of the portfolio against its benchmark, as well as by the relative allocation of duration over various sector buckets between portfolio and benchmark.

For instance, a manager may choose to increase the active duration contribution of a particular sector if they believe that securities in that sector will show significant decreases in yield. If this yield movement occurs, the portfolio sector will outperform its benchmark counterpart. Duration asset allocation decisions therefore allow a more nuanced response to perceived investment opportunities than do global-level duration decisions.

An active duration allocation position is slightly more challenging to implement than a market allocation position. To express a market allocation view for a particular country, sector or security type is simply a matter of ensuring that the market weight of that sector is changed by buying appropriate securities and selling others. In contrast, there exist several ways to take an active duration position:

- by overweighting a sector with the same duration as that of the benchmark;
- by keeping sector market weights the same between portfolio and benchmark, and increasing the duration of the securities held in the required sector;
- by using some combination of the above.

A duration allocation decision may also imply a market weight decision, whether intentional or otherwise. This will affect the return made by carry, so trade-offs may have to be made between the effects of active duration allocation decisions on curve returns, and their effects on carry returns. For an example, see the discussion on carry return later in this chapter.

Duration attribution has close parallels to the Brinson-Fachler algorithm, which breaks down active returns into asset allocation returns and stock selection returns. Negative duration contribution corresponds to market weight, and change in yield corresponds to return:[1]

$$r_i^{AA} = (w_i^P - w_i^B)(R_i - R) \tag{14.2}$$

$$r_i^{SS} = (r_i - R_i)w_i^P \tag{14.3}$$

where

- r_i^{AA} is the asset allocation return for sector i;
- r_i^{SS} is the stock selection return for sector i;
- w_i^P is the weight of sector i in the portfolio;
- w_i^B is the weight of sector i in the benchmark;
- R_i is the return of sector i in the benchmark;
- R is the return of the benchmark.

14.1.4 Modified duration and spread duration

Recall that a fixed income security can have two measures of interest rate sensitivity, denoted by *modified duration* and *spread duration*. Modified duration measures the security's sensitivity to movements in the risk-free curve. Spread duration measures the security's sensitivity to changes in the OAS.

A portfolio is often managed in terms of one particular type of duration. The algorithm described in this book applies equally to modified duration

[1] For simplicity, I have combined the interaction term with the stock selection term. For further information on this point, see Chapter 3.

and credit spread duration attribution. In the latter case, simply substitute credit spread durations for modified durations throughout.

14.2 RETURN OF A SINGLE FIXED INCOME SECURITY

The major drivers of return for a fixed income security are conveniently summarised as *carry*, *curve* and *credit*.

Carry return is generated by the passage of time, and is driven by coupon payments and capital gains or losses in the security's price. Carry return is closely approximated by $y\delta\tau$, where y is the security's yield to maturity and $\delta\tau$ is the elapsed time.

Curve return is generated by movements in the risk-free curve. Market return is closely approximated by $-MD\delta y_{RF}$, where MD is the modified duration of the security and δy_{RF} is the change in the risk-free curve at the security's maturity. This change in yield is often decomposed further into:

- changes due to parallel and non-parallel curve movements;
- changes due to parallel, twist and curvature curve movements;
- changes at individual maturity points, or key rates.

Credit return is generated by movements in the credit spread, which is the amount of yield change that is not accounted for by changes in the risk-free curve. It is closely approximated by $-MD_S\delta y_{CS}$, where MD_S is the spread duration of the security and δy_{CS} is the change in the bond's credit spread.

These are all bottom-up effects, which means that their returns can be combined at the security level to give aggregated returns at the portfolio level.

14.3 CALCULATING DURATION RETURNS

Following Fischer (1998), we define the *duration weight* $\widetilde{w_i}$ of security i in a portfolio as

$$\widetilde{w_i} = \frac{w_i MD_i}{MD^p} \tag{14.4}$$

where w_i is the market weight of the security, MD_i is its modified duration and MD^p is the modified duration of the portfolio.[2] Duration weight has the property that

[2] The sector's spread duration weight is calculated in the same way, but using spread duration for the security and portfolio rather than modified duration.

$$\sum_{i \in P} \tilde{w}_i = 1 \tag{14.5}$$

The duration weight $\widetilde{W}^C$ of a country C is then given by the sum of the duration weights for securities from that country:

$$\widetilde{W}^C = \sum_{i \in C} \tilde{w}_i \tag{14.6}$$

A country's contribution to duration in a portfolio is the product of the country's duration weight and the portfolio's modified duration:

$$\sum_{i \in C} w_i MD_i = \widetilde{W}^C MD^p \tag{14.7}$$

Ignoring convexity effects, the total active return of a portfolio against its benchmark can then be written

$$\begin{aligned} R_P - R_B = & \left(\delta\tau \sum_{i \in P} w_i^P y_i^P - \sum_{i \in P} \tilde{w}_i^P MD_i^P \delta y_i^P \right) \\ & - \left(\delta\tau \sum_{i \in B} w_i^P y_i^B - \sum_{i \in B} \tilde{w}_i^B MD_i^B \delta y_i^P \right) \end{aligned} \tag{14.8}$$

where the first term in each bracket is the carry return, and the second is the duration return. Here, for each sector i:

- w_i^P and w_i^B are market weights;
- $\tilde{w}_i^P$ and $\tilde{w}_i^B$ are duration weights;
- y_i^P and y_i^B are yields to maturity;
- δy_i^P and δy_i^B are changes in yields to maturity;
- MD_i^P and MD_i^B are modified durations.

$\delta\tau$ is the elapsed time, and P and B refer to the portfolio and benchmark, respectively. Note that the aggregated changes in yield δy_S should be calculated using duration contribution weights, rather than simple market weights, as yield changes may differ between security or sector. For a fuller explanation of this point, see Appendix F.

$$\delta y_S = \frac{\sum_{i \in S} w_i MD_i y_i}{\sum_{i \in S} w_i MD_i} \tag{14.9}$$

The duration allocation framework introduces an additional market direction term, reflecting the additional degree of freedom available from taking global duration positions.

14.3.1 Duration asset allocation

Duration asset allocation (or relative return effect) R^{DAA} measures the return generated by the excess modified duration of a sector and the change in yield (or spread) of the sector against that of the benchmark. It is given by

$$R_i^{DAA} = -(w_i^P MD_i^P - w_i^B MD_i^B)(\delta y_i^B - \delta y^B) \quad (14.10)$$

$$= -(\tilde{w}_i^P MD^P - \tilde{w}_i^B MD^B)(\delta y_i^B - \delta y^B) \quad (14.11)$$

This return is analogous to the asset allocation return term (3.1) in the Brinson analysis, as it measures the effect of a particular sector having different duration contributions between portfolio and benchmark.

If the portfolio manager has made duration allocation decisions at several levels, the duration asset allocation return made at each level may be calculated as shown later in this chapter.

14.3.2 Duration stock selection

Stock selection (or instrument effect) return R^{DSS} is given by

$$R_i^{DSS} = -\tilde{w}_i^P MD^P(\delta y_i^P - \delta y_i^B) \quad (14.12)$$

This return is analogous to the stock selection return (3.2) in the Brinson analysis. The aggregated yield changes δy_i may be broken down further into return generated by factor-specific movements in the portfolio's yields, such as parallel and non-parallel curve shifts, or sector curve and security-specific credit movements.

14.3.3 The market direction effect

The market direction effect R^{DIR} measures return generated by the aggregate spread duration difference:

$$R_i^{DIR} = -\tilde{w}_i^P \delta y^B (MD^P - MD^B) \quad (14.13)$$

This term has no analogue in the Brinson framework, as it represents a source of risk that is not present in equity portfolios. A useful way to see this is to consider the portfolio's duration weights, which are analogous to market weights in the Brinson model. In a market allocation framework, portfolio sector weights always have to add up to one, but no such constraint exists for duration.

14.3.4 Multiple levels of attribution

Duration asset allocation return can be decomposed further into returns from several levels of duration allocation decision, if this reflects the manner in which the portfolio was managed.

Consider an arbitrary sector S. The benchmark's yield change δy_S^B for that sector is given by

$$\delta y_S^B = \frac{\sum_{i \in S} w_i^B \delta y_i^B}{\sum_{i \in S} w_i^B} \tag{14.14}$$

where w_i^B is the weight of security i and δy_i^B is its change in yield over the calculation period.

Recall that, for each subsector in S, the duration asset allocation return is given by

$$R_i^{DAA} = -(\tilde{w}_i^P MD^P - \tilde{w}_i^B MD^B)(\delta y_i^B - \delta y^B) \tag{14.15}$$

This return can be broken down into asset allocation return at sector and subsector levels. Suppose that the asset allocation decision is not made in one step, but instead involves calculating the return made by first taking decisions at the sector level, and secondly at the level of individual subsectors. Since

$$\delta y_i^B - \delta y^B = (\delta y_i^B - \delta y_S^B) + (\delta y_S^B - \delta y^B) \tag{14.16}$$

the last term in (14.15) can be expanded to give

$$\begin{aligned} R_i^{DAA} = & -(\tilde{w}_i^P MD^P - \tilde{w}_i^B MD^B)(\delta y_i^B - \delta y_S^B) \\ & - (\tilde{w}_i^P MD^P - \tilde{w}_i^B MD^B)(\delta y^S - \delta y_S^B) \end{aligned} \tag{14.17}$$

The first term is the relative return at the lower level; it uses return of the benchmark for the current sector as the reference yield.

The second term has limited meaning at the subsector level. However, if aggregated over sector S, it gives the overall asset allocation return for the sector.

There is one remaining step to be taken before these results can be used. The results of lower asset allocation decisions taken after the first, top-level allocation decision must take into account the return generated from all previous decisions, and remove it.

Therefore, we cannot simply repeat the process in the previous step using duration contributions aggregated over each security type, because the duration contributions of each security in the managed portfolio result from *two* nested allocation decisions, not one. To measure the return added by duration allocation at Level 2 requires that the allocation return made at Level 1 be excluded from the result.

This works as follows. After the first set of duration asset allocation returns have been calculated, the benchmark duration contributions are rescaled so that their sum over each Level 2 sector equals the sum of the portfolio duration contribution weights in that same sector. In other words, at Level 1 the portfolio-level duration contributions are made equal to the benchmark-level duration contributions. This removes the effects of the top-level allocation decision. The process is identical to that described in Section 3.4, but applied to duration contributions instead of market values.

Within each sector, the ratio of the portfolio duration contributions remains the same, so we can still measure the effect of duration allocation decisions made within that sector. What we have removed is the impact of the higher-level decisions, as required. The new duration contributions can now be used to calculate the returns due to the second-level duration allocation decision.

The need for this readjustment is not always obvious, as the totals over each source of risk are the same whether or not the correction is applied. However, the weight-adjusted returns convey a truer picture of the sources of return in the portfolio.

Example

Consider the portfolio and benchmark shown in Table 14.2, which have holdings in two sectors (A, B) and four subsectors (S1, S2, S3, S4). Duration allocation decisions are made first at Level 1, and then at Level 2; weights, duration and yield changes at security and sector levels are shown in Tables 14.2 and 14.3.

Table 14.2 **Sector weights, durations and yield changes**

Level 1	Level 2	w_P	w_B	MD_P	MD_B	δy_P	δy_B
A	S1	40.0%	30.0%	3.4	2.4	1%	–3%
A	S2	30.0%	10.0%	5.3	1.4	2%	3%
B	S3	10.0%	50.0%	1.2	0.5	5%	4%
B	S4	20.0%	10.0%	0.5	6.0	–2%	1%
TOTAL		100.0%	100.0%	3.17	1.71	1.1%	1.5%

At Level 1, the aggregated values from this table are calculated as follows.

Assuming initially that all duration asset allocation decisions are made at Level 2 (in other words, in terms of allocations to S1, S2, S3 and S4), the duration asset allocation returns are as shown in Table 14.4, where the first term is given by $(40\% \times 3.4) - (30\% \times 2.4) \times (-3.0\% - 1.5\%)$.

Conversely, if we assume that the duration allocation decision is first made at Level 1 and then at Level 2, the calculation is now spread across two levels. First, the return due to allocation at Level 1 is calculated.

Table 14.3

Aggregated sector weights, durations and yield changes

Level	w	W	md	MD	dy	DY
A	70.0%	40.0%	4.21	2.15	1.0%	–2.0%
B	30.0%	60.0%	0.73	1.42	0.0%	4.0%

Table 14.4

Single-level duration allocation returns

Sector	r^{DAA}
S1	–2.88%
S2	2.175%
S3	–0.325%
S4	0.250%
TOTAL	–0.78%

Table 14.5

Two-level duration allocation returns

Sector	r_0^{DAA}	r_1^{DAA}
S1	–6.27%	–0.96%
S2		6.525%
S3	–1.26%	–0.065%
S4		1.25%
TOTAL	–7.53%	6.75%

Here, the allocation returns are calculated using the aggregated quantities in Table 14.3. For instance, the duration asset allocation return for Sector A is given by $(70\% \times 4.21 - 40\% \times 2.15) \times (-2.0\% \times 1.5\%) = -6.27\%$.

To calculate the returns at Level 2, simply use the supplied weighted duration differences between sectors, times the difference between the change in yield and the change in yield for that sector. In this case, the duration allocation return for Sector 1 is given by $(40\% \times 3.4) - (30\% \times 2.4) \times (-3.0\% + 2.0\%) = -0.96\%$. Table 14.5 shows the full set of results.

The sum of the two duration allocation decision returns is -0.78%, as expected.

14.3.5 Carry return

The sum of the effects discussed so far only measures the returns generated by duration allocation effects, which are generated by movements in the underlying yield curves. A fuller discussion includes the role played by carry return, which can be equally important in an attribution context.

When managing a fixed income portfolio on the basis of duration allocation, a number of trade-offs come into play. By taking a particular duration position, the manager may also have taken an implicit market weight position, and this will affect the active carry return in addition to the return arising from duration allocation. Conversely, the portfolio may have been managed primarily with regard to carry, leaving the interest rate risks relatively uncontrolled.

In some cases it may be appropriate to report the sources of active return in terms of duration allocation for interest rate positioning, and market allocation for carry. In effect, this splits the analysis up into two steps:

- Carry return, decomposed into asset allocation and stock selection returns.
- Duration return, decomposed into duration asset allocation, duration stock selection and market positioning returns.

The sum of the two sets of effects will equal the overall active return.

14.3.6 Fixed income effects

Fixed income returns that are generated by changes in yield can be included in this framework within the duration stock selection term.

For instance, if changes in yield in equation (14.12) are due to parallel, non-parallel and credit shifts movements in the sector's underlying curve, then the change in yield due to these effects may be calculated and a stock selection return calculated for each.

14.3.7 Nested duration allocation with fixed income effects

This section shows a detailed worked example of duration asset allocation attribution working at multiple levels, with market allocation used for attribution of carry return, and fixed income effects included at the security level. Information is provided at the security level so that the reader can see how and where effects are aggregated.

Such an analysis assumes that a security-level fixed income attribution analysis has already been run, and that the non-carry return of each security has been decomposed into shift, twist and credit components. In practice there would also be a residual return, which measures the difference between the return observed in the market and that calculated from known risk factors. The analysis might include other returns due to factors such as convexity and prepayments.

Table 14.6 **Raw data for duration attribution, summarised at sector levels**

Security	Country	Sector	w	W	MD_p	MD_b	y	δy_{shift}	δy_{twist}	δy_{credit}	δy_{total}
AP	UK	Industrial	5%	13%	5.158	5.158	4.60%	–0.95%	0.04%	0.90%	–0.01%
BP	UK	Industrial	0%	13%	5.395	5.395	4.04%	–0.95%	0.76%	–0.41%	–0.60%
CP	UK	Industrial	44%	23%	5.870	5.870	3.88%	–0.95%	–0.93%	–0.37%	–2.25%
LP	UK	Finance	8%	5%	2.253	2.253	3.40%	–0.95%	–0.36%	0.88%	–0.43%
MP	UK	Finance	13%	8%	3.348	3.348	2.78%	–0.95%	0.67%	0.83%	0.55%
XP	USA	Government	5%	10%	6.848	6.848	5.50%	–0.95%	–0.98%	–0.42%	–2.35%
YP	USA	Government	10%	11%	5.247	5.247	4.60%	–0.95%	–0.06%	0.89%	–0.11%
ZP	USA	Government	15%	17%	6.077	6.077	5.10%	–0.95%	–0.35%	0.25%	–1.04%
		Industrial	49%	49%			4.12%				
		Finance	21%	13%			3.02%				
		Government	30%	38%			5.06%				
	UK		70%	62%			3.89%				
	USA		30%	38%			5.06%				
	TOTAL		100%	100%			4.33%				

Security-level returns are calculated from the standard expression

$$r = y\delta\tau - MD\delta y \qquad (14.18)$$

where y, δy and MD are supplied in Table 14.6, and $\delta\tau = 1/12$, or one month (see Table 14.7). The aggregate and active portfolio returns are also shown in Table 14.8.

Table 14.7

Security-level returns

Security	r
AP	–3.54%
BP	1.63%
CP	2.93%
LP	–0.50%
MP	1.30%
XP	6.66%
YP	–5.38%
ZP	2.00%

Table 14.8

Overall returns

Source	Return
r^P	1.34%
r^B	0.92%
Excess	0.42%

The calculation of active returns falls naturally into two categories: *carry* return and *curve* return.

14.3.8 Carry return

For completeness, we calculate carry return both in terms of performance contribution and in terms of market asset allocation.

The active carry return contribution generated by security i is given by

$$C_i^{carry} = (w_i^P - w_i^B)y_i\tau \qquad (14.19)$$

and the sum of these terms equals the overall active carry return. This quantity (–0.2165%) is shown in column *Active carry* in Table 14.9.

Table 14.9 **Carry allocation and selection returns**

Stock	Adjusted weight	Active carry	Country allocation	Sector allocation	Carry selection
AP	13.000%	–0.0307%			–0.0307%
BP	13.000%	–0.0438%			–0.0438%
CP	23.000%	0.0680%			0.0680%
LP	8.077%	0.0085%			–0.0002%
MP	12.923%	0.0116%			0.0002%
XP	7.895%	–0.0229%			–0.0133%
YP	8.684%	–0.0038%			0.0050%
ZP	13.421%	–0.0085%			0.0067%
Industrial	55.3%			–0.0012%	
Finance	14.7%			–0.0046%	
Government	38.0%			0.0000%	
UK			–0.0030%		
USA			–0.0049%		
SUBTOTAL			–0.0078%	–0.0058%	–0.0081%
TOTAL		–0.02165%			–0.02165%

This return is also the sum of the asset allocation returns and the stock selection returns.

The first level of asset allocation return, which takes place at country level, is run using the standard Brinson expression

$$r_i^{AA} = (w_i - W_i)(R_i - R)$$

and the weights and returns aggregated up to this level. For instance, asset allocation return contribution for the UK sector was

$$r_{AA}^{UK} = (70\% - 62\%) \times (3.89\% - 4.33\%) \times \frac{1}{12} = -0.0030\%$$

The next level of asset allocation at sector level proceeds as before, save that the benchmark weights are now adjusted using the weights from the previous step. For instance, the asset allocation return contribution from weighting the UK industrial sector was

$$r_{AA}^{UK\ Industrial} = (49.0\% - 55.3\%) \times (4.12\% - 3.89\%) \times \frac{1}{12} = -0.001\%$$

where the 49% is the portfolio weight of the UK Industrial sector, the 55.3% is the benchmark weight of the industrial sector (49.0%) times the adjustment factor of (70.0% / 62.0%), the 4.12% was the yield of the industrial sector and the 3.89% was the yield of the upper-level sector – in this case, the UK.

Finally, stock selection return is given at the security level by

$$r_i^{SS} = (w_i^P - \tilde{w}_i^B)y\delta\tau \tag{14.20}$$

where $\tilde{w}_i^B$ is the adjusted benchmark weight. For instance, the stock selection return for security ZP is given by

$$r_{SS}^{ZP} = (15.0\% - 13.421\%) \times 5.10\% \times \frac{1}{12} = 0.007\%$$

where the 13.421% is the benchmark weight for this security (17.0%), times the weight of the Government sector in the portfolio (30%), divided by the weight of the same sector in the benchmark (38.0%).

Results for both sets of calculations are shown in Table 14.10, together with the adjusted benchmark weights at levels where they are used. As expected, the sum of the active returns from the two levels of asset allocation plus the sum of the stock selection returns at security level equals the overall active return from carry.

14.3.9 Curve return

The returns from duration allocation decisions are calculated in much the same way, except that there is another global source of return (*market*

Table 14.10

Duration allocation returns

Stock	Adjusted duration	Market direction	Country AA	Sector AA	SS	Duration	Twist	Credit
AP	0.70				0.490%	−0.037%	0.235%	0.292%
BP	0.73				−1.136%	−0.062%	−0.351%	−0.723%
CP	1.41				0.562%	0.099%	−0.129%	0.592%
LP	0.18				−0.001%	0.000%	−0.001%	0.000%
MP	0.43				0.000%	0.000%	0.001%	−0.001%
XP	0.53				−0.248%	−0.016%	−0.156%	−0.076%
YP	0.45				−0.076%	0.007%	−0.035%	−0.048%
ZP	0.80				0.070%	0.009%	0.041%	0.020%
Industrial	3.03			−0.003%				
Finance	0.42			−0.024%				
Government	1.78			0.000%				
UK			0.005%					
USA			−0.049%					
SUBTOTAL		−0.054%	−0.044%	−0.027%	−0.340%	0.000%	−0.395%	0.055%
TOTAL		−0.054%	−0.044%	−0.027%	−0.340%			

direction), we use duration contributions rather than market weights, and there are three sources of security return instead of one.

14.3.10 Market direction

The modified durations of portfolio and benchmark are given by the sum of their respective duration contributions:

$$MD^P = \sum_i w_i^P MD_i^P = 5.235\%$$

$$MD^B = \sum_i w_i^B MD_i^B = 5.398\%$$

The change in yield of the benchmark is given by

$$\delta Y^B = \sum_i w_i^B \delta y_i = 0.363\%$$

The market direction return is therefore given by

$$r^{MD} = -(5.235\% - 5.398\%) \times 0.363\% = 0.059\%$$

14.3.11 Duration allocation

Duration allocation at the top (country) level is given by

$$r_{DAA} = -(w_i^P MD_i^P - w_i^B MD_i^B)(\delta y_i^B - \delta y^B)$$

For instance, the duration allocation return contribution from the UK is given by

$$r^{DAA} = -(3.456 - 3.102) \times (-0.347\% - 0.333\%) = -0.003\%$$

where the first term measures the active duration contribution from the UK, and the second measures the difference in yield change between the UK and the benchmark overall.

At the lower (sector) level, duration allocation return is calculated in a similar way, but using adjusted benchmark duration contributions. The contribution from the UK/Industrial sector is

$$r^{DAA} = -(2.841 - 3.03) \times (-0.364\% - 0.347\%) = -0.001\%$$

where the duration contribution from benchmark is given by the contribution from UK/Industrial, times the sum of duration contributions for the portfolio at the Industry level, divided by the sum of duration contributions for the benchmark at the same level:

$$\tilde{w} = 2.722 \times \frac{2.841}{2.722} = 2.841$$

14.4 DISCUSSION

14.4.1 Van Breukelen attribution

The duration allocation approach is closely related to the van Breukelen algorithm (van Breukelen, 2000), which also decomposes active return of fixed income portfolios into overall duration, asset allocation and market selection terms.

However, in the van Breukelen approach the yields of the securities are assumed to be the market's risk-free yields, allowing close integration with the Karnosky-Singer framework. No account is taken of convexity, so security returns are given by the expression

$$r = c - MD\delta y \tag{14.21}$$

where r is the return, c the risk-free return, MD the modified duration and δy the change in yield.

14.4.2 Presenting duration options to users

The ability to run multiple types of asset allocation analysis, in tandem with bottom-up fixed income analyses, allows a wide range of attribution models to be run, such as:

- pure bottom-up fixed income attribution (no asset allocation returns);
- market asset allocation and stock selection reports (standard Brinson);
- global duration, spread duration allocation and selection reports (duration allocation or spread duration allocation report);
- Brinson hybrid model, including returns from other fixed income effects that contribute to changes in the yield, such as curve reshaping and sector curve movements;
- spread selection hybrid model, including fixed income effects.

Part 4

ATTRIBUTION ON FIXED INCOME SECURITIES

15. Bonds

16. Money market securities

17. Inflation-linked securities

18. Futures

19. Annuities and amortising securities

20. Swaps

21. Options and callable bonds

22. Collateralised and securitised debt

15

Bonds

15.1 Introduction

15.2 Bond pricing formulae

15.3 Types of bonds

15.4 Repos

15.1 INTRODUCTION

The structure and attribution treatment of bonds was covered in some detail in Chapter 6. This chapter shows some of the other guises in which bonds appear in performance measurement.

The fundamental idea behind a bond is that it is a temporary transfer of capital from the investor to the issuer of the bond that is repaid at a given date in the future, called the maturity date. To compensate the investor for making the loan, the bond makes regular interim cash flows, called *coupons*, to the investor.

The details vary between issuer. For instance:

- the settlement period, which includes the length of time between a bond paying a coupon and the investor receiving the funds, can vary;
- the interval between coupon payments can vary during the first or last period, depending on when the bond was issued and its maturity date;
- some bonds issue coupons that change over time, according to a stated timetable;
- other bonds include embedded options that give the issuer the right to redeem the bond early.

Bonds have a long history as a financial instrument, with the British Government financing much of the cost of the Napoleonic wars through bond issuance paying coupons of around 4% a year. Mr Darcy's ten thousand a year implied he had £250,000 invested in the Funds, an enormous sum for Georgian England.

15.2 BOND PRICING FORMULAE

In general, the price P of a bond is given by the sum of its discounted cash flows:

$$P = \frac{c}{(1 + y_1)^{t_1}} + \frac{c}{(1 + y_2)^{t_2}} + \cdots + \frac{1 + c}{(1 + y_n)^{t_n}} \tag{15.1}$$

where

- c is the bond's coupon;
- t_i is the time between the present and the date of cash flow i, measured in years;
- y_i is the discount yield for cash flow i.

This formula assumes that appropriate yields are available for each cash flow. In practice, this can be difficult as there is no standard yield curve for any market. For this reason, and to ensure consistency of pricing between buyers and sellers, many central banks publish explicit pricing formulae for standard bonds that assume a constant yield over all maturities. For instance, the price of an Australian long-dated debt security is priced using an expression of the form[1]

$$P = v^{(f/d)}(g(1 + a_n) + 100v^n)$$

where

- $v = 1/(1 + i)$, where i is the bond's annual percentage yield to maturity divided by 200;
- f is the number of days from settlement to the next coupon date;
- d is the number of days in the half year ending on the coupon date;
- c is the interest payment per \$100 face value at the next coupon date;
- g is the annual coupon rate divided by 2;
- n is the number of half-years between the next coupon date and maturity;
- $a_n = (1 - v^n)/i$.

These pricing formulae can look formidable, but they are always based on closed-form variants of (15.1). Most of their technical detail specifies rounding conventions, coupon timing, settlement conventions and decimal places, so that if two parties agree on a yield when buying or selling a bond, they can also agree on the price.

15.3 TYPES OF BONDS

15.3.1 Sovereign debt

Sovereign debt usually refers to bonds issued by sovereign countries, which can in principle always raise capital by levying taxes.

For most of the last century, sovereign debt was one of the safest investments possible. However, there have been occasional defaults by sovereign governments due to revolution (Russia, 1917), war (Nazi Germany, 1945) or financial mismanagement (Argentina, 1990; Russia, 1998), and in recent years many governments have had their risk-free 'AAA' rating downgraded by one or more of the major ratings agencies. This means that, in theory, there is a possibility that these countries might default on their debt.

[1] Special rules apply when the bond has a maturity of less than six months.

The chances of this actually happening are perceived as remote, because of the catastrophic effects such an event would have on the global financial system.

Sovereign debt generates return from yield and sovereign curve movements. Some noise in the bond's returns may arise from liquidity effects. For instance, a 30-year bond that has just been issued is typically heavily traded, but it may be harder to find a counterparty for last year's 30-year bond, which is now a 29-year bond, and so no longer a reference issue.

15.3.2 Corporates

A corporate bond has the same structure as a sovereign bond, but is issued by a company rather than a country. This means that the same pricing and attribution techniques can be used for both. A corporate bond may be less creditworthy than a sovereign bond, and in this case return from changes in credit spreads may make a significant contribution to return.

Quite often, corporate bonds contain one or more embedded options. These are discussed in Section 15.3.7. Sovereign and corporate bonds without embedded options or other features are often referred to as *vanilla bonds*.

15.3.3 Perpetuals

A perpetual bond pays regular coupons but never matures. In other words, it never repays its principal but generates a cash stream in perpetuity.

The price P of a perpetual bond is given by

$$P = \sum_{i=1}^{\infty} \frac{c}{(1 + y)^i} = \frac{c}{y} \tag{15.2}$$

where c is the bond's coupon and y is its yield to maturity.

Perpetual bonds never generate any pull-to-par return, as their maturity date is always infinitely far away. As a result, their yield to maturity is always the same as their running yield.

15.3.4 Munis

A municipal (or *muni*) is a bond issued by a local government or one of its agencies. The income generated by a muni bond is often exempt from taxes, in which case the yield and coupon will be higher than an equivalent corporate bond. For instance, if the tax rate is t and the market yield is y, the effective yield will be $y/(1 - t)$, reflecting the additional income for the bondholder that will not be paid in tax.

Munis commonly have embedded options. In addition, they often have much lower credit ratings than government debt with a similar structure because of the higher risks they carry. For instance, at the time of writing the City of Detroit has just filed for bankruptcy protection, and its bonds are in default.

15.3.5 Semi-government bonds

Semi-government bonds (or *semis*) are issued by Australian states, rather than the Australia federal government. They typically have slightly lower credit ratings than Australian sovereign debt (currently AAA) and so pay slightly higher yields. Their pricing and treatment is otherwise identical to Australian sovereign Commonwealth Government Loan bonds.

15.3.6 Zero coupon bonds

A zero coupon bond (or *zero*) is a government or corporate bond that has a single cash flow paid at maturity. Zero coupon bonds with maturities of more than two years are relatively rare.

Zeros with shorter maturities are called *bank bills* (see Chapter 16).

The time to maturity of a zero coupon bond is always equivalent to the bond's duration, as there are no coupons to distort the duration calculation.

15.3.7 Callable and puttable bonds

A callable bond is a bond that contains an embedded option, allowing it to be *called* by the issuer. This means that on predefined *call dates* the issuer can return the investor's funds and cancel the bond.

This is usually not a welcome event for the bondholder, since it only makes sense to call a bond if interest rates are expected to remain lower than the bond's coupon. In this case, the issuer can save money by calling the bond and issuing a new one at a lower coupon. However, the bondholder will then have to reinvest their funds at the lower prevailing rate of interest, which will reduce their income.

To compensate the bondholder for this *reinvestment risk*, a callable bond pays a higher yield than a non-callable bond with similar structure. The extra yield generated by the presence of the embedded call option is called the *option-adjusted spread*.

Since the maturity of a callable bond is uncertain, it can be difficult to estimate its modified duration and hence its interest rate sensitivity. In practice, it is usually fairly clear whether such a bond will be called or not, depending on the current level of the yield curve. If a bond is likely to be called, its maturity date can be set to the next call date; otherwise, use the supplied maturity date.

Uncertainty about whether a bond will be called may cause its maturity date and modified duration to vary widely. This can in turn lead to large attribution effects and (in particular) generate extra residual return. It may be useful to assign any residual for such securities to a separate category where it can be monitored.

When running attribution on callable bonds, I recommend:

- decomposing carry return into risk-free, credit and OAS returns, so that the extra return generated by the bond's optionality can be measured;
- using the expected call/maturity date to calculate the bond's maturity;
- assigning any residual to a category called 'Bond optionality' or similar.

Puttable bonds are similar, except that the optionality feature works to the advantage of the bondholder, who can choose whether to redeem the bond at a range of agreed dates. In this case the OAS is negative, since the reinvestment risk is borne by the bond-issuer.

15.4 REPOS

A repo agreement (or *repo*) is a short-term sale of a bond, together with an agreed repurchase in the future, in order to raise short-term cash. Repos are generally regarded as money-market instruments and are covered in Chapter 16.

16

Money market securities

16.1 Introduction
16.2 Money market yield curves
16.3 Money market curve decomposition
16.4 Cash
16.5 Bank bills and discount securities
16.6 Accrual securities
16.7 Floating rate notes
16.8 Interest rate and credit risk
16.9 FRN types
16.10 Yields and discount margins
16.11 FRN durations
16.12 Decomposing the return of an FRN
16.13 Yield curve attribution
16.14 Attribution with complete data
16.15 Attribution with incomplete data
16.16 Treatment of FRNs in commercial systems
16.17 FRNs and securitisation

16.18 Currency forwards

16.19 Repurchase agreements (repos)

16.20 Money market benchmarks

16.1 INTRODUCTION

This chapter covers attribution techniques for securities with maturities of less than a year, the prices of which are affected by movements in short-term interest rates. These include *cash*, *discount securities*, *accrual instruments*, *floating rate notes*, *repos* and *forwards*.

16.2 MONEY MARKET YIELD CURVES

When running attribution on money market instruments, the reader should be aware that standard curve data may be quite inaccurate for this purpose, simply because there can be fine detail in this part of the curve that is lost if one takes a broad-brush view over all maturities. For instance, the Nelson-Siegel function is designed to model gross features of the curve over maturities out to 50 years using a small number of parameters. For this reason, the same function may not model money market–specific curves accurately unless specifically fitted to the shorter part of the curve.

For attribution on a money market portfolio, where investment decisions have been made in terms of expected curve movements at low maturities, it may be preferable to use specific high-resolution curves in preference to those used for longer-dated portfolios, even though they refer to the same market.

Fortunately, money market yield curves are particularly simple to construct. As the majority of instruments traded at these maturities pay no coupons, their market yields are identical to their zero coupon yields, so a zero coupon curve can be constructed from the yields of a representative set of securities trading at various maturities.

If the yield curve is sufficiently accurate, short-term rates such as the base rate and the Fed Funds rate may be read from the appropriate curve using interpolation. Use of a single curve as the central source of reference rates for all securities can be a time-saving short cut, compared to the potential effort required to supply and update them separately.

16.3 MONEY MARKET CURVE DECOMPOSITION

Typically, it is not necessary to look at money market yield curves in terms of shift, twist and curvature unless the manager is running the portfolio with a focus on these types of curve movement. More usually, a money market portfolio will focus on credit, so it is these returns that should be highlighted in the attribution report.

16.4 CASH

In principle, cash is a simple asset type to model. In practice, tracking down exactly how much cash is held in a portfolio often presents accounting headaches and can require a disproportionate amount of effort by the performance analyst.

Assuming continuous compounding, the return r_{cash} generated by a cash holding is given by

$$r_{cash} = (1 + y)^t - 1 \quad (16.1)$$

where

- y is the deposit yield;
- t is the elapsed time as a fraction of a year.

By definition, cash carries no interest rate or credit risk, so its return arises entirely from carry. Cash always has zero modified duration and convexity.

In practice, interest rates used in the calculation of interest return may be:

- zero (for settlements);
- the overnight or Fed Funds rate, if funds are borrowed or lent between large banks;
- the tom/next (tomorrow/next) rates for trades executed tomorrow, delivery on next business day;
- the official bank rate, or repo rate, the interest rate charged by a central bank for overnight lending;
- the inverse repo rate, the rate at which banks deposit funds with a central bank.

Although the price of cash is unaffected by interest rate changes, its presence will affect the interest rate sensitivity, and hence the modified duration of a portfolio. For instance, *cash drag* occurs when part of the capital in a managed fund has not been invested in revenue-generating assets. The market value of the assets remains unchanged, but the interest rate sensitivity of the portfolio is lessened.

Example: cash accrual

Suppose the AUD base rate is 3.5%. The continuously compounded return for an AUD cash deposit over six months is

$$r_{cash} = (1 + 0.035)^{\frac{6}{12}} - 1 = 0.017349$$

16.5 BANK BILLS AND DISCOUNT SECURITIES

Discount securities include zero coupon bonds, bank bills, letters of credit and promissory notes. While the label may vary, the underlying structure of these securities is identical.

A discount security generates a single cash flow at maturity. The present value of the security is therefore the discounted value of this future cash flow at the present time.

The duration of a discount security is therefore exactly the same as its time to maturity.

Although discount securities do not pay coupons, they do generate carry return. This can sometimes cause confusion, for if a security pays no coupon, how can the passage of time generate return? The reason is that carry return is the sum of two returns: running yield and pull to par. Although running yield is zero for a security that does not pay coupons, the pull to par return need not be. As the maturity date of the security comes closer, the market price must converge to the face value, and this generates return even if interest rates remain unchanged.

The price p of a discount security is given by

$$p = \frac{F}{(1 + y)^t} \qquad (16.2)$$

where

- F is its face value;
- y is the yield to maturity;
- t is the time to maturity, in years.

Since there is only one cash flow to consider, only one point on the yield curve matters when pricing or performing attribution, and this makes attribution on discount securities particularly simple. For instance, suppose that the YTM of a bank bill is 3.6% at the start of a month and 3.9% at the end; 0.2% of this movement is due to parallel shifts in the curve, and 0.1% is due to other curve movements.

A discount security is sufficiently simple to price that we can perform attribution from first principles. Consider a bill with a maturity date of 31 December 2012 and a face value of 100. On 1 January 2012, its yield to maturity is 4.00% and it has 365 days left until maturity. On 8 January 2012, its yield has dropped to 3.95% and it has 358 days left to run.

The price p_0 at the start of period is

$$p_0 = \frac{100}{(1 + 0.040)^{365/365}} = 96.15385$$

and the price p_1 at the end of the period is

$$p_1 = \frac{100}{(1 + 0.0395)^{358/365}} = 96.27160$$

The overall return of the security over this interval is given by

$$r = \frac{(96.27160 - 96.15385)}{96.15385} = 0.001225$$

Using this pricing formula, the return of the security can be broken down into market effects and time effects. The return due to changes in yield can be derived by pricing the security at the same date but with different yields:

$$p_i = \frac{100}{(1 + 0.0395)^{365/365}} = 96.20010$$

Using the same p_0 and p_1 as above, the return due to the passage of time is given by

$$r_t = \frac{(96.20010 - 96.15385)}{96.15385} = 0.000481$$

and the return due to changes in yield by

$$r_y = \frac{(96.27160 - 96.20010)}{96.15385} = 0.000744$$

The total return is $0.000481 + 0.000744 = 0.001225$, as before.

Compare this to the results given by the perturbational attribution equation $r = y\delta t - MD\delta y$, where the first term approximates the return due to the passage of time, and the second the return due to changes in yield. The yield at the start of the interval is 4.00%, the duration is just 1.000 (the time to maturity in years) and the modified duration is given by

$$MD = \frac{D}{(1 + y)} = \frac{1.000}{(1 + 0.04)} = 0.961538$$

Using these values, the return due to the passage of time is given by

$$r_t = 7/365 \times 4.00\% = 0.000767$$

and the return due to changes in yield by

$$r_y = -0.961538 \times (3.95\% - 4.00\%) = 0.000481$$

Both values are close to those derived from first principles.

16.6 ACCRUAL SECURITIES

Accrual securities are very similar to discount securities in terms of return and risk, but are structured slightly differently. Instead of selling at a discount and maturing at face value, they are issued at face value and mature at face value plus interest. Their return is therefore given by the expression presented earlier for discount securities.

16.7 FLOATING RATE NOTES

A floating rate note, or FRN, is structurally identical to a bond, but with the important difference that its coupon varies according to market conditions. FRNs are among the most complex type of money market security.

The coupon on an FRN is set to a money market reference rate such as 3-month LIBOR or the Fed Funds rate, plus a fixed increment called the reset margin. The coupon is reset at specific intervals, typically at the start of a coupon payment interval. The coupon reset interval is usually quarterly, but can also be semi-annual or monthly.

Floating rate notes tend to be long-dated and are therefore closer to coupon-paying bonds in structure. However, they are usually regarded as money market securities as they have no exposure to longer-dated interest rates.

The reason is that an FRN can be regarded as a zero coupon bond with a face value equal to the sum of its principal and the next coupon payment (for a more detailed pricing treatment, see below). Suppose that an FRN has a face value of 100, its coupon has just been paid and the reset rate is r. The next coupon is payable in six months. Then the value of the future cash flow is $100 \times (1 + r/2)$, but this will be discounted at the same rate, so the FRN's current market price remains unchanged at 100. In other words, its price is not affected by the reset rate.

Any decrease in value for an FRN due to increasing interest rates is thus compensated for by rising coupon payments. Unlike a bond, for which prices fall when interest rates rise, FRN prices are generally unaffected by changes in interest rates. They can therefore form a useful alternative investment to bonds in a rising interest rate environment.

If credit conditions are unchanged, the price of the FRN will revert to par on each coupon reset date. However, this seldom happens in reality. Usually, the creditworthiness of the FRN has changed, so the price will be a little above or below par on the reset date.

Example

On 9 November 2012, the European Investment Bank (EIB) issued an FRN with maturity date 22 February 2017 and a quarterly coupon set to 3-month LIBOR plus 20bp.

16.8 INTEREST RATE AND CREDIT RISK

Because the FRN's price is largely determined by the level of the next coupon, its modified duration is always close to zero. FRNs are therefore relatively immune to interest rate risk. This is why FRNs are regarded as money market instruments, despite their long maturities.

Unless you are focusing on the shortest part of the yield curve where maturities are a year or less, interest rate returns generated by FRNs may safely be ignored for attribution. In practice, the main source of risk and return for an FRN is credit risk. FRNs are usually issued by companies with below investment grade ratings[1] and have average credit ratings around B, so their returns are largely driven by widening or tightening of credit conditions.

16.9 FRN TYPES

Many types of FRN exist, including perpetual, variable rate, structured, reverse, capped, floored, collared, step-up recovery, range, corridor and leveraged. They are mostly differentiated on the basis of how their coupons are calculated:

- A stepped FRN has its reset margin changed at different times during the security's lifetime.
- A capped FRN has a maximum coupon payment value.
- A floored FRN has a lowest coupon payment.
- A reverse FRN's coupon payment moves in the opposite direction to the reference rate. For instance, its coupon might be set as reset margin minus LIBOR.
- A callable FRN has an embedded option, allowing the issuer to repurchase the FRN at times of low interest rates and reissue the debt as fixed rate bonds.
- A variable rate note is an FRN for which the reset margin itself is variable.

16.10 YIELDS AND DISCOUNT MARGINS

Fixed coupon bonds can be compared using their yield to maturity, which allows their respective return if held to maturity to be compared, independently of structural features such as coupons and tenor.

[1] At the date of writing (December 2012), the US Treasury has announced it will sell floating-rate notes. Historically low interest rates are decreasing the appeal of treasury bonds at auction, which carry a fixed coupon and will go down in value if rates increase. Floating rate notes will maintain their value if and when rates increase, and so will be more attractive to investors. Presumably these FRNs will carry the same high credit rating as US Treasury bonds.

Since the FRN's cash flows cannot be calculated in advance, YTM is not normally used to assess FRNs. Instead they are compared using a measure called the *discount margin*, which measures spread relative to the reference rate, and hence expected return. This spread is the sum of the reset margin, defined when the FRN is issued, and the credit spread that compensates the FRN's holder for its credit risk. Discount margins apply only to FRNs, and the yield of the FRN is the sum of the reference rate and the discount margin.

To understand the discount margin, consider the return made by the owner of the security due to the pull-to-par effect, over and above the return made by coupon payments. If the FRN is bought at less than its maturity value, extra return will be made over the security's lifetime as its price converges to par at maturity. The discount margin is this return, plus the reset margin; it can be thought of as the option-adjusted spread for an FRN.

The simple margin (SM) of an FRN measures its effective spread, which is a simple approximation to the discount margin. It is given by

$$SM = \frac{100}{P}\left(\frac{100 - P}{M} + r\right) \tag{16.3}$$

where

- P is the FRN's clean price;
- M is the FRN's time to maturity, in years;
- r is the reset margin.

The FRN's discount margin is measured in a similar way, but involves discounting future cash flows by the current reference rate plus margin. The FRN's price is then calculated and compared to the market value, and the margin is repeatedly adjusted until a value is found that equates the market price to the sum of the discounted cash flows. Since discount margins are usually supplied for attribution, I do not describe this process in further detail; see Fabozzi and Mann (2000) for more information.

16.11 FRN DURATIONS

Unlike a bond, an FRN has *two* duration measures, reflecting its exposure to both interest rates and discount margins:

- *Interest rate duration* measures the FRN's sensitivity to changes in interest rates, as discussed earlier. The interest rate duration is closely approximated by the time to the next coupon, which is usually a fraction of a year. FRNs therefore have relatively low modified durations.

- *Spread duration* measures the FRN's sensitivity to changes in the discount margin. Spread duration is typically much larger than interest rate duration, and is measured by calculating the modified duration of the FRN in the same way as that of a vanilla bond, using all its cash flows. An FRN's returns are typically driven by changes in the discount margin, reflecting the fact that spread durations are much higher than interest rate durations for this asset class.

16.12 DECOMPOSING THE RETURN OF AN FRN

The price P of an FRN per \$100 face value is given by a rather complex expression that involves various reference rates, reset and discount margins, the terms and conditions of the security, and the current date. The details are given in Appendix B.

While it is possible to use this expression to run attribution on an FRN by repricing at each valuation date and examining the effect of changing each parameter, this requires a significant amount of data. Fortunately, there is a much simpler way to treat FRNs in an attribution framework. To a high degree of accuracy, the return r of an FRN is given by

$$r = y\delta t - MD_S\delta DM \tag{16.4}$$

or, splitting the yield into reference return and discount margin

$$r = R_T\delta t + DM\delta t - MD_S\delta DM \tag{16.5}$$

where

- y is the yield of the FRN;
- δt is the elapsed time, as a fraction of a year;
- MD_S is the spread duration;
- δDM is the change in the discount margin;
- R_T and DM are as defined above.

Note that I have not included return due to changes in the interest rates, since this is usually negligible. In practice, (16.5) replicates the returns of an FRN very accurately. For attribution purposes, it is much easier to calculate the FRN's spread duration than it is to reprice the FRN. Even if you are using a first-principles approach elsewhere in your attribution analysis, it is preferable to use (16.5) for FRNs.

16.13 YIELD CURVE ATTRIBUTION

Since the FRN's return depends on short-term interest rates and discount margin, the shape of the yield curve at longer maturities has little effect on the security's returns. For this reason, it is seldom necessary to decompose returns into parallel and non-parallel shifts when running attribution on FRNs; a single measure of yield shift is often all that is required. In the context of a portfolio containing other types of security, it is perfectly permissible to show an FRN's returns as the sum of carry return and a security-specific (credit) return, and to assume curve change return is zero.

16.14 ATTRIBUTION WITH COMPLETE DATA

Suppose that the spread duration, the reference rate and the discount margin are all available on a daily basis. The FRN's yield will then be the sum of the reference rate and the discount margin, and attribution can proceed as above.

16.15 ATTRIBUTION WITH INCOMPLETE DATA

Suppose that the only daily market data available apart from the return of the FRN is a risk-free yield curve. In this case we can still run attribution, but with slightly less detail than in the previous case.

First, note that the reference rates used to price FRNs are very closely related to particular maturities on the yield curve. For instance, 3-month LIBOR rate and 3-month CD rates are closely correlated, as are the Federal Funds rate and the 6-month treasury bill yield. A yield curve that is accurate at the short end will supply reference rates that are easily accurate enough for attribution.

Secondly, the yield of the FRN is the sum of its reference rate and its discount margin. A yield curve will supply the reference rate, which is read from the appropriate maturity on the yield curve, but not the discount margin, which is a function of the day-to-day creditworthiness of the security. Then we can write the reference return of the FRN as the first term in equation (16.5), and assign the rest of the return to discount margin return.

16.16 TREATMENT OF FRNs IN COMMERCIAL SYSTEMS

The main difficulty with running attribution on FRNs is that they do not fit into a conventional bond attribution framework. Their dependency on changes in the discount margin rather than yield requires an extra term in the attribution equation, which is often unavailable in commercial systems.

Should this be the case, the suggested treatment is to set up an FRN as follows:

- Set the yield to be the reference rate for the FRN, plus the margin. For instance, in the above example this will be LIBOR plus 20 basis points. Reference rates are not usually volatile, so it may be sufficient to reset the rate each time a coupon is paid.
- Set the modified duration to zero. This ensures that there will be no market return, and all remaining return from the FRN will be assigned to the residual bucket.
- Relabel the residual bucket as 'Discount margin'.

This approach will give exactly the same results as for the full treatment, except that the yield return will be understated because it will not show the full carry return due to the extra yield from the discount margin. However, one might argue that this is actually more accurate, because it aggregates all returns arising from the discount margin (carry and duration return) into one figure.

16.17 FRNs AND SECURITISATION

FRNs often appear in securitisation tranches (see Chapter 22). While the details of the securitisation may be complex, attribution on a tranche that has been structured as an FRN is identical to attribution on a stand-alone FRN.

16.18 CURRENCY FORWARDS

A currency forward locks in the price at which a given amount of currency can be bought or sold at a given date in the future. Assuming continuous compounding, the cost F of a forward is given by

$$F = Se^{(r_d - r_f)t} \tag{16.6}$$

where

- S is the amount to hedge, in base currency;
- r_d is the domestic (base) interest rate;
- r_f is the foreign (local) interest rate;
- t is the period over which the forward contract is active.

A forward can be regarded as two continuously compounded bank bills, one long the base currency and the other short the local currency, with the cash flows from settlement arising at the maturation of the contract.

Forwards are usually used for hedging against adverse currency movements for multi-currency portfolios and for hedging equity and fixed income benchmarks. Their use in attribution is covered in more detail in the section on Karnosky-Singer attribution in Chapter 4.

16.19 REPURCHASE AGREEMENTS (REPOs)

A repo agreement (or *repo*) is a short-term sale of a bond, together with an agreed repurchase in the future, in order to raise short-term cash. The difference between the sale and repurchase prices can be interpreted as a rate of return, called the *repo rate*. A repo therefore behaves like a secured deposit rather than a set of transactions.

A reverse repo is the opposite of a repo. If bank A engages in a repo agreement with bank B, then bank B has entered into a reverse repo with bank A.

Term repo agreements can be made for a fixed term of between one day and a year. Conversely, an open repo agreement does not have a set maturity date on which the position is unwound.

The various types of repo are particularly simple to treat in an attribution framework. Since the returns made by investing in this asset class are similar to a cash deposit at the repo rate, all repo return can be treated as simple interest. As a result, repos should never show any residual in an attribution report.

It may be useful to split out repos from other asset classes in an attribution report, to emphasise that the return they generate is entirely different to other sources of return, such as carry and risk-free curve movements.

16.20 MONEY MARKET BENCHMARKS

Money market benchmarks tend to be very straightforward in design. For instance, the UBSW Bank Bill Index is simply formed of 13 bank bills that mature on successive weeks. As the shortest-dated bills mature, new longer-dated bills enter the index.

17

Inflation-linked securities

17.1 Introduction

17.2 Overview of the inflation-linked bond market

17.3 What is an inflation-linked bond?

17.4 The Canadian model for inflation-linked debt

17.5 Inflation ratios

17.6 Real yields and nominal yields

17.7 Pricing an inflation-linked bond

17.8 Real yield term structure

17.9 Pricing an inflation-linked bond

17.10 Modified duration and return of inflation-linked gilts

17.11 Break-even yields in attribution

17.12 Inflation swaps

17.13 Practical considerations

17.1 INTRODUCTION

Inflation-linked securities present some additional challenges for the attribution analyst compared to vanilla sovereign and corporate bonds, because of their dependence on inflation rates and real, rather than nominal, yields.

This chapter presents an overview of what inflation-linked securities are and how they are priced, highlights some of their major differences compared to related asset classes and presents an attribution framework that can be used for the majority of inflation-linked bonds.

Inflation-linked bonds are also referred to as index-linked bonds or just linkers, and the reader will often find these terms used interchangeably in the marketplace.

17.2 OVERVIEW OF THE INFLATION-LINKED BOND MARKET

In the twentieth century, inflation-linked bonds were exclusively issued by sovereign governments, but many are now offered by corporate and other entities. From 2011 to 2012, inflation-linked issuance made up 23% of the total gilts offered in the UK and more than 10% of issuance by the US Federal Reserve. Countries that have issued inflation-indexed debt now include the United States, the United Kingdom, France, Germany, Italy, Sweden, Canada, Australia, Israel and Japan.

Reasons for issuing inflation-linked debt include:

- the high and volatile levels of inflation seen in Latin America in the 1960s and 1970s;
- demonstrating commitment to disinflationary policies;
- capitalising on inflationary expectations;
- encouragement of long-term inflation hedges for liabilities such as pensions.

Inflation-linked bonds and related securities, such as inflation swaps, are common, and any attribution system should be able to measure the specific types of return generated by this asset class.[1]

[1] The first inflation-linked bonds were probably issued in Massachusetts around 1780 during the Revolutionary War. Massachusetts' currency had depreciated to the extent that the American soldiers were losing large amounts of their income to inflation, resulting in low morale and occasional mutiny. To address this situation, the state government defined a price index based on a portfolio of items and that were each worth about £1 at the time: five bushels of corn, 68 4/7 pounds of beef, 10 pounds of wool and 16 pounds of shoe leather. Troops were then paid a fixed multiple of the value of this basket (Shiller, 2003).

17.3 WHAT IS AN INFLATION-LINKED BOND?

An inflation-linked bond is a bond that has its interest and principal payments indexed against inflation, using a measure such as the General Index of Retail Prices (RPI) in the UK or the Consumer Price Index (CPI) in the United States. The index is typically based on a complex mixture of assets that represents the cost of living in Western societies.

As the inflation index rises, the bond's principal rises in proportion. Since coupons are calculated as a proportion of the bond's principal, any coupons also change in line with inflation. For instance, suppose a bond is issued with $100 face value and a 5% coupon. The CPI then rises 60% over the security's lifetime. In this case, the principal rises to $160, so the coupon payable at maturity will also have risen by 60%, and the payment at maturity will be $160. However, the principal and coupon are still $100 and 5% in real terms, whereas the value of a non-indexed bond will have fallen to $100/1.6 = 62.5% of its initial purchasing power.

The holder of such a bond therefore expects their investment at least to be immunised against inflation, and to generate a known, predictable return relative to the current rate of inflation. The bond's market-quoted real yield measures the bond's guaranteed rate of return over and above that of inflation if held to maturity.

Therefore, inflation-linked bonds can be used in a number of different ways. They both allow investors to hedge their assets against the effects of inflation, and to take speculative positions on changes in inflation rates and real yields. The attribution analyst's task is to measure these inflation-generated returns, in addition to returns from other sources of risk such as carry, credit and changes in the market's term structure.

17.4 THE CANADIAN MODEL FOR INFLATION-LINKED DEBT

Inflation-linked bonds pay periodic coupons that are set to the product of a nominal coupon rate and the inflation index. The majority of such bonds follow the *Canadian model* (Deacon et al., 2004) where daily inflation is measured as the ratio of the inflation index over two successive months, lagged by three months. I follow this convention in the remainder of this chapter, but there are some exceptions of which the reader should be aware:

- UK inflation-linked gilts issued before 2005 used an inflation ratio that was constant over each calendar month.
- Australian indexed annuity bonds are a stream of cash flows indexed to inflation, without any principal payment at maturity. These can be modelled as an inflation-linked bond minus a zero coupon inflation-linked bond.

17.5 INFLATION RATIOS

Inflation-linked securities use various forms of inflation ratio to measure the day-to-day effects of inflation.

The current rate of inflation will not be known on the date that the security is traded, because of the time and effort required to collect and collate the index. Instead, recent inflation measurements are used instead to calculate an indicative daily inflation rate.

For example, consider a UK inflation-linked gilt with a three-month indexation lag. The daily index ratio is defined as follows:

$$IR_t = RPI_T + \left(\frac{t-1}{T}\right)(RPI_{T+1} - RPI_T) \qquad (17.1)$$

where

- IR_t is the (calculated) index ratio at time t;
- RPI_T and RPI_{T+1} are the (published) applicable RPI values for the first day of the month three months ago, and the RPI value for the first day of the next month after that date, respectively;
- t is the calendar date at which the ratio is to be calculated;
- D is the number of days in the current month.

The applicable starting RPI used in this formula is the published RPI for the calendar month falling three months earlier. For instance, to calculate an index ratio during January 2012, the values used should be for October and November 2011. By convention, the result is rounded to the fifth decimal place.

Example

The RPI index ratio for 5 January 2012 uses the RPI factors for October (238.0) and November (238.5). Its value at this date is

$$IR_t = 238.0 + \frac{4}{31}(238.5 - 238.0) = 238.06452$$

17.6 REAL YIELDS AND NOMINAL YIELDS

A common point of confusion arising when discussing inflation-linked bonds is the meaning of yield. In the following sections I present the terms *real yield*, *nominal yield* and *break-even yield*.

17.6.1 Real yield

For inflation-linked bonds, trades and revaluations are made on the basis of *real yield*.

Real yield measures the return that will be generated over and above inflation if the bond is purchased now and held to maturity. Real yield is similar to nominal yield in that it measures the return of the bond if held until maturity, but dissimilar in that nominal yield does not take inflation into account, which will erode the value of the bond. The term real yield is used because it is a measure of the true, or real, growth in the bond's purchasing power over its lifetime.

The real yield of an inflation-linked bond is always known, because it is quoted in the marketplace.

A fixed-coupon bond also has a real yield, but this can be measured only after the bond matures, since this is the first point at which the cumulative effects of inflation on principal and interest on the bond's return can be measured.

17.6.2 Nominal yield

Fixed-coupon bonds and inflation-indexed bonds both have a nominal yield.

For the fixed-coupon bond, the nominal yield is the same as its yield to maturity.

For the inflation-indexed bond, the nominal yield is given by the *Fisher equation*, which states that the nominal interest rate y is the sum of the real interest rate r and the inflation rate i:

$$y = i + r \tag{17.2}$$

17.6.3 Break-even yield

The break-even inflation rate (BEIR) is the rate of inflation for which the nominal yield on an index-linked bond is the same as the nominal yield of a conventional bond having the same maturity. In other words, it is the rate of inflation above which an inflation-linked investment will outperform a fixed-coupon investment. Therefore, the break-even rate represents the market's consensus on future inflation. Break-even rates are published for a range of countries and maturities on a daily basis in the *Financial Times* and on Bloomberg.

For instance, at the time of writing the yield on 10-year US notes was 1.6%, and the yield on 10-year TIPS was −0.8%. The 10-year US breakeven rate was therefore 1.6% −(−0.8%) = 2.4%, indicating that the market expects average annual US inflation of 2.4% over the next 10 years.

Similar measures can be calculated for other maturities to generate an *inflation term structure*, showing the market's inflationary expectations over a range of timescales.

At a given maturity, the break-even yield y_b is the difference between the nominal yield y_n and the real yield y_r:

$$y_b = y_n - y_r \tag{17.3}$$

If future inflation is higher than the level implied by the current break-even level, then inflation-linked securities will give a better rate of return than ordinary gilts, and vice versa. Break-even rates therefore present an additional source of return for portfolio managers, and the attribution analysis framework in this chapter allows the returns of an inflation-linked bond to be decomposed into returns made by break-even yields and real yields.

Depending on the investment strategy, managers of inflation-linked funds may prefer to see returns either on a total return basis or on a nominal plus break-even return basis.

17.7 PRICING AN INFLATION-LINKED BOND

A fixed-coupon bond requires only a nominal yield for its price to be calculated. In contrast, an inflation-linked bond requires two sources of information:

- its real yield;
- the inflation rate.

If the inflation-linked bond's real yield is positive, it is outperforming inflation. At the time of writing (January 2013) many real yields on inflation-linked securities were negative, implying that expected inflation is higher than Treasury bond yields. The implication is that holders of these inflation-linked bonds are accepting a return on their investment that is lower than inflation. This is not the same as a negative absolute return; the bond's return is still positive, but its return is not keeping pace with inflation.

One reason investors are willing to accept this poor performance is that this negative real return is known and certain. The bond is government guaranteed, so the risks of default or other credit events are minimal.

17.8 REAL YIELD TERM STRUCTURE

Some central banks publish real yield curves, showing expected real yields as a function of maturity date. Real yield curves should always be used for attribution of inflation-linked bonds, as they may have a different shape and behaviour to the nominal term structure.

The Bank of England also publishes an implied inflation curve, showing the term structure of inflation implied from relative yields of gilts and inflation-linked securities. This indicates expected levels of inflation at various dates in the future, as implied by the bond markets.

If the effects of changes in the shape of the real curve need to be measured, real yield curves will be required for attribution analysis.

17.9 PRICING AN INFLATION-LINKED BOND

The pricing formula for an inflation-linked bond is identical to that of a vanilla bond, save that real yields are used rather than nominal yields. The price of a UK index-linked gilt, paying two coupons a year, is

$$P = w^{\frac{r}{s}}\left[d_1 + d_2 w + \frac{cw^2(1 - w^{n-1})}{2(1 - w)} + 100w^n\right] \tag{17.4}$$

where

- P is the real dirty price per £100 nominal;
- c is the coupon per £100 nominal;
- r is the number of calendar days from the settlement date to the next coupon date;
- s is the number of calendar days in the full coupon period in which settlement occurs;
- n is the number of quasi-coupon periods from the next coupon period to maturity;
- $w = \dfrac{1}{1 + y/2}$, where y is the real yield.

Note that the market price must be indexed using the inflation ratio, shown in the previous section.

Alternatively, an inflation-linked bond can be priced off the real yield curve using the expression

$$P = \sum_{n=1}^{N} \frac{c}{(1 + y_{n,t})^n} + \frac{100}{(1 + t_{N,t})^N} \tag{17.5}$$

where c has the same meaning as above, $y_{n,t}$ is the real yield for the n th cash flow at maturity t and N is the number of outstanding coupons.

Example

A 1.875% coupon bond, maturing on 22 November 2022, is purchased on 5 January 2012 at a real yield of −0.60698%. The settlement date is 6 January and the real dirty price is £128.18180 per £100 nominal.

The RPI factor on the date the bond was issued was 205.658. Therefore, the price must be indexed by multiplying by the ratio of the inflation index on this date (238.06452) to the RPI factor on the date the bond was issued (205.658), giving an actual price of

$$P = \frac{238.06452}{205.658} \times £128.18180 = £148.38966$$

17.10 MODIFIED DURATION AND RETURN OF INFLATION-LINKED GILTS

In the current context, modified duration has a slightly different meaning to that for bonds without inflation indexation. Here, modified duration is a measure of the bond's price sensitivity to changes in its real yield. However, the Fisher equation states that the nominal yield of a bond is given by the sum of the real yield and the inflation return, so a modified duration calculated from the above pricing equation will not take inflation returns into account.

Running attribution on an inflation-linked bond therefore requires a slight modification to the usual expression. In addition to the usual returns generated by the passage of time and by movements in real interest rates, we also have a known return generated by the index ratio:

$$r = y\delta t - MD\delta y + \left(\frac{IR_t}{IR_{t-1}} - 1\right) \tag{17.6}$$

where

- r is the inflation-linked bond's return;
- y is the real yield to maturity;
- δt is the elapsed time;
- MD is the modified duration with respect to real yields;
- δy is the change in real yield;
- IR_{t-1} and IR_t are the applicable inflation ratios at the start and end of the current interval, respectively.

The third term is required because the return due to inflation has been removed from the returns due to market movements. In a conventional bond, inflation and investment returns are already combined in the form of the nominal yield.

This term is sometimes called *inflation carry*, but it is more properly a separate source of return unrelated to carry, and should always be displayed separately.

Equation (17.6) is the appropriate perturbational attribution equation to use for inflation-linked bonds.

Example

Table 17.1 **Attribution on a 1.875% 2022 UK Index-linked gilt**

Date	*P*(£)	*Y*	*MD*	*IR*	r_M	$y \times \delta t$	$-MD \times \delta y$	*I*	r_C
26/02/2010	116.2892	1.0529%	15.85	217.85000	0.624%	0.009%	0.540%	0.069%	0.621%
01/03/2010	115.9989	1.0687%	15.85	218.00000	–0.250%	0.003%	–0.250%	–0.001%	–0.250%
02/03/2010	117.3599	0.9952%	15.86	217.99680	1.173%	0.003%	1.170%	–0.001%	1.167%
03/03/2010	117.228	1.0024%	15.86	217.99360	–0.112%	0.003%	–0.110%	–0.001%	–0.113%
04/03/2010	118.0385	0.9590%	15.87	217.99030	0.691%	0.003%	0.690%	–0.001%	0.690%
05/03/2010	116.4612	1.0441%	15.84	217.98710	–1.336%	0.009%	–1.350%	–0.004%	–1.344%
08/03/2010	115.6543	1.0881%	15.82	217.97740	–0.693%	0.003%	–0.700%	–0.001%	–0.694%
09/03/2010	116.4658	1.0441%	15.83	217.97420	0.702%	0.003%	0.700%	–0.001%	0.699%
10/03/2010	115.9734	1.0709%	15.82	217.97100	–0.423%	0.003%	–0.420%	–0.001%	–0.423%
11/03/2010	115.2677	1.1096%	15.81	217.96770	–0.609%	0.003%	–0.610%	–0.001%	–0.610%
12/03/2010	115.9593	1.0720%	15.81	217.96450	0.600%	0.009%	0.590%	–0.004%	0.598%
15/03/2010	116.4787	1.0439%	15.81	217.95480	0.448%	0.003%	0.440%	–0.001%	0.446%
16/03/2010	117.3341	0.9977%	15.82	217.95160	0.734%	0.003%	0.730%	–0.001%	0.732%
17/03/2010	118.0434	0.9597%	15.83	217.94840	0.605%	0.003%	0.600%	–0.001%	0.603%
18/03/2010	118.2596	0.9482%	15.83	217.94520	0.183%	0.003%	0.180%	–0.001%	0.182%
19/03/2010	118.6702	0.9266%	15.83	217.94190	0.347%	0.008%	0.340%	–0.004%	0.347%
22/03/2010	119.2222	0.8973%	15.83	217.93230	0.465%	0.002%	0.460%	–0.001%	0.464%
23/03/2010	119.3475	0.8907%	15.83	217.92900	0.105%	0.002%	0.100%	–0.001%	0.105%
24/03/2010	118.9461	0.9121%	15.82	217.92580	–0.336%	0.002%	–0.340%	–0.001%	–0.337%
25/03/2010	119.251	0.8959%	15.83	217.92260	0.256%	0.002%	0.260%	–0.001%	0.256%
26/03/2010	119.684	0.8732%	15.82	217.91940	0.363%	0.007%	0.360%	–0.004%	0.362%
29/03/2010	120.8872	0.8101%	15.84	217.90970	1.005%	0.002%	1.000%	–0.001%	1.001%
30/03/2010	120.2612	0.8430%	15.83	217.90650	–0.518%	0.002%	–0.520%	–0.001%	–0.520%
31/03/2010	121.2847	0.7894%	15.84	217.90320	0.851%	0.002%	0.850%	–0.001%	0.848%
01/04/2010	121.796	0.7699%	15.83	217.90000	0.422%	0.011%	0.310%	0.099%	0.420%

Source: Compiled with data from the UK Debt Management Office, http://www.dmo.gov.uk

Table 17.1 provides an example of this expression's use in practice. Here

- P is market price;
- Y is yield to maturity;
- MD is modified duration;
- IR is inflation ratio;
- r_M is market return, calculated from market price and coupon payments;
- I is inflation carry;
- r_C is calculated return, using (17.6).

17.11 BREAK-EVEN YIELDS IN ATTRIBUTION

This equation can be extended further to measure the effects of changes in the break-even rate. Denoting y_n as the nominal yield and $y_b = y_n - y_r$ as the break-even yield and substituting into equation (17.6), the attribution equation becomes

$$r = y_r \delta t - MD(\delta y_n - \delta y_b) + \left(\frac{IR_t}{IR_{t-1}} - 1 \right) \qquad (17.7)$$

In addition to the carry and inflation return terms, the market return term is now split into two new terms, one driven by changes in the nominal yield (the market return) and one driven by changes in the break-even yield (the inflation expected return).

Whether it is useful to calculate break-even returns in this way depends on the investment approach taken by the portfolio manager.

For instance, an index-linked fund with an index-linked benchmark is managed by forecasting movements in the real yield curve, so an attribution report should present returns in terms of curve changes. Break-even and nominal risk do not form part of the investment strategy, so there is no need to display returns at this level of detail.

Conversely, a trader who wants to minimise duration risk but take exposure to break-even spreads might buy a long nominal bond and sell an inflation-linked bond with the same duration. Here, the attribution report should show real yield returns broken down into nominal and break-even returns, as the trader is taking explicit inflation bets in their portfolio.

17.12 INFLATION SWAPS

An inflation swap is an elegant way of taking exposure to inflation risk.

The simplest (and most common) inflation swap is an exchange of cash flows at maturity. The holder of such a security pays a fixed amount at maturity but receives an amount indexed to inflation over the life of the swap, and the value of the swap at times before maturity is determined by movements in inflation since inception. For more details on how to treat swaps in an attribution framework, refer to Chapter 20.

17.13 PRACTICAL CONSIDERATIONS

- *Pricing* – If attribution is run using an explicit pricing scheme, inflation-linked bonds can use the same pricing formula as vanilla bonds, but their price and coupons must be indexed to the appropriate value. If a perturbational scheme is used, an inflation term must be added to the fundamental attribution equation.
- *Yield data* – Inflation-linked bonds require real yields rather than nominal yields.
- *Inflation data* – Depending on the approach used, price indices and inflation ratio time series must be provided.
- *Risk data* – Typically the duration measure on an inflation-linked bond is the real duration, or the sensitivity of the bond's price to parallel shifts in the real yield curve.
- *Presentation* – Since conventional bonds and inflation-linked bonds show different risks, their returns should be shown in separate categories on an attribution report. This applies to return from both carry and curve movements, since the shape and movements of the curves driving the two markets may be quite different, even though they refer to the same currency.

18

Futures

18.1 Introduction

18.2 How futures work

18.3 Attribution on bond futures

18.4 Futures contracts on other fixed income securities

18.5 Heuristics for dealing with futures

18.1 INTRODUCTION

Futures contracts on bonds, or *bond futures*, are not complex, but tend to cause more difficulties in attribution analysis than any other asset class. The reasons include:

- their often substantial effective weights in managed funds, meaning that their contributions to return and residuals are typically much greater than individual stocks;
- the cheapest-to-deliver feature of bond futures contracts;
- ways in which optionality and noise in the price of the futures contract can distort attribution results.

For these reasons, any attribution scheme must treat futures on fixed income securities with especial care – and even then futures often generate substantial residuals. At the end of this chapter, I suggest some pragmatic ways to help treat this asset class.

18.2 HOW FUTURES WORK

A bond futures contract replicates the behaviour of a physical bond, including contribution to profit and loss, without the requirement to trade a physical security. Bond futures are designed to form a highly liquid market, allowing positions to be set up and unwound quickly and cheaply. The future acts as a proxy for the underlying bond by delivering the same exposure with very small transaction costs.

In addition, a short position can be taken in a bond future relatively easily. This is much harder to transact with a physical bond, which typically requires trading in the repo market or buying a put option.

Like futures on currencies or commodities, a bond futures contract promises delivery of a bond at a certain date in the future.[1] Bond futures trade in the form of standardised contracts, with delivery in March, June, September and December.

Unlike the commodities markets, however, the owner of a bond futures contract does not know in advance precisely what bond they will receive at maturity. Rather than a single known bond, the seller of the contract can deliver one of a number of bonds from a predefined pool. For instance, at the time of writing the UK Long Gilt contract is based on a bond with maturity between 8.75 and 13 years, and a nominal coupon of 6% (the *nominal* bond). This means that if you own a long gilt contract and hold it to maturity, you will receive a bond with a maturity between these limits. The coupon

[1] The exception are the Australian and New Zealand markets, where the cash equivalent of the bond is delivered; see Appendix C.

will probably not be 6%, but the yield will be adjusted to the yield of the nominal bond, using a published quantity called the *conversion factor*. The price of the bonds in the pool will vary, so the seller of the contract will usually deliver the cheapest security, known as the *cheapest to deliver* (CTD).

There are several good reasons why it makes sense to make delivery from a pool of bonds, rather than a single instrument.

One is that the availability of any individual bond issue is limited. If a futures contract was based on one single bond, and liquidity became poor, then liquidity in the futures contract would become poor too.

Another is to avoid the possibility of a *squeeze*, where a speculator buys a large quantity of both the futures contract and the underlying bond. As the delivery date for the futures contract approaches, other market participants who are short the contract would need to buy them back at higher prices. The threat of such a situation would discourage traders from taking short positions and drive down liquidity.

However, the use of the CTD bond does imply some extra complexity for the attribution analyst. One of the most important is that the CTD can change during the lifetime of the futures contract. I cover this case in the following section.

18.2.1 Contracts

Many countries have active bond futures exchanges on which standardised bond and bill contracts are traded.

Bond futures contracts typically trade using standardised expiration or maturity dates. The maturity month is denoted using the codes H, M, U, Z, with the year following the month. For instance, the code for the US 30-year T-Bond contract maturing in December 2013 is USZ3.

If a fund wants to keep a futures position beyond the maturity date of the contract, the manager will typically sell the existing contracts a few weeks before they mature and buy contracts for the following contract. This is called *rolling over*.

Do not confuse the maturity date of the contract with the maturity date of the underlying bond. These dates will be completely different. In particular, the maturity date of the contract is independent of the interest-rate sensitivity of the future.

Exchanges often introduce new contracts if market research shows sufficient market appetite. The coupon of contracts can also change according to market conditions. For instance, during October 2012 the notional coupon on the UK long gilt was revised downwards from 6% to 4% for the March 2012 and subsequent contracts, reflecting the lower average coupons of bonds on issue.

18.2.2 The theoretical price of a future

At any given time, a bond future is associated with an underlying CTD bond, which is the bond that will be delivered at the maturity of the contract.

For attribution purposes it is necessary to know the details of this bond, which has an associated *conversion factor* by which the price of the contract is multiplied to ensure that its yield to maturity on the delivery day of the contract equals to the notional coupon of the contract. However, for reasons shown subsequently, the conversion factor is not required when running attribution. The CTD is available from sources such as Bloomberg (page DLV) or futures exchanges.

The theoretical price of a bond future is closely related to that of its CTD. Broadly speaking, this is the price of the physical bond (including accrued interest), plus financing costs, minus any coupon and reinvestment income accrued received during the life of the contract. More precisely,

$$P_{future} = \frac{(1 + rt)P_{bond} - \sum_{i=1}^{N} C_i(1 + rt_{i,del}) - AI_{del}}{CF} \quad (18.1)$$

where

- P_{future} is the futures price;
- P_{bond} is the (dirty) bond price, including accrued interest;
- r is the repo rate applicable to the bond future;
- t is the fraction of a year to the maturity of the contract;
- C_i is the ith coupon;
- N is the number of coupons paid between the current date and the maturity date of the contract;
- $t_{(i,del)}$ is the fraction of a year between coupon i and the maturity date of the contract;
- AI_{del} is the accrued interest payable on the bond on the maturity date of the contract;
- CF is the bond conversion factor.

This is a rather formidable formula, so here is a worked example.

Example

On 18 January 2013, the CTD bond for the 30-year Government of Canada bond future (LGB) was the Canadian 5% 1 June 2037. The clean price of this CTD is \$109.31 per \$100 face value, and the conversion factor is 1.1691. What was the theoretical price of the June future?[2]

[2] This example is from the brochure '30-year Government of Canada Bond Futures', published by the Bourse de Montréal, www.m-x.ca.

On January 18, the previous coupon date was 1 December. There are therefore 48 days of accrued interest due on a semi-annual coupon payment of 2.5%, so on a nominal face value of \$100,000, the CTD bond costs

$$\$100{,}000 \times (109.31/100) + 48/183 \times 0.025) = \$109{,}965$$

This is known as the *dirty price* of the bond.

There are 164 days from settlement to the futures maturity date. The financing costs of holding this position to the futures maturity date using the repo rate are

$$\$109{,}965 \times 0.0495 \times 164/365 = \$2446$$

The income received during the holdings period includes a coupon paid 29 days before the future matures, together with interest paid on that coupon at the repo rate:

$$\$2500 + (\$2500 \times 0.0495 \times 29/365) = \$2510$$

The total costs of the bond position are therefore

$$\$109{,}965 + \$2446 - \$2510 = \$109{,}901$$

Subtract the accrued interest generated on the bond between next coupon (1 June) and futures delivery gives

$$\$109{,}901 - (\$100{,}000 \times 0.05 \times 29/365) = \$109{,}591$$

Divide the result by the conversion factor of 1.1691 (which is constant over the future's lifetime, and is typically published on the exchange website) to get the final theoretical price of \$93,739, or \$93.739 per \$100 face value.

The market price of the futures contract on this date was \$93.74 per \$100 face value, so there is a very small arbitrage opportunity.

More generally, to find the theoretical price of a bond future:

- start with the dirty (including accrued interest) price p of the underlying CTD bond;
- calculate the financing costs of the bond

$$f = p \times r \times \delta T$$

  where r is the repo rate, and δT is the fraction of a year to run before the expiration of the futures contract;

- calculate the income i of the bond during the contract's lifetime. i is the accrued interest owing on the bond at expiration of the contract, times the repo rate;
- if a coupon is to be paid between now and the expiration of the futures contract, add this to the financing costs.

Since there is an explicit relationship between the theoretical and the market price of the future, it is, in principle, possible to arbitrage this relationship. Traders who buy a bond and simultaneously sell the futures contract, and close out positions at the expiry of the contract, are engaging in *cash and carry* trading. The difference between the cash price and the futures price is called the *basis*, and traders who arbitrage price differences between the price of the CTD and the future are *basis trading*.

18.2.3 Data required to price a bond futures contract

In addition to the usual quantities required to price a vanilla CTD bond, a futures contract also requires levels of the repo rate and the bond conversion factor:

- The repo rate is relatively stable during the contract's lifetime and may be approximated as a constant, or as the risk-free rate.
- The bond conversion factor is known at the time the contract is issued and remains constant throughout the lifetime of the contract.

The conversion factor simply rescales all futures prices by a constant amount. If we wish to measure the return of the future rather than its absolute price, it is not necessary to source this quantity, as it will not affect the attribution returns.

More explicitly, if the price of the future at time t is $CF \times P_t$, then the return of the future over the interval $[t, t + 1]$ will be

$$r = \frac{CF \times P_{t+1} - CF \times P_t}{CF \times P_t} = \frac{P_{t+1} - P_t}{P_t} \tag{18.2}$$

In other words, the conversion factor drops out and is not needed.

18.2.4 Changes in the CTD

If there are large changes in the level of the yield curve during the lifetime of a contract, the CTD bond can change. In very active markets, the CTD can change several times in a day.

While this can cause difficulties for arbitrage traders, changes in the CTD seldom present much of a problem for attribution analysts. As long as the supporting software allows effective dating capabilities for security modelling, a change in the CTD simply involves redefining the structural parameters of the underlying bond (coupon, maturity).

Some commercial attribution systems require the user to maintain all bonds in the delivery bucket for each futures contract held, together with the data required to price these securities, in order to ensure that every bond future is linked to its correct CTD.

In my experience, this is a great deal of work. Although there may be cases where the CTD changes during the lifetime of a contract, this only happens relatively rarely, and the user may prefer to monitor such occurrences manually.

18.3 ATTRIBUTION ON BOND FUTURES

There are several ways in which a bond future can be treated in an attribution scheme.

A first-principles approach will use formula (18.2) for a futures price. In general terms, one might reprice the future under a range of yield curve scenarios, and calculate the resulting returns.

An alternative route is to consider the theoretical price F of a bond futures contract

$$F = (S - PV)(1 + r)^t \tag{18.3}$$

where

- S is the spot price of the bond;
- PV is the present value of the coupons payable by the bond during the life of the futures contract;
- r is the risk-free rate at the futures maturity;
- t is the life, in years, of the futures contract.

Assuming that there are no coupons payable between the present time and the maturity of the contract, we can calculate the return of the futures contract as follows.

Denote the price of the futures contract F_t at time t as

$$F_0 = S_0(1 + rt_0) \tag{18.4}$$

and

$$F_1 = S_1(1 + rt_1) \tag{18.5}$$

Then the return of the futures contract R_F is given by

$$R_F = \frac{F_1 - F_0}{F_0} = \frac{S_1(1 + rt_1) - S_0(1 + rt_0)}{S_0(1 + rt_0)} \tag{18.6}$$

Assuming $S_0 \approx S_1$, $rt \ll 1$ gives

$$R_F \approx \frac{S_1 - S_0 + S_1rt_1 - S_0rt_0}{S_0} \tag{18.7}$$

or

$$R_F \approx R_B - r\delta t \tag{18.8}$$

Ignoring convexity, the perturbational equation for the return R of a bond is

$$R = y \times \delta t - MD \times \delta y \tag{18.9}$$

Using this expression in (18.8) gives

$$R_F = (y - r) \times t - MD \times \delta y \tag{18.10}$$

where

- R_F is the bond future's return;
- y is the yield to maturity of the CTD;
- r is the risk-free rate;
- δt is the elapsed time;
- MD is the modified duration of the CTD;
- δy is the change in the yield to maturity of the CTD.

This is the same expression for the return of a vanilla bond, with the single difference that the carry return term has been modified by subtracting the risk-free rate. The holder of a bond future should expect their carry return to be lessened because they are in effect borrowing the cost of the underlying security in order to have it delivered at the contract expiration date. The reduction in carry return reflects this borrowing cost. Therefore, (18.10) *is the perturbational equation for a bond future, and should be used in place of* (18.9) *for all assets of this type.*[3]

18.3.1 Sensitivity to risk numbers

One difficulty with the perturbational approach to attribution on futures is that the results rely heavily on the accuracy of the supplied risk numbers.

Consider a bond future with a modified duration of six years, a yield to maturity of 1% at the start and end of a 1-day period, and a zero repo rate. Over this day the return of the future will be

$$r = \frac{1\%}{365} = 0.0027\%$$

There is no return due to duration as yields are unchanged.

[3] Note that Australian and New Zealand bond futures do not generate any carry return. This case is described in more detail in Appendix C.

Now suppose that the yield to maturity at the end of the interval is incorrectly quoted as 1.01%, or 1 basis point above the true value. In this case the future return will be

$$r = \frac{1\%}{365} - 6 \times (1.01\% - 1.00\%) = -0.0573\%$$

or nearly 6 basis points away from the true value. Given that long-dated futures of this type often have a large effective exposure in many portfolios, one should take especial care to ensure yields for this asset class are as accurate as possible. For instance, if the future has 20% effective exposure in a portfolio and a yield 10 bp away from the true value, it will contribute $5.7 \times 10 \times 0.2 = 11.5$ basis points to the portfolio's residual, which is substantial and can in some cases exceed the returns from all other effects combined.

18.3.2 Noise in the attribution calculation

Given that the relationship between the futures price and the CTD is so close, it is worth asking how any noise (or *basis*) can appear at all. Causes of residual in a futures attribution calculation include:

- noise in the attribution calculation for the CTD bond;
- optionality implied by the choice of which contract to deliver;
- US traders can choose when in the month they want to deliver the underlying bond to the contract owner.

These factors can (and do) affect the pricing levels of a bond future. However, the details are highly technical and make little difference to the overall report. For more information, see Burghardt et al., 2005.

The net result is that attribution residuals frequently occur on bond futures, even with completely accurate data on the current CTD bond. They are largely unavoidable, and the attribution analyst should be able to explain why they arise.

18.3.3 Other pitfalls

Some institutions hedge their portfolios using a probability-weighted price for bond futures. Since the CTD is not known in advance, the probability of the various deliverable bonds becoming the CTD at the contract's maturity is calculated and a weighted price calculated, along with probability weighted analytics (yield, modified duration, convexity).

This yield is not suitable for attribution, since it does not measure the yield of the cheapest to deliver but is the yield of a basket of securities that might become the CTD. The CTD's yield and maturity should always be used for attribution.

18.4 FUTURES CONTRACTS ON OTHER FIXED INCOME SECURITIES

While bonds are the most common underlying instrument for fixed income futures, futures contracts are also available on a range of other security types. These include Eurodollars, bank bills and interest rate swaps.

Interest rate futures are a particularly simple asset class. The price P of a short sterling contract is given by

$$P = 100 - y \tag{18.11}$$

where y is the interest rate at expiry at the expiration date of the contract. For instance, if a short sterling future is trading at a price of 94.880, this implies the 3-month LIBOR rate will be 5.12% at the maturity date of the future.

In an attribution framework, these securities may be modelled as follows. Since $\delta P = -\delta y$, we have

$$r = \frac{\delta P}{P} = -\frac{\delta y}{100 - y} \tag{18.12}$$

where r is the return of the future and δy is the future's change in yield.

Note that there is no carry term, and that no use is made of modified duration. Interest rate futures should therefore be treated differently to conventional securities in an attribution framework, as the usual perturbational equation does not apply.

Since the calculation is exact, residuals should never be generated for this asset class.

The future's yield should be read from the appropriate part of the yield curve. For instance, since the above security is priced off a 3-month LIBOR rate, yields should be read at the 3-month point (note that this will require conversion from zero rate to forward rate, since Eurodollar yields are actually forward yields).

18.5 HEURISTICS FOR DEALING WITH FUTURES

Given that a future is designed to behave like an idealised bond, it should be possible to treat it in the same way.

If bond futures are generating large attribution residuals, one possible solution is to assign this residual to 'duration', because curve movements are what drive most of the future's return. The client is happy because futures residuals automatically drop to zero, and the attribution report now reflects the underlying investment strategy without being polluted by bad analytics data.

19

Annuities and amortising securities

19.1 Introduction

19.2 Prepayments

19.3 Mortgage-backed securities

19.1 INTRODUCTION

An amortising security is superficially similar to a bond, in that it is issued by a borrower who intends to repay the funds to the lender via scheduled payments. Unlike a bond, however, the principal of the loan is repaid over the lifetime of the loan rather than as a single bullet payment at the bond's maturity.

The best-known amortising security is a mortgage on a house. Typically, the mortgage is structured so that the lender makes equal payments over the lifetime of the loan. These payments are made up of repayments of principal and interest. At the outset, the payments go almost entirely to paying off interest, but as the principal reduces the proportions change until near the end of the security's lifetime the payments are almost entirely directed to principal reduction.

The cash flow structure of an amortising bond is therefore very different to that of a vanilla bond with a similar maturity:

- The modified duration of the amortising bond is much shorter than that of the bond, since its cash flows are uniformly distributed over all payment dates, rather than being concentrated around the bond's maturity date. The interest rate sensitivity of an amortising bond's price is therefore lower than that of a bond with the same maturity date.
- The credit rating of an amortising bond tends to be higher than that of a vanilla bond, since repayments of principal are made throughout the bond's lifetime rather than at a date in the far future, thereby reducing the risk to the lender.

The expression for an amortising bond's payments is relatively straightforward:

$$A = P\frac{i(i+1)^n}{(1+i)^n} - 1 = P\left[\frac{i+1}{(i+1)^n} - 1\right] \quad (19.1)$$

where

- A is the periodic payment amount;
- P is the principal;
- i is the periodic interest rate;
- n is the total number of payments over the lifetime of the loan.

Here the periodic interest rate refers to the amount per interval. For instance, if the bond pays 6% per year but payments are due monthly, then the relevant interest rate is $6\%/12 = 0.5\%$.

The total return of amortising securities is complicated slightly by the paydown of principal over the security's lifetime. See Chapter 12 for a discussion of this topic.

19.2 PREPAYMENTS

A common feature of many such loans is the ability to make early payments towards the principal of the loan. If even a modest amount can be added to the principal payment in the first few years of the loan, its lifetime can be drastically reduced.

The ability to make prepayments, or to repay the debt earlier, is a valuable feature for the borrower, since it allows more flexibility in how the debt is treated and the ability to refinance at lower rates should interest rates drop during the term of the loan. The ability to make prepayments is equivalent to the borrower holding an embedded call option.

Securities that are based on such loans are more complex than vanilla bonds or callable bonds, because of the presence of both variable cash-flows and an embedded option.

19.3 MORTGAGE-BACKED SECURITIES

A mortgage-backed security (or MBS) is a legal entity that pools together a group of mortgages into a single tradeable entity. The cash flows from each individual mortgage are aggregated by the administrating body into regular coupons, and any prepayments are returned to the MBS holder.

Many of the same terms that are used to describe other interest rate securities can also be used for MBS, as they have maturity dates, coupons, interest rate and credit risk, and yield. The major points to note are as follows:

19.3.1 Yield and risk

The ability to make early repayment on the principal means that the purchaser carries extra risk.

For instance, suppose an MBS is issued at 10%. A naïve purchaser of the MBS may expect to receive around 10% a year on their principal.

However, if interest rates fall to 2% there will be a flood of refinancing by mortgage holders. The purchaser of the bond will receive most or all of the invested capital back much earlier than expected, and then find that it can only be invested at 2% – a drastic drop in return.

To compensate the investor for this reinvestment risk, MBS pay a higher yield than bonds with similar credit ratings. There are various ways to put a price on reinvestment risk, including treating the MBS as a mixture of a bond and an option, or (more accurately) by considering various pathways over which interest rates can develop and their effect on the price of the security. This topic is covered further in Chapter 21.

19.3.2 Convexity

The presence of an option in an MBS often leads such securities to have *negative convexity*. The reason is that if interest rates fall, there will be more incentive for the mortgage-holders to refinance. The holder of an MBS will be paid off faster than expected, and the price of the MBS will not rise as quickly as the price of a bond without the embedded option.

Whether this is a problem depends on the investor's strategy and view of interest rates. The effects of negative convexity are offset to some degree by the higher yields paid by an MBS.

19.3.3 Interest rate sensitivity

Unlike a vanilla bond, where the main cash flows are concentrated at maturity, the cash flows of an MBS are distributed over a wide range of maturities. The dependence of an MBS's price on interest rates is therefore much more complex than a vanilla bond, and this can make use of simple interest rate risk measures, such as modified duration, misleading.

For portfolios where MBS represent only a small proportion of the interest rate risk, this may not matter. For portfolios that have a large exposure to such securities, it may be preferable to use interest rate measures such as key rate durations to analyse the sensitivity of the portfolio to curve movements at individual maturities.

19.3.4 Prepayment models

While it is seldom possible to make any firm predictions about future prepayment streams for an individual mortgage stream, one can make use of external research to model prepayments for pools of mortgages.

One of the most widely used models is that published by the Public Securities Association (PSA). The main features of the model, which is based on extensive observations of real borrowers, are that prepayment rates start at zero when the mortgage is first issued, then rise for the first 30 months of the mortgage, and are constant thereafter.

This incorporates the views that during the first few years of a mortgage, borrowers:

- are less likely to move to a different home;
- are less likely to refinance;
- cannot afford to make additional payments.

The standard PSA model assumes that repayments rise linearly over the first 30 months to a maximum annualised prepayment level of 6% and stay constant thereafter. This 6% level is known as 100% PSA. If repayment rates rise to 9%, the corresponding PSA rate is 9%/6% × 100% = 150% PSA.

The presence of prepayments can drastically affect the cash flow patterns of an MBS; see, for instance, Fabozzi (2001).

Any change in the repayment rate will therefore affect the price, and hence the return, of the MBS, and it is possible in principle to assign a return to changes in this factor. An amortising bond can be seen as a special case of an MBS for which the repayment rate is zero. Some managers make heavy use of prepayment models to price and manage their MBS holdings. The rate at which the MBS will be paid down is forecast using a wide range of inputs.

Attribution on more complex prepayment models will require custom software that can, at the least, allow the user to input prepayment rates, or allow the model to be integrated into the code. Such models are highly specialised and fall outside the scope of this book.

20

Swaps

20.1 Introduction
20.2 Two-leg swaps
20.3 Single-leg swaps
20.4 Modelling swaps
20.5 Types of swap
20.6 Credit default swaps

20.1 INTRODUCTION

Swaps are often presented as complex and impenetrable financial instruments that only rocket scientists can understand. In fact the attribution of their return is rather straightforward if one has a basic grasp of the security types described in previous chapters.

20.2 TWO-LEG SWAPS

Perhaps the most common swap encountered is a vanilla interest rate swap.

The easiest way to picture this instrument is as a portfolio that has:

- bought a bond with fixed coupons and a given maturity date;
- sold a floating rate note with the same maturity date and face value.

In essence, a swap is an agreement for two counterparties to swap cash flow streams, although in practice the principal is seldom exchanged. Naturally, one has to have confidence that the other side in the agreement will keep their side of the bargain.

The maturity payments cancel out at maturity, so the owner of the swap will receive a stream of fixed coupons, and pay a stream of floating coupons throughout the lifetime of the swap. The two cash flow streams are called the legs of the swap: one floating, one fixed.

Most swaps are traded OTC (over the counter) and so are tailored to the individual requirements of the customer. If a perturbational approach to attribution is used, the risk numbers of the two legs must typically be calculated by the performance analyst or be supplied, on a custom basis, from a data vendor.

Why might one want to own such a security? The classical case is that of a home owner who is concerned that interest rates may rise, and wants to lock in fixed payments. In this case a swap will do exactly what they want. If the yield curve is positively sloped, the fixed payments will be higher than their current floating payment, but the monthly payment will then be constant regardless of how interest rates change subsequently.

More generally, a swap can be an excellent way to take tailored exposure to movements in yield curves in a very liquid market.

Most, if not all, swaps can be modelled as two stand-alone securities with opposite exposures. For instance, a zero coupon inflation-linked swap is a zero coupon bond (which makes one payment at maturity) and an inflation-linked bond (which makes inflation-linked payments). In this case, the maturity payout may be non-zero if the principal payment is indexed against inflation.

Swaps are highly liquid and are traded in huge volumes. They define a term structure called the *swap curve*, which is usually slightly higher than the sovereign curve because of the slightly higher risks of dealing with non-sovereign counterparties in the marketplace. A manager who wants to take interest risk may choose to do so entirely in terms of customised swaps tailored to match their risk profile. This is seldom possible in the sovereign bond market without extra effort and liquidity concerns.

As long as one knows the terms and conditions of the swap, they present little difficulty for the attribution analyst in the framework described here.

20.3 SINGLE-LEG SWAPS

Some accounting systems record swaps in terms of their fixed leg only, assuming that the interest rate risk of the floating leg is sufficiently low that it will make little contribution to return, and that the floating leg's return will come entirely from yield.

If the swap is modelled as a vanilla bond, the swap's return may be much higher than this assumption warrants because of its leverage. Some ways the market uses to handle this are:

- set up a cash offset with the same market value as the floating leg;
- adjust the various returns on a pro-rata basis so the overall return equals the accounting value;
- assign all residual return to parallel curve shift, since this is usually the main driver of swap return.

Swaps are usually designed to have a market value of zero when they are set up. This means that if treated as single-leg instruments, their very high leverage can present difficulties for the performance analyst. When modelled as distinct securities, swaps are an excellent candidate for the use of performance contribution rather than raw performance in an attribution report.

20.4 MODELLING SWAPS

The simplest way to model a swap in a fixed income portfolio is to treat each leg as a separate fixed income security. In this case there will be no issues with high leverage. Ideally, the attribution report should be able to group the two legs together using a sector classification scheme that links both legs of the swap together, usually by name.

More sophisticated attribution systems have the capability to define subportfolios at various levels of depth. Here, the swap can be set up as an independent subportfolio and treated as a stand-alone security.

20.5 TYPES OF SWAP

Other types of swap include:

- a *total return swap* – an exchange of cash flows between the total return of an asset such as an equity or bond index (including capital growth and coupons, or dividends) and another source of regular interest payments, such as a bond or an FRN;
- a *currency swap* – an exchange of cash flows between two loans or bonds in different currencies;
- a *basis swap* – an exchange of cash flows between two floating rate notes.

All these cases can be treated in an attribution framework by modelling the swap legs as distinct securities.

20.6 CREDIT DEFAULT SWAPS

Despite their name, credit default swaps (or CDS) follow a rather different pattern to the other types of swaps described in this chapter.

The buyer of a CDS makes regular payments to a counterparty. In return, they receive a payout if a nominated security defaults or undergoes a credit event. A CDS is therefore a type of insurance against the value of a bond falling due to default.

The pricing of CDS securities can involve some complex mathematics. However, for attribution purposes their treatment is very straightforward. Since their pricing is almost entirely determined by credit, their return should be assigned to this risk category.[1]

[1] CDS carry a very small sensitivity to changes in the term structure due to premium payments over the security's lifetime. However, for most practical purposes this curve return may be ignored.

21

Options and callable bonds

21.1 Introduction

21.2 Measuring yield on bonds with embedded options

21.3 Optionality in practice

21.1 INTRODUCTION

A bond with an embedded call has the property that, on certain dates, the issuer can withdraw the bond and return the principal, plus any accrued interest, to the purchaser. For the bondholder, this means that their funds, which were safely invested, will now have to be invested somewhere else.

This *reinvestment risk* adds extra uncertainty for the bondholder. To compensate for the possibility of lower future income, a bond with a call option trades at a higher yield than a similar security with no optionality.

Conversely, a bond with an embedded put allows the bondholder to exchange the bond for cash at any time and to reinvest it at a higher rate if market conditions allow, so the bond issuer pays a lower yield.

Therefore, bonds with optionality will have an extra component of yield due to this feature, and the attribution analyst may wish to show the return due to this additional yield in its own category on an attribution report.

Various types of embedded option are available:

- An *American* option allows the bond's issuer to repurchase the security at any time after issue. This results in maximum uncertainty for the bond's owner, so pays the highest excess yield.
- A *Bermudan* option allows the issuer to buy the security back at certain given dates in the future, often on the same dates as coupon payments.
- A *European* option allows the issuer to buy the bond back at one predetermined date during the bond's lifetime. This type of option carries the least uncertainty for the bondholder, and so pays the lowest excess yield.

The holder of such a security cannot know at the time of purchase if or when the option will be triggered, so the future cash flows – and hence the current price – of the security must be subject to some modelling of future market conditions.

21.2 MEASURING YIELD ON BONDS WITH EMBEDDED OPTIONS

In this section we cover some of the measures of yield used for bonds with optionality.

21.2.1 Yield to worst

Unlike a vanilla bond, the date at which a callable bond will be redeemed is not known in advance. To calculate the YTM for such a bond, it is necessary to choose a *redemption date* in advance. The market convention is to take the most pessimistic assumption possible, which leads to the lowest return for the investor:

- If the bond is priced above par, the first possible redemption date is chosen. The reason is that interest rates have fallen, so the bond issuer will wish to exercise their option as soon as possible and issue a new bond at the prevailing lower rate.
- If the bond is priced below par, the last possible redemption date is chosen, because rates have risen and the issuer is paying less than the market rate for funds by leaving the bond uncalled.

The yield to maturity calculated under this assumption is called the *yield to worst*, as it is the lowest possible yield that the investor can receive from holding the bond. Naturally, if the actual redemption date differs from either of these assumptions, this calculated yield is of little use.

The yield to worst will always be lower than the security's actual yield to maturity.

Yield to worst is seldom used in performance attribution. It is more useful when assessing the relative risks of different, comparable bonds.

21.2.2 Yield to call

Suppose a callable bond is trading above par, or that its market price is above its face value. In this case, its coupon will be higher than current interest rates. The bond's issuer may then decide to call the bond at the next call date.

To take account of this when calculating the bond's expected yield, the redemption date is assumed to be the next call date, rather than the maturity date. The resulting yield is called the *yield to call*.

In the opposite case where a bond trades below par, its coupon will be below current interest rates, so there will be little incentive for the issuer to redeem the bond early. The redemption date will then be the bond's final maturity date, and the yield to call will be equal to the yield to maturity.

For callable bonds, yield to call is a more accurate guide to the actual yield available than yield to maturity. If available, it should be used in preference to yield to maturity; but note that option-adjusted spread (see below) is preferable to either.

A similar measure, called *yield to put*, exists for puttable bonds.

21.2.3 Option-adjusted spread and duration

Neither of the measures described above is ideal to measure the expected yield of a bond with embedded options, as they make no estimate of when the bond will actually be called. A more sophisticated approach uses the idea of *option-adjusted spread*.

While a full account of the technique is outside the scope of this book, the basic idea is to build a model of how interest rates evolve over the lifetime of the bond, and calculate the value of the embedded option at each point. This allows the calculation of a unique price for the bond at the current date.

This price will be lower than the price of an equivalent bond without call features, so its yield will be higher. Option-adjusted spread is a flat (equal across all maturities) spread that is added to the risk-free curve such that the sum of the security's cash flows, priced using this new curve, equals the market price. In other words, it is a measure of the extra yield provided by the embedded option.

For bonds that have simple embedded options (i.e., without prepayment), the OAS is entirely due to the embedded option, so it is relatively straightforward to calculate the carry return generated by the option; it is just the OAS, minus any credit spread due to the bond, times the elapsed time. A more complex model is required for securities where prepayments can occur.

OAS is preferable to yield to call for attribution purposes, because it models the way in which interest rates may move in the future, rather than just using a snapshot of the bond's current price. In other words, it makes some reasonable assumptions about when the bond will actually be called, and so provides a more accurate picture of the bond's true yield, as well as explicitly splitting out the return from optionality. However, it is much more complex to calculate, and values of OAS may be difficult to acquire.

Just as spread duration measures the sensitivity of a security's price to credit spread, option-adjusted duration (OAD) measures sensitivity to changes in option-adjusted spread. Some software systems describe all modified duration as OAD, even for securities with no optionality.

Your institution probably has its own model for calculation of OAS; there is no unique, globally accepted way to calculate it. If your attribution system also supplies a means of calculating OAS, consider whether the (probably different) values you will be using will cause problems.

The main reason I do not go into the construction of OAS in depth is that, most probably, your clients will already have values of this measure that were used to make the investment decisions in your portfolio. If you have a value available for OAS, use it. Otherwise, you may wish to try to integrate the pricing model used into your attribution system, if technically possible (and it may not be).

21.3 OPTIONALITY IN PRACTICE

Perhaps the most complex part of modelling a callable bond is specifying its call provisions. In addition to its coupon, maturity, credit rating and coupon frequency, you will also need to supply the type of its embedded option, the call dates and the price at which the bond is to be repurchased. For a perturbational attribution approach, you will need to provide modified duration, OAD, the changes in yield from the sovereign curve, and any change in credit spread or OAS.

In either case it may be preferable to calculate OAS externally, and provide OAS as an external input to your attribution system, together with YTM and return. In practice this will require close integration between your performance data and your risk data, which may present challenges.

Should you use OAS in your reports? If the information is available, yes; the presence of the option is generating extra yield for the security, above what is required by the probability of default, and this makes extra return for the holder.

If OAS is not available, one has two courses:

- Attempt to calculate it oneself. This requires access to some type of pricing model. Models can vary greatly in complexity.
- Ignore the presence of the option and treat the callable bond as a vanilla bond with the same credit rating. In this case, return due to optionality will be written to the residual bucket, since the option-free bond's yield will be lower than its actual value. This will result in some inaccuracy, first because the return due to the passage of time will be lower than the actual figure, and secondly because the bond will be priced slightly differently.

22

Collateralised and securitised debt

22.1 Introduction
22.2 Securitisation
22.3 Collateralised debt
22.4 Attribution on securitised debt

22.1 INTRODUCTION

Collateralised and securitised debt forms some of the more complex types of instrument traded in the fixed income markets. Fortunately, it is seldom necessary to delve into their details in order to treat them in attribution reports.

22.2 SECURITISATION

Securitisation is the process of pooling various types of debt, such as residential and commercial mortgages, car loans and credit card debt, into new types of liquid security such as bonds and pass-through securities. The most commonly encountered securitised bond is a mortgage-backed security, which, as the name implies, is backed by a pool of residential mortgages.

Since the bond is based on the cash flows from a large number of mortgages, the risk of any one mortgage defaulting is low, so risk-averse investors will prefer to invest in the securitised debt rather than the underlying issues. The securitised debt can also be sold in smaller parcels than would be possible with the underlying debt, increasing the number of potential investors in the security.

22.3 COLLATERALISED DEBT

A collateralised debt obligation, or *CDO*, is a pool of financial assets with varying characteristics that generate revenue over time. These assets are typically bonds, mortgages or other types of security but may also include tranches from other issued CDOs. In other words, they are securities that are securitised on other assets, rather than physical assets in their own right.

The CDO repackages the cash flows from these assets into different *tranches* that can be sold on to investors. The tranches are structured so that the most creditworthy tranches have first claim on the cash flows and underlying collateral if any of the assets default. As a result, these *senior* tranches are assigned a higher credit rating than the *mezzanine*, *junior* and *toxic waste* tranches, which offer progressively higher yields to compensate the purchaser for their additional default risk.

The appeal of CDOs for the issuer is that they offer a way to parcel up debt that would not be otherwise saleable, either for reasons of creditworthiness or liquidity.[1] Their appeal to the buyer is that they also offer higher yields than corporate debt with the same credit rating.

---

[1] In the aftermath of the 2010 global financial crisis, many commentators compared CDOs to sausages: tasty, but one is better off not knowing their ingredients.

Many types of CDOs have been traded in the marketplace, depending on their underlying asset class. Table 22.1 shows some of the most commonly encountered.

Table 22.1

Types of CDO

Acronym	Type	Collateral
CLO	Collateralised loan obligation	Leveraged bank loans
CBO	Collateralised bond obligation	Leveraged fixed income securities
CSO	Collateralised synthetic obligation	Credit derivatives
SFCDO	Structured finance CDO	Structured products such as asset-backed securities and mortgage-backed securities
CRECDO	Commercial Real Estate CDOs (CRE CDOs)	Commercial real estate assets
CBO	Collateralised bond obligations	Corporate bonds
CIO	Collateralised Insurance Obligations	Insurance contracts
CDO^2	CDO-squared	Tranches issued by other CDOs
CDO^n	CDOn	Tranches issued by other CDO^2, at (possibly) many levels

22.4 ATTRIBUTION ON SECURITISED DEBT

For the attribution analyst, the main concern with these security types is knowing what cash flow structure should be used to model the difference tranches. Fortunately, they almost always follow the standard patterns of a bond or FRN. Given the pricing and cash flows of each tranche, the techniques described earlier in the book can be used to include such securities into an attribution report.

Part
5

ATTRIBUTION IN PRACTICE

23. Popular attribution models
24. Reporting

23

Popular attribution models

23.1 The Campisi model

23.2 Duration attribution

23.3 The Tim Lord model

23.4 Key rate attribution

23.5 Top-down attribution

In this chapter I describe a number of widely used fixed income attribution models. Attribution approaches are often described in terms of one or other of these models.

23.1 THE CAMPISI MODEL

The Campisi model was first proposed in a paper published by Stephen Campisi (Campisi, 2000). It is perhaps the simplest possible security-level model for fixed income attribution (see Figure 23.1).

Breakdown of effects in the Campisi model

Figure 23.1

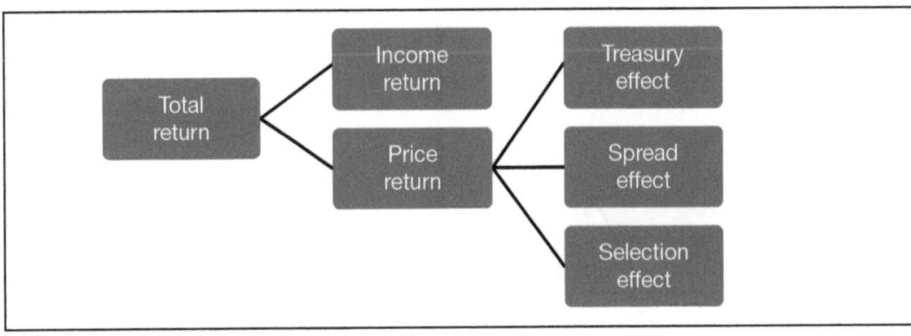

The Campisi model can be applied at the portfolio, sector or security levels.

- *Income return*: Campisi's original paper describes income return as generated by coupons; specifically, as the average annual coupon divided by the average beginning market price. This is actually running yield, as it omits any pull-to-par effects.
- *Treasury effect* combines the returns from parallel and non-parallel curve movements into one source of return, given by $-MD\delta y_{treasury}$. The change in treasury yield $\delta y_{treasury}$ is given by the change in the treasury curve at the tenor point equal to the duration of the portfolio.
- *Spread effect* is the effect of changes in the average spread δy_{spread}, given by $-MD\delta y_{spread}$. Treasury and spread durations are assumed to be equivalent.
- *Selection* or *security-specific* return is given by total return, minus the sum of the previous three effects.

There is no residual term. Any unexplained returns are aggregated into selection effect.

23.2 DURATION ATTRIBUTION

The duration model provides slightly more information than the Campisi model. Treasury effects, which are returns generated by changes in the level of the sovereign curve, are decomposed into returns made by parallel movements in the curve (*duration return*), and those from non-parallel movements (*curve return*) (see Figure 23.2). Modified duration measures sensitivity to both types of yield movement, so this effect gives its name to the model.

As noted in Chapter 10, the definition of how parallel curve movements should be calculated varies widely between practitioners.

There is no formal definition of the duration model in the attribution literature, but it is one of the most widely used.

Figure 23.2 **Duration attribution**

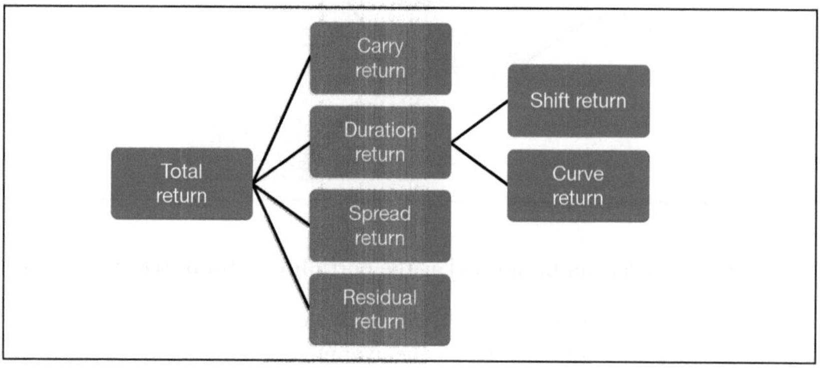

23.3 THE TIM LORD MODEL

The Tim Lord model is similar to the Campisi and Duration models, but includes a number of more detailed effects (Lord, 1997; Figure 23.3).

- *Income* return is given by change in accrued interest and other income cash flows. As with the Campisi model, this is more correctly described as the return due to running yield. Unlike the Campisi model, pull-to-par and roll-down effects are measured here as *calendar returns* (see below).
- *Duration* return is defined as price return due to changes in the treasury par curve, measured as the product of the negative modified duration of each security times the change in yield of its duration matched treasury (a synthetic treasury bond with the same modified duration as the target bond).

Figure 23.3

Tim Lord attribution

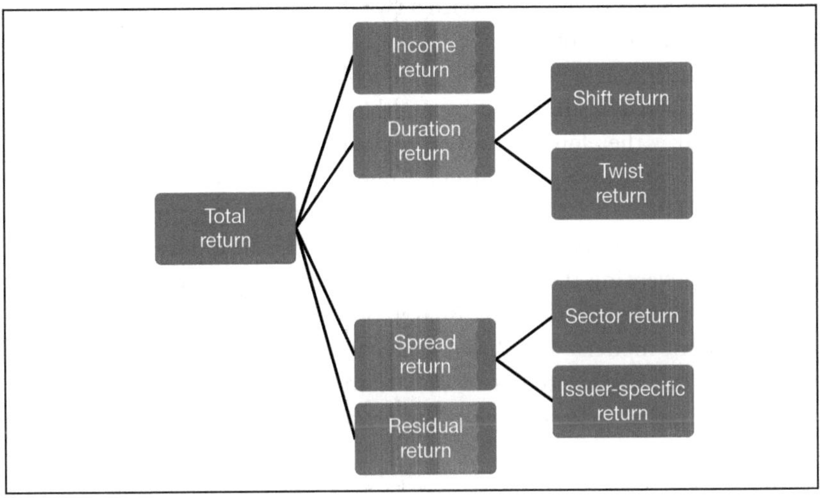

- *Shift* return is generated by parallel shifts in the treasury curve. The shift is measured at the five-year maturity point on the curve.
- *Twist* return is the portion of return generated by non-parallel shifts in the treasury curve.
- *Spread* return is further decomposed into sector return and issuer-specific return.
- *Sector* return is calculated by recording the change in spread for the security's defined sector, which is the average OAS change for all benchmark securities in that category.
- *Issuer-specific* return is the difference between spread return and sector return.
- *Residual* return is any remaining return that is unexplained by the sum of the previous effects.

Lord notes that the model can generate substantial residuals if a security's pricing model is wrongly specified. However, this is easily addressed if the attribution system can use specialised pricing models, rather than a one-size-fits-all approach.

Most security-based models are variants of the Tim Lord approach.

23.4 KEY RATE ATTRIBUTION

Modified duration measures the sensitivity of price to changes in overall levels of interest rates. For instance, if the yield curve moves downwards by 10 basis points, a bond with a 10-year modified duration will generate a return of 100 basis points, but a bond with a two-year modified duration will generate only 20 basis points.

A *key rate duration* measures the price sensitivity of a security to a change in its yield curve at a single maturity, rather than to movements in the curve as a whole. It is therefore well suited to detailed analysis of the return of securities with cash flows spread over a range of maturities, such as amortising bonds and MBS, since the returns of these securities are affected by movements at many points on the curve, rather than being dominated by the curve level governing the value of the main principal payment.

Key rate duration attribution usually follows the same pattern as Campisi and Tim Lord models. The difference is that returns from changes in the yield curve are represented as returns from different maturities along the yield curve, rather than from global movements such as shift and twist (see Figure 23.4).

Figure 23.4 **Key rate attribution**

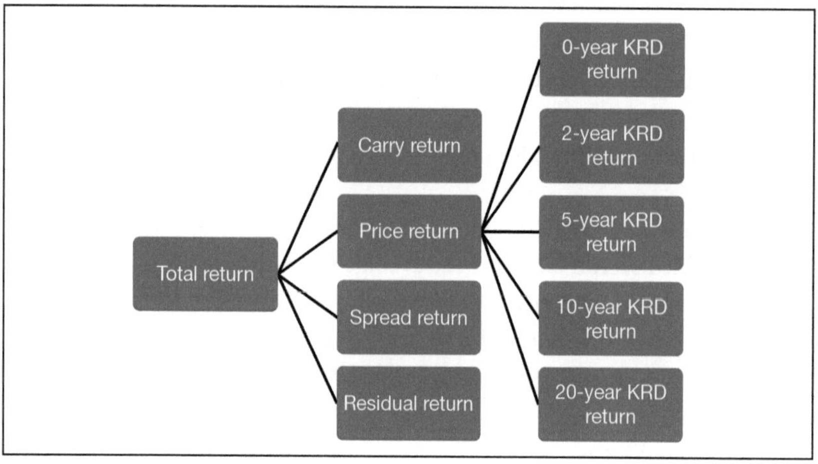

23.5 TOP-DOWN ATTRIBUTION

Top-down (or mixed, or balanced) attribution forms a useful approach to attribution on fixed income portfolios where over- or underweighting of sectors forms part of the investment process, in addition to fixed income investment decisions (see Figure 23.5). Top-down attribution forms a combination of the successive portfolio methodology, of which Brinson attribution is the simplest example, and the successive spread methodology, which underlies the various models shown earlier. The approach is described in the GRAP paper (Groupe de Recherche en Attribution de Performance, 1997).

Figure 23.5

Top-down attribution

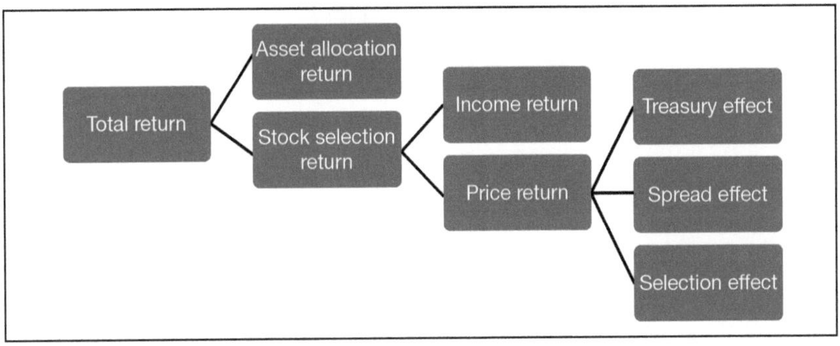

In practice, the results from a top-down attribution are the same as for one of the previous analyses, but with an additional asset allocation term. Results are usually presented down to the sector level only.

24

Reporting

24.1 Treatment of residuals

24.2 Unattributed return

24.1 TREATMENT OF RESIDUALS

Residuals are a fact of life in attribution. Even for the most liquid securities, it is most unlikely that there will be a perfect match between the price as calculated from market curves, and the market price.

The consumer of attribution reports should therefore be deeply suspicious of a report that claims zero residual return. On many occasions, residual return may be redefined as credit return, but this should always be made clear to the user.

The best way to treat residuals is to accept that they convey useful information and that they act as a check that pricing accuracy lies within acceptable limits.

24.2 UNATTRIBUTED RETURN

A very useful technique for business-as-usual reporting is to use an *unattributed* return bucket on attribution reports.

New securities enter portfolios all the time. Usually, these are based on existing patterns, such as corporate bonds or swaps. However, particularly in the fixed income markets and for larger investors, new security types may often need to be included in a portfolio even if they are not types that are included in the current security library, and so cannot be priced by the attribution application.

In this case the analyst has three courses of action:

- Halt all production attribution reporting until the security can be modelled correctly. This is seldom a practical option, especially as an entirely new security type may require a new build of the underlying software.
- Attempt to represent the new security as an existing type. This may work in the short term but is seldom a satisfactory solution.
- Place its return contribution into an *unattributed* bucket. This indicates that the attribution system cannot yet handle this asset type, so its contribution to report is placed into a separate category where it may be monitored.

Essentially, this approach defers solution of the problem. As long as its performance contribution is small, the presence of this new security will not substantially affect the overall conclusions of the attribution report, which tells the story of which global risks affected the portfolio's absolute or active returns. Attribution reporting can then proceed as usual until the security can be modelled in the correct form.

In most cases, the third approach will be preferable to halting the production of attribution reports until the security has been classified.

Afterword

This book has presented much of the background material required to understand and implement attribution, a business-critical technique that continues to offer effective routes to increased profits and funds under management.

The installation and deployment of an industrial-strength attribution system that meets all stakeholder requirements is a major undertaking that requires substantial IT and budget resources as well as time, money and expertise.

Unfortunately, existing systems remain expensive and difficult to use. The business risk in setting up attribution remains high, with many highly visible failed projects.

The Flametree attribution engine has been designed to address these problems by offering virtually all the attribution models described in this book in ready-to-run form, as a stand-alone application, as a compiled library, as source code, via our bureau service, or via one of our industry partner platforms.

The engine offers one of the widest range of attribution methodologies currently available from any vendor, and includes balanced, hybrid and duration weighted allocation models as well as a full range of fixed income attribution effects.

In addition, our data-light architecture allows both equity and fixed income attribution to be run using the results of your existing performance measurement software, without compromising on depth of analytics or instrument coverage.

For more information on new developments and functionality, demonstrations, testimonials, licensing and consulting, please contact Flametree Technologies at sales@flametreetechnologies.com, or visit our web site at www.flametreetechnologies.com.

Appendices

A. A summary of the Karnosky-Singer attribution model

B. Explicit pricing of an FRN

C. Attribution on Australian and New Zealand bond futures

D. Parametric and non-parametric yield curve models

E. Replicating the return of a hedged benchmark

F. Duration-weighted yields

G. Combining duration allocation returns

H. Sources of yield curve data

APPENDIX A

A summary of the Karnosky-Singer attribution model

- The user of forwards to hedge a portfolio's FX exposures can significantly change the conclusions of of an attribution analysis.
- In addition to the weights of the physical and forwards portfolios, the FX returns and the risk-free returns are also required to run accurate attribution.

Two sets of weights are used for the portfolio, reflecting its market and hedge exposures. If there is no hedging in position, the two sets of weights are identical.

Denote the weights of the unhedged portfolio sectors as w_i^P and the weights of the hedged portfolio sectors as w_i^H. Then the forward weights are given by $w_i^P - w_i^H$, and the sums of the weights obey

$$\sum_i w_i^P = 1 \tag{A.1}$$

$$\sum_i w_i^H = 1 \tag{A.2}$$

$$\sum_i (w_i^P - w_i^H) = 0 \tag{A.3}$$

Assuming continuous compounding, the return of the hedged portfolio R^P is given by

$$R^P = \sum w_i^P(r_i^P - c_i) + \sum_i w_i^H(c_i + f_i) \tag{A.4}$$

where w_i^P and w_i^H are as above, r_i^P is the portfolio local currency return, c_i is the risk-free return and f_i is the currency return of sector i, respectively. Similarly, the return of the (unhedged) benchmark R^B is given by

$$R^B = \sum w_i^B(r_i^B + f_i) \tag{A.5}$$

Two intermediate quantities are needed to calculate Karnosky-Singer returns: the *base return* and the *return premium*.

The base return B_i is the sum of the FX return and the risk-free return, and represents the return one might expect by holding assets in a particular market sector without making any investment decisions. The aggregated base return $\overline{B}$ is given by

$$\overline{B} = \sum_i w_i^B B_i \tag{A.6}$$

The return premium P_i is the benchmark return minus the risk-free return, and represents the real return generated by the market. The aggregated return premium $\overline{P}$ is given by

$$\overline{P} = \sum_i w_i^B P_i \tag{A.7}$$

Then the market or asset allocation return R_{AA} is given by

$$R_{AA} = \sum_i (w_i^P - w_i^B)(P_i - \overline{P}) \tag{A.8}$$

the currency return R_C by

$$R_C = \sum_i (w_i^H - w_i^B)(B_i - \overline{B}) \tag{A.9}$$

and the stock selection return R_{SS} by

$$R_{SS} = \sum_i w_i(r_i^P - r_i^B) \tag{A.10}$$

The sum of these three returns is the active return of the portfolio against the benchmark $R_P - R_B$.

APPENDIX B

Explicit pricing of an FRN

The price P of an FRN per \$100 face value is given by the expression

$$P = 100 \times \left[\frac{(R_T + M)\frac{d}{365} + \frac{M - DM}{4}a_n + 1}{1 + (r + TM)\frac{f}{365}} \right] \qquad \text{(B.1)}$$

where

- R_T is the reference rate at the last coupon reset date T;
- M is the reset margin;
- DM is the discount margin;
- r is the zero rate at the next coupon payment date;
- d is the number of days in the current interest period;
- f is the number of days from settlement date to next coupon date;
- $a_n = (1 - v^n)/i$;
- $v = 1/(1 + i)$;
- $i = (S + DM)/n$;
- S is the annual swap rate from settlement to maturity of the FRN;
- n is the number of interest periods to maturity at the next coupon date.

Quarterly coupons and a 365-day year are assumed.

The expression is easier to understand if each term is examined separately:

- $(R_T + M)\frac{d}{365}$ is the next coupon payment;
- $\frac{(IM - TM)}{4}a_n$ is the present value, at the next coupon date, of the difference between the reset margin and the current discount margin, for all future payments, as an annuity (a series of equal payments at regular intervals);
- $1 + (r + TM)\frac{f}{365}$ discounts the values of these payments back to the present.

APPENDIX C

Attribution on Australian and New Zealand bond futures

The Australian and New Zealand markets treat futures on bonds slightly differently to other countries. Since the maturity of the underlying bond is always a constant, set interval, there is no carry return from this asset class.[1] The return R_F of an Australian or New Zealand bond future is given by

$$R_F = -MD\delta y \tag{C.1}$$

where MD is the future's modified duration, and δy is its change in yield. A fixed income attribution system that models futures should be able to handle this asset type as a special case.

Australian bond futures are quoted in terms of '100-yield', and this quantity is called 'price'. For instance, a 'price' of 95.675 actually means a yield of 4.325%. The price of the underlying nominal CTD is quite different, which can be confusing.

Since Australian bond futures always have a fixed number of coupons to maturity (6 for 3-year bonds, 20 for 10-year bond futures) their pricing is particularly simple:

$$P = \frac{\left(\frac{c}{2}\right)\cdot(1 - v^{20})}{i} - 100 \cdot v^{20} \tag{C.2}$$

where

- $i = \frac{y}{2}$;
- $v = \frac{1}{1 + i}$;
- y is yield to maturity;
- c is coupon rate, currently 6% for AUD bond futures.

[1] 'For ASX Treasury Bond futures, the pricing formula can be simplified because there is always an exact number of half years to maturity, and hence there is no requirement to calculate accrued interest.' (*A guide to the pricing conventions of ASX Interest Rate Products*, www.sfe.com.au)

The price from this formula should be used for calculating effective exposures and risk measures. For instance, the modified duration of an Australian 10-year bond future can be calculated using

$$MD = \frac{P(y + \delta) - P(y)}{\delta P(y)} \qquad \text{(C.3)}$$

where $\delta \ll 1$, and $P(y)$ is as defined above.

APPENDIX D

Parametric and non-parametric yield curve models

D.1 PARAMETRIC CURVE MODELLING

In this case the form of a yield curve is assumed to follow a particular pattern that can be modelled by a mathematical function with a small number of parameters. These parameters can then be supplied in place of the raw curve data.

The best-known parametric model for yield curve modelling is from Nelson and Siegel (1987) who proposed the following expression for a curve's yield at an arbitrary maturity τ:

$$y(\tau) = \beta_0 + \beta_1\left[\frac{1 - e^{-\tau/\lambda}}{\tau/\lambda}\right] + \beta_2\left[\frac{1 - e^{-\tau/\lambda}}{\tau/\lambda} - e^{-\tau/\lambda}\right] \tag{D.1}$$

- The four parameters β_0, β_1, β_2 and λ define the curve.
- This function matches a wide range of yield curve behaviours, such as sloped, flat, curved, inverted and humped.
- Virtually any curve observed in the marketplace can be fitted to a Nelson-Siegel function, using least-squares or similar techniques.
- The value of β_0 is the asymptotic (or long) yield as τ becomes very large.
- $\beta_0 + \beta_1$ is the short (or spot) rate.
- β_1 represents the difference between the short- and long-term rates, which may be interpreted as the *slope* of the curve.

D.2 SPLINE MODEL

A spline model typically fits a first or second order polynomial between successive curve data points. There are many refinements on this approach that include considerations such as ensuring the curve is globally smooth.

APPENDIX E

Replicating the return of a hedged benchmark

E.1 INTRODUCTION

This appendix outlines a way to construct a set of FX hedging positions for a hedged benchmark so that its overall return is identical to its vendor-supplied return.

Benchmark providers supply security-level returns in both local and base currency returns, from which it is straightforward to calculate the aggregate, unhedged return of the benchmark.

However, things become less clear when hedging is taken into account. Hedging involves adding a number of forward or FX holdings so that the currency risk is hedged away. Unfortunately, the details of the calculation (and the forward and FX rates) are seldom made available by the benchmark vendor, who will typically only supply the top-level hedged benchmark return. To model hedged benchmarks for attribution requires the user to supply a set of hedge trades so that the overall return is correct.

E.2 THE RE-HEDGING ALGORITHM

The algorithm works by constructing an artificial currency hedge at each date, and by adjusting the returns of the currencies by a small amount.

- Calculate the weights of the various securities in the benchmark by currency sector. The sum of these sector weights will be 100%.
- Set the weights of the currency hedges to be the negative of the currency sector weight, for all except the base currency sector, which is assigned a weight of 100% − (*sector weight*). The sum of these hedge weights will be 0%.
- Calculate the FX returns for each sector. This is the ratio of the base currency and the local currency returns.

- Calculate the overall return of the hedge as the sum-product of the hedge weights and the FX weights. This return, plus the unhedged return of the benchmark, should be close to the hedged benchmark return.
- Adjust the returns of all sector weights up or down by a small multiplicative factor until the overall return of the hedged benchmark is correct.

E.3 WORKED EXAMPLE

As an example, Table E.1 shows the calculation on the Citigroup World Global Bond Index, hedged into GBP.

On the 17 November 2011, the details of the calculation were as follows:

Table E.1 **Benchmark forward hedging**

Currency	Weight	Hedge	FX	Hedge contribution
AUD	0.962%	−0.962%	−0.718%	0.00690%
CAD	1.988%	−1.988%	−0.086%	0.00171%
CHF	0.311%	−0.311%	−0.056%	0.00018%
DKK	0.642%	−0.642%	−0.131%	0.00084%
EUR	27.325%	−27.325%	−0.131%	0.03577%
GBP	6.026%	93.974%	0.000%	0.00000%
JPY	33.020%	−33.020%	−0.058%	0.01920%
MXN	0.596%	−0.596%	−0.471%	0.00281%
MYR	0.354%	−0.354%	−0.203%	0.00072%
NOK	0.207%	−0.207%	−0.516%	0.00107%
PLN	0.485%	−0.485%	−0.250%	0.00122%
SEK	0.421%	−0.421%	−0.170%	0.00072%
SGD	0.261%	−0.261%	−0.144%	0.00038%
USD	27.403%	−27.403%	−0.013%	0.00347%
TOTAL	100.000%	0.000%		0.07496%

The return of the unhedged benchmark was 0.00305% and the return of the artificial hedge was 0.07496%, implying a total return of 0.07801%. This was close, but not identical, to the published return of 0.07870%.

To correct this, define a quantity f, which is close to one, and multiply all currency returns used in the hedge calculation by this amount until the sum of the unhedged return and the hedge portfolio match the published return.

On any given day, denote the return of the unhedged benchmark as u, the return of the artificial hedge as h, and the published hedge return as H. Then

$$H = u + (f \times h) \tag{E.1}$$

which implies

$$f = \frac{H - u}{h} \tag{E.2}$$

In the above example $u = 0.00305\%$, $h = 0.07478\%$, $H = 0.07870\%$, giving a value of

$$f = \frac{0.07870\% - 0.00305\%}{0.07478\%} = 1.0115$$

To ensure that the return of the hedged benchmark equals the published return on any particular date, simply multiply the hedge holdings on that day by f.

E.4 FRACTIONAL HEDGING

A manager sometimes has a mandate to use a partially hedged benchmark. In this case, part but not all of the currency risk is hedged away. The market convention is to talk '50% hedging', '100% hedging' and so on.

The above example demonstrates 100% hedging. To apply 50% hedging to a portfolio, simply multiple the factor f by the desired fraction. For instance, the above benchmark can be 50% hedged by multiplying each of the synthetic forward lines by $0.5 \times f$.

E.5 DISCUSSION

This approach makes some fairly sweeping assumptions – in particular, that we can recreate the hedge using spot FX positions instead of forwards, that the hedge is rebalanced against the benchmark every day, and that there are no interest effects in the hedge.

Nevertheless, given that index vendors often supply minimal information about the methodology or instruments used for hedging, these assumptions are generally permissible, especially as the simulated hedge returns are close to the true returns.

APPENDIX F

Duration-weighted yields

Why use the expression

$$\delta y = \frac{\sum_{i \in C} w_i MD_i \delta y_i}{\sum_{i \in C} w_i MD_i} \quad \text{(F.1)}$$

instead of the more obvious

$$\delta y = \frac{\sum_{i \in C} w_i \delta y_i}{\sum_{i \in C} w_i} \quad \text{(F.2)}$$

to calculate a sector yield?

The reason is that the yield calculated by (F.1) does not work if the curve change is non-parallel, or (equivalently) if not all the δy_i are the same. A suitable value for δy will give the same result whether treating the portfolio as a single security, or as an ensemble of many. In other words,

$$MD^P \delta y^P = \sum_{i \in P} w_i MD_i \delta y_i \quad \text{(F.3)}$$

Since

$$MD^P = \sum_{i \in P} w_i MD_i, \quad \text{(F.4)}$$

the result follows.

APPENDIX G

Combining duration allocation returns

To see that the sum of the market duration allocation, market duration selection and market direction terms is in fact the active market return, expand equations (14.11–14.13) to give

$$\begin{aligned} R_i^{DAA} &= -\tilde{w}_i^P MD^P \delta y_i^B + \tilde{w}_i^B MD^B \delta y_i^B \\ &\quad + \tilde{w}_i^P MD^P \delta y^B - \tilde{w}_i^B MD^B \delta y^B \end{aligned} \tag{G.1}$$

$$R_i^{DIR} = -\tilde{w}_i^P MD^P \delta y^B + \tilde{w}_i^P MD^B \delta y^B \tag{G.2}$$

$$R_i^{DSS} = -\tilde{w}_i^P MD^P \delta y_i^P + \tilde{w}_i^P MD^P \delta y_i^B \tag{G.3}$$

Summing the terms and rearranging gives

$$\begin{aligned} R_i^{MARKET} = &-(\tilde{w}_i^P MD^P \delta y_i^P - \tilde{w}_i^B MD^B \delta y_i^B) \\ &-(\tilde{w}_i^P MD^P \delta y^B - \tilde{w}_i^P MD^P \delta y^B) \\ &-(\tilde{w}_i^P MD^P \delta y_i^B - \tilde{w}_i^P MD^P \delta y_i^B) \\ &-(\tilde{w}_i^B MD^B \delta y^B - \tilde{w}_i^P MD^B \delta y^B) \end{aligned} \tag{G.4}$$

The second and third terms on the RHS are zero. Summing over i gives

$$\begin{aligned} R^{MARKET} = &-\left(\sum_i \tilde{w}_i^P MD^P \delta y_i^P - \sum_i \tilde{w}_i^B MD^B \delta y_i^B \right) \\ &+ \delta y^B MD^B \sum_i (\tilde{w}_i^P - \tilde{w}_i^B) \end{aligned} \tag{G.5}$$

Since

$$\sum_i \tilde{w}_i^P = \sum_i \tilde{w}_i^B = 1 \tag{G.6}$$

the last term in (G.5) also reduces to zero, and the result follows.

APPENDIX H

Sources of yield curve data

This appendix supplies a list of web sites from which sovereign yield curve data is currently available for free (Table H.1). The list is not exhaustive, and new sources of yield data may become available from other sites.

Yield curves from countries that are not on this list, and industry sector curves, will probably require a commercial data vendor subscription.

The raw data from these sites are supplied in many different file formats, including CSV, XML and Excel. In addition the structures of the various web sites often change over time, so the paths and names of files of interest may require occasional updates.

Table H.1

Sources of yield curve data

Country	Issuer	Web site
UK	Bank of England[a]	www.bankofengland.co.uk
Europe	European Central Bank	www.ecb.europa.eu
US	Federal Reserve	www.federalreserve.gov
Japan	Japanese Ministry of Finance	www.mof.go.jp
Australia	Reserve Bank of Australia	www.rba.gov.au
Canada	Bank of Canada[b]	www.bankofcanada.ca
Thailand	Thai Bond Market Association	www.thaibma.or.th

[a] Current and historical data on UK yield curves includes data on government curves, real yield curves and implied inflation curves.
[b] Currently, Canadian curve data is only supplied with a three-month lag.

Bibliography

Bacon, C. (2008). *Practical portfolio performance measurement and attribution, 2nd edition*. Wiley Finance.

Barber, J.R. & M.L. Copper. (1996). Immunization using principal component analysis. *Journal of Portfolio Management* 23. 99–106.

van Breuleken, G. (2000). Fixed income attribution. *The Journal of Performance Measurement* Summer. 61–68.

Brinson, G. & N. Fachler. (1985). Measuring non-US equity portfolio performance. *Journal of Portfolio Management* Spring. 73–76.

Brinson, G., G. L. Beebower & L. R. Hood. (1986). Determinants of portfolio performance. *Financial Analysts Journal* July-August. 39–44.

Brown, P.J. (1994). *Constructing and calculating bond indices*. Probus.

Burghardt, G.D., T.M. Belton, M. Lane & J. Papa. (2005). *The treasury bond basis, 3rd ed.* McGraw-Hill.

Campisi, S. (2000). Primer on fixed income attribution. *The Journal of Performance Measurement* 4 (Summer). 14–25.

Carino, D. (1999). Combining attribution effects over time. *Journal of Portfolio Management* Summer. 5–14.

Choudhry, M. (1994). *Analysing and interpreting the yield curve*. Wiley Financial.

Colin, A. (2007). A new approach to the decomposition of yield curve movements for fixed income attribution. *Journal of Portfolio Management*.

Colin, A., F. Bardoux & M. Cubilie. (2006). A Brinson model alternative: an equity attribution model with orthogonal risk contributions. *Journal of Portfolio Management* Summer. 59–62.

Colin, A. M. (2005). *Fixed income attribution*. Wiley Finance.

Davies, O. & D. Laker. (2001). Multiple-period performance attribution using the Brinson model. *Journal of Performance Measurement* Fall. 12–22.

Dawkins, R. (1976). *The selfish gene*. Oxford.

Deacon, Derry Mirfendereski] Deacon, M., A. Derry & D. Mirfendereski. (2004). *Inflation-indexed securities: Bonds, swaps, and other derivatives (2nd edition)*. Wiley Finance.

Fabozzi, F.J. (2001). *The handbook of mortgage-backed securities, 5th edition*. McGraw-Hill.

Fabozzi, F.J. (2012). *The handbook of fixed income securities, 8th edition*. McGraw-Hill.

Fabozzi, F.J. & S.V. Mann. (2000). *Floating-rate securities*. Frank J. Fabozzi Associates.

Fischer, Cunha F., B. (1998). Performance attribution for an emerging market external-debt portfolio. *'Portfolio Strategies', JP Morgan Emerging Markets Research* September.

Frongello, A. (2002). Linking single period attribution results. *Journal of Performance Measurement* 10–22.

Groupe de Recherche en Attribution de Performance. (1997). Synthèse des modèles d'attribution de performance.

Karnosky, D. S. & B. Singer. (1994). *Global asset management and performance attribution*. The Research Foundation of the Institute of Chartered Financial Analysts.

Laker, D. (2003). *Karnosky Singer attribution: a worked example*. Barra.

Lord, T. (1997). The attribution of portfolio and index returns in fixed income. *The Journal of Performance Measurement*. 2, 45–57.

Menchero, J. (2000). An optimized approach to linking attribution effects over time. *Journal of Performance Measurement* 36–42.

Nelson, C.R. & A.F. Siegel. (1987). Parsimonious modeling of yield curves. *The Journal of Business* 60(4), 473–489.

Phoa, W. (1998). *Advanced fixed income analytics*. Frank Fabozzi Associates.

Record, N. (2003). *Currency overlay*. Wiley Finance.

Shiller, R. J. (2003). The invention of inflation-linked bonds in early America. Working Paper 10183, National Bureau of Economic Research December.

UK DMO. (2005). Formulae for calculating gilt prices from yields, 3rd edition, UK Debt Management Office. http://www.dmo.gov.uk/.

Index

3-month LIBOR, 197

accrual instrument, 193
accrual securities, 197
accrued interest, 113
accurate intraday contributions, 18
active carry, 163
active return, 25
additive aggregation, 20
allocation returns, 31, 283
American option, 243
amortising bond, 231, 234, 258
amortising security, 231
annual compounding, 88
annual coupon, 114, 255
arithmetic compounding, 69
arithmetic smoothing, 76
asset allocation, 3, 4, 6, 19, 29, 30, 31, 43
attribution
  on bond futures, 224–7, 273–4
  break-even yields in, 215
  with complete data, 201
  on credit portfolios, 145
  equity, 6
  on Euro bond portfolios, 143–4
  fixed income, 6
  with incomplete data, 201
  multiple levels of, 169–71
  portfolios, 3
  return and, 4–5
  risk, types of, 3–4
  securities and, 3
  on securitised debt, 250
  strategy tagging and, 4–5
  types of, 5–6
Australian bond futures, 273–4

balanced attribution, 157–9, 258
bank bill future, 227
bank bills, 97, 195–6
bank rate, 194
barbell strategy, 151
base currency return, 51
base rate, 193
base return, 63, 269
base and return premiums, 63–4
basis, 223
basis swap, 239
basis trading, 223
BEIR *see* break-even inflation rate
benchmark, 3, 14, 23
Bermudan option, 243
bond, 85–6, 185–9
bond futures, 219–26, 224–7
  risk numbers, sensitivity to, 225–6
bond futures contracts, 219–20, 223
bond pricing formulae, 185–6
bond yield, 88–9
bonds, 85–6, 185–9
  maturities, 87
  modified duration of, 89
  pricing, 88
  return of, 90–1
  types of, 186–9
bond's market return, 98
bootstrapping, 97
bottom-up attribution models, 31–2, 163
'bottom-up' investment process, 31
break-even inflation rate (BEIR), 210
break-even yields, 210–11, 215
Brinson attribution, 29–38, 44–5, 159
  asset allocation, 29–30
  bottom-up attribution, 31–2
  Brinson risks, hedging, 32

Brinson attribution (*continued*)
  hedged portfolio, 60–3
  sector classification, 30
  single-level, 33–8
  stock selection, 31
  successive portfolio attribution, 44–5
  top-down attribution, 32
Brinson expression, 176
Brinson, Gary, 29
Brinson-Fachler model, 33–4, 35, 37–8, 165
Brinson-Hood-Beebower model, 34–5, 38
bullet payment, 106, 231
bullet security, 132
business as usual, 263
butterfly, 131

calendar returns, 256
call date, 188
callable bond, 86, 113, 188–9, 244, 245–6
callable FRN, 198
Campisi model, 255
Canadian model, 208
capped FRN, 198
Carino, D., 74
Carino smoothing, 73–6
carry, 89, 92, 115
carry returns, 88–9, 90, 92, 113, 115–16, 166, 171–2, 174–6
  carry-based investment strategies, 113–14
  decomposed, 116, 117–20
carry-based investment strategies, 113–14
cash, 194
cash and carry, 223
cash drag, 194
cash flows, 17–18
cash flow structure, 231
cash offsets, 20–2
CDO *see* collateralised debt obligation
CDS *see* credit default swaps
central banks, 134
cheap/dear effects, 119
cheapest to deliver (CTD), 220, 223–4, 226, 227
classification structure, 19
CMOs *see* collateralised mortgage obligations
Colin-Cubilié-Bardoux attribution, 133
collateralised debt obligation (CDO), 249–50
collateralised mortgage obligations (CMOs), 149
compliance, 26
composite benchmark, 24
compounded returns, 14
compounding interval, 14
Consumer Price Index (CPI), 208
continuous compounding, 51, 88, 194
contracts, 220
conversion factor, 220
convexity, 150–2, 233
  effects, 120
  and price, 150
  trading, 150–1
corporate bond, 137, 138, 139, 187
counterparty, 56, 187, 239
coupon reset interval, 197
coupons, 87
CPI *see* Consumer Price Index
credit attribution, 145
credit carry return, 118
credit curves, 99
credit default swaps (CDS), 239
credit effects, 91
credit event, 239
credit ratings, 138–40
credit return, 92, 142, 166
credit risk, 198
credit spread return, 91
credit spreads, 91, 137–8
creditworthiness, 138, 153
cross terms, 69–70
CTD *see* cheapest to deliver
cubic interpolation, 96
currency attribution, 51–5
  base currency return, 51
  forwards contract, 56–7
  hedge returns, measuring, 59–60
  hedging and risk, 57–8
  Karnosky-Singer attribution model, 65
  local currency return, 51
  naïve attribution, hedged portfolio, 58–9
  portfolio hedging, 55–6
  unhedged portfolios, 52–5
currency exposures, 51, 56
currency forward, 202–3
currency futures contract, 56

currency option, 56
currency risk, 56, 57
currency swap, 239
current/running yield, 114–15, 117–18
curvature, 98
curve flattening trade, 98
curve movement, 166
curve return, 92, 166, 176, 178
curve shifts taxonomy, 128–9
  duration and curvature, 129–30
  key rate duration returns, 132–3
  no sovereign curve effects, 129
  principal component analysis, 131–2
  shift, twist and curvature, 130–1
  undecomposed curve return, 129
curve twist, 127–8

data vendors, 134
date, 220
debt restructuring agreement, 86
default, 91, 188, 239
delivery, 219, 220
deposit yield, 194
derivative, 20
dimensionality reduction, 131
dirty price, 222
discount margins, 198–9
discount securities, 195–6
discount yields, 97
discounted cash flows, 88
dividend, 15, 16, 86
duration allocation, 163–9
duration allocation return, 177–8
duration allocation risk, 164
duration asset allocation, 168
duration attribution, 256–7
duration matched treasury, 256
duration options, 179
duration returns, 166–8, 256
duration risk, 163
duration stock selection return, 172
duration weight, 166–7
duration-based asset allocation, 164–5
duration-weighted yields, 281

effective exposure, 21
embedded call, 243
embedded option, 243, 245–6
embedded put, 243
equity attribution, 6
  basic concepts, 29
  Brinson attribution, 29–38
  multiple-level asset allocation, 38–42
  off-benchmark securities, 43
  security-level attribution, 45–7
  successive portfolio attribution, 43–5
equity attribution models, 163
Euro bond portfolios, 143–4
  attribution with country curves, 144
  attribution without country curves, 144
Eurobond, 51
Eurodollar future, 227
European option, 243
Excel, 74
exchange rate risk, 3
existing portfolios, 134
expiration date, 56

face value, 85–7
factor analysis, 6
Fed Funds rate, 193, 194, 197
Fisher equation, 210, 213
fixed income attribution, 6, 103
fixed income effects, 172
fixed income returns, 172
fixed income risks, 85–92
  bond, 85–6
  bond yield, 88–9
  carry return, 88–9
  credit effects, 91
  maturities and, 87
  prices and yields, 89
  pricing conventions, 86–7
fixed income securities, 3
fixed-coupon bonds, 198, 210, 211
flat yield curve, 96
flattening, 98
floating rate note (FRN), 193, 197
  decomposing, 200
  durations, 199–200
  explicit pricing of, 271
  and securitisation, 202
  treatment of, in commercial systems,
    201–2
  types, 198
floored FRN, 198

foreign exchange return, 79
forwards, 3, 193
forwards contract, 56–7
fractional hedging, 279
frequency of compounding, 14
FRN *see* floating rate note
fundamental attribution equation, 104
futures basis, 223
futures contracts, 219
  fixed income securities and, 227
futures margin, 20
futures offset, 20
FX exposure, 56

General Index of Retail Prices (RPI), 208
geometric aggregation, 20
geometric compounding, 72
geometric smoothing, 76–9
government bonds, 188
government debt, 137

hedge, 3
hedge position, 56
hedged benchmark, 277–9
hedged portfolio
  Brinson attribution, 60–3
  naïve attribution, 58–9
hedging, 4, 57–8, 279
heuristics, 227–8
highly leveraged securities, 18
high-yield portfolio, 113
hybrid models, 179

immunisation, 99
implied inflation curve, 211
income return, 255, 256
inflation, 3, 106, 119, 207
inflation carry, 213
inflation carry return, 119
inflation data, 216
inflation rate, 208, 209
inflation ratios, 209
inflation swaps, 215–16
inflation term structure, 210
inflation-linked bond, 211, 212–13
inflation-linked bond market, 207
inflation-linked debt, 208
inflation-linked gilts, 213–15
inflation-linked securities, 207–16, 208
interaction, 35, 36
interest rate duration, 199
interest rate exposure, 163
interest rate future, 227
interest rate risk, 3
interest rate sensitivity, 233
interest rate swap future, 227
interest rates, 95–6, 198
interpolation, 96
intraday performance, 18
inverse repo rate, 194
inverted yield curve, 96
investment strategy, 3, 4
issuer-specific return, 257

junior tranche, 249
junk bonds, 138

Karnosky-Singer attribution model, 65, 269–70
key rate attribution, 257–8
key rate duration (KRD) returns, 132–3
  first principles, 133–4
  perturbational, 133
key rates, 258

LDI *see* liability-driven investment
letter of credit, 195
leverage, 238
liability-driven investment (LDI), 26
LIBOR, 198
linear interpolation, 96
linker, 207
liquidity, 119, 142, 153, 220
liquidity return, 153
local currency return, 51
lower-level asset allocation returns, 40–2

managed fund, 3
market direction effect, 168
market direction return, 178
market exposure, 20
market interest rate, 86
market noise, 120
market price, 86
market return, 90

market value attribution, 29
market weight attribution, 29
maturity, 87, 95
maturity date, 85, 86
MBS *see* mortgage-backed security
mezzanine tranche, 249
mixed attribution, 258
modelling swaps, 238
modern portfolio theory, 24
modified duration, 165–6
money market, 193
money market benchmarks, 203
money market curve decomposition, 193
money market securities, 193–203
money market yield curves, 193
money-weighted return, 16
Monte Carlo simulation, 25
mortgage, 231
mortgage-backed security (MBS), 149, 232–4
multiple-level asset allocation returns, 40
muni bond, 187–8

NAV *see* Net Asset Value
negative convexity, 233
negative interest rate, 88
negative real yield, 211
Nelson-Siegel function, 193
nested duration allocation, 172
Net Asset Value (NAV), 23–4
net present value, 88
New Zealand bond futures, 273–4
noise, 226
nominal yield, 114, 210
non-bond securities, 120
non-parallel shift, 98–9
non-zero price return, 23
notional cash, 20

OAD *see* option-adjusted duration
OAS *see* option-adjusted spread
off the run, 153
off-benchmark securities, 43
on the run, 153
option-adjusted duration (OAD), 244–6
option-adjusted spread (OAS), 244–6
option-adjusted spread (OAS) curve, 142
optionality, 189, 226, 245

overnight rate, 194
over-the-counter (OTC) instruments, 26

par, 87
par curve, 96, 97
parallel movement, 98, 99
parallel shift, 124–7
parallel shift, yield curve, 98
parametric curve modelling, 275
pass-through security, 249
paydown return, 149–50
payment frequency, 137
performance, 13
performance contribution, 17, 18, 60, 263
performance measurement, 13–26
  active return and, 25
  benchmark and, 24–5
  cash flows and, 17–18
  cash offsets and, 20–2
  compounded returns and, 14
  edge cases and, 22
  external returns and, 22–4
  liability-driven investment and, 26
  money-weighted return and, 16
  portfolio returns and, 17, 20
  return concept and, 13–14
  sector returns and, 19
  security transactions and, 17–18
  stochastic attribution and, 25–6
  time-weighted return and, 15–16
periodic interest rate, 231
perpetual bond, 187
perturbational equation, 103–7
portfolio returns, 17, 20
portfolios, 3
pragmatism, 79
prepayment models, 233–4
prepayments, 232
presentation, 216
price return, 23
pricing, 216
pricing conventions, 86–7
pricing formula, 97
pricing securities, 103
principal, 85
principal component analysis (PCA), 131–2

probability-weighted price, 226
profit and loss, 13
promissory note, 195
PSA *see* Public Securities Association
Public Securities Association (PSA), 233–4
pull-to-par effect, 199
pull-to-par return, 153
pull-to-parity effect, 117–18
purchasing power, 208
puttable bonds, 188–9

rate of return, 14, 15, 114
raw pricing functions, 107
real yield, 209–10
real yield curve, 211
real yield term structure, 211–12
redemption date, 244
redemption yield, 115
re-hedging algorithm, 277
reinvestment risk, 119
repayment of principal, 137
repo, 189, 193, 203
repo agreement, 189, 203
repo effects, 120
repo rate, 194, 203
reset date, 197
reset margin, 197, 198
residual return, 257
residuals, 107–8, 263
return, concept of, 13–14
return contribution, 71
return premium, 269
revaluation, 15, 18
reverse FRN, 198
reverse repo, 203
riding the yield curve, 152
risk, 232
risk data, 216
risk numbers, 107
risk-free carry return, 118
risk-free curve, 129
risk-free yield, 91
rolldown, 152–3
rolldown return, 153
rolling over, 220
RPI *see* General Index of Retail Prices
running/current yield, 114–15, 117–18

sector carry return, 118
sector classification, 30
sector, concept of, 19
sector curve allocation, 143
sector curve return, 118
sector curves, 99, 137, 140–1
  attribution returns and, 142–3
  constraints, on shape, 141–2
  option-adjusted spread (OAS), 142
sector returns, 19, 257
sector weights, 19
securitisation, 249
securitised debt, 250
security spread curve, 142–3
security transactions, 17–18
security-level attribution, 45–7
  asset allocation, multiple levels of, 46–7
  Brinson model, 45–6
  stock selection and interaction terms, combined, 46
security-specific carry return, 118
selection return, 259
selection/security-specific return, 255
semi-annual coupon, 86
semi-government bonds, 188
senior tranche, 249
sensitivity measure, 98
shift return, 257
shift/twist/butterfly (STB) analysis, 132
simple margin, 199
simple yield, 114
single fixed income security, 166
single-leg swaps, 238
single-level asset allocation returns, 39
single-level Brinson attribution, 33–8
  Brinson-Fachler model, 33–4, 37–8
  Brinson-Hood-Beebower model, 34–5, 38
  interaction return, 35–7
smoothing algorithms, 69–80
  Carino smoothing, 73–6
  cross terms, 69–70
  foreign exchange return, 79
  geometric smoothing, 76–9
  internally consistent return contributions, 71
  path-independence, 71–2

sovereign bond, 187
sovereign curve attribution, 123–4
sovereign curve risk, 3
sovereign debt, 137, 186–7
spline model, 275
spot curve, 97
spread duration, 200
spread duration, interest rate sensitivity, 165–6
spread effect, 255
spread return, 257
squeeze, 220
stand-alone portfolios, 108
steepening, 98
stepped FRN, 198
stochastic attribution, 25–6
stock selection, 168
stock selection returns, 42, 158
strategy tagging, 4–5
successive portfolio attribution, 43–5
swap curve, 238
swap leg, 239
swaps, 237–9
  modelling, 238
  single-leg, 238
  two-leg, 237–8
  types of, 239
swing return, 23–4

tax effects, 119
term structure, 96
theoretical price, of bond future, 221–3
Tim Lord model, 256–7
time-weighted return and, 15–16
top-down attribution, 258–9
top-down investment process, 32
top-level asset allocation returns, 40
total return swap, 239
trading return, 22–3
treasury bond yields, 211
treasury effect, 255
twist return, 257
two-leg swaps, 237–8

unattributed return, 263
unhedged portfolios, 52–5
  Karnosky-Singer attribution, 65

vanilla bond, 238, 243
variable rate note, 198

yield to call, 244
yield curve attribution, 200–1
yield curve data, 134, 285
yield curve models, 275
yield curves, 95–9, 123–4
  credit spreads, 99
  interest rates and, 95–6
  interpolation and, 96
  non-parallel shift, 98–9
  par curves, 97–9
  parallel movements in, 98
  zero curves, 97–9
yield data, 216
yield to maturity (YTM), 115
  in attribution reports, 120
  an inflation-linked bond, 119
  pros and cons of, 116
yield to put, 244
yield to worst, 243–4
yields, 198–9, 232
  current, or running yield, 114–15
  measure for attribution, 116–17
  nominal yield, 114
  for non-bond securities, 120
  simple yield, 114
  types of, 114–15
  yield to maturity, 115

zero coupon bonds, 97, 188
zero curves, 141
zero-coupon sector curves, 141